Facebook®

FOR

DUMMIES®

3RD EDITION

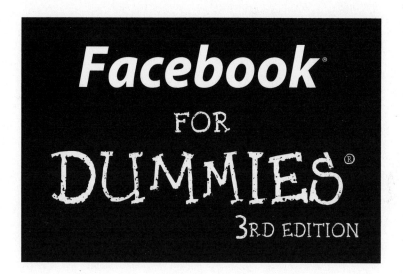

by Carolyn Abram and Leah Pearlman

WILEY

Wiley Publishing, Inc.

Facebook® For Dummies® 3rd Edition

Published by
Wiley Publishing, Inc.
111 River Street
Hoboken, NJ 07030-5774

www.wiley.com

WILEY

About the Authors

Carolyn Abram: One of the first Facebook users on the west coast, Carolyn took her English degree from Stanford University (Class of 2006) and decided the best career move was to get paid to be on Facebook all day long. At Facebook from 2006 to 2009, Carolyn is currently studying fiction writing at California College of the Arts in San Francisco. Originally from Ardsley, New York, Carolyn resides in California. Her hobbies include hiking, writing, enjoying sunshine, mocking her friends, and playing Ultimate Frisbee.

Leah Pearlman: Leah graduated with a degree in computer science from Brown University, where she first signed up for Facebook to find out the name of a boy in a class. Typical. She spent two years at Microsoft learning the product management ropes (seriously, there are ropes) before becoming a Product Manager for Facebook. Since joining, she has worked on a wide range of projects including messaging and the Inbox, News Feed, Pages, and Ads. She currently works on Facebook's Internal Communications team. Her hobbies include such pretentious sounding activities as yoga, snowboarding, writing, and playing Ultimate Frisbee.

Authors' Acknowledgments

First and foremost, we'd like to thank Blake Ross, double agent and ghost writer extraordinaire. We also could never have started (or finished) this book without the help of everyone at Wiley: Steve Hayes, Nicole Sholly, Blair Pottenger, as well as everyone listed on the other side of this page. We don't have space to list by name everyone on the Facebook team we'd like to thank; everyone who makes Facebook such a great product to write about, and use.

Leah gives her personal thanks to Mom and Dad for the endless supply of you-can-do-its and nose-to-the-grindstone-kiddos. Special shout-out to brother DJ, nephew Collin, and Uncle Marc for graduating from newbie to Facebook-JV, without the help of this handy how-to. Thanks Maggie and Emily for your sisterly and BFF-erly love, respectively. An obvious, yet totally genuine thanks to Carolyn; if you had an Awesome button, I'd press it. Finally, thank you, spell-check; without ewe nothing eye right wood make any cents.

Carolyn gives her personal thanks to Eric (nee Boyfriend), Mom and Dad, Becca and Matt, Charlotte, Grandma and Grandma. Thank you friends for all of the support over the last year. Lastly, to Leah: If you had any of the following buttons, I'd press them: Awesome, Awkward, and Spell Check.

In closing, we'd like to thank the millions of Facebook users around the world who are busy connecting, organizing, and generally having fun on Facebook. Keep on signin' on.

Publisher's Acknowledgments

We're proud of this book; please send us your comments at http://dummies.custhelp.com. For other comments, please contact our Customer Care Department within the U.S. at 877-762-2974, outside the U.S. at 317-572-3993, or fax 317-572-4002.

Some of the people who helped bring this book to market include the following:

Acquisitions, Editorial

Project Editor: Nicole Sholly

Executive Editor: Steve Hayes

Copy Editor: Melba Hopper

Technical Editor: Claudia Snell

Editorial Manager: Kevin Kirschner

Editorial Assistant: Amanda Graham

Sr. Editorial Assistant: Cherie Case

Cartoons: Rich Tennant
(www.the5thwave.com)

Composition Services

Project Coordinator: Sheree Montgomery

Layout and Graphics: Carl Byers, Ashley Chamberlain

Proofreaders: John Greenough, Nancy L. Reinhardt

Indexer: Galen Schroeder

Publishing and Editorial for Technology Dummies

    Richard Swadley, Vice President and Executive Group Publisher

    Andy Cummings, Vice President and Publisher

    Mary Bednarek, Executive Acquisitions Director

    Mary C. Corder, Editorial Director

Publishing for Consumer Dummies

    Diane Graves Steele, Vice President and Publisher

Composition Services

    Debbie Stailey, Director of Composition Services

Contents at a Glance

Introduction *1*

Part I: Getting Started with Facebook *7*

Chapter 1: The Many Faces of Facebook 9
Chapter 2: Adding Your Own Face to Facebook 29
Chapter 3: Finding Your Way Around Facebook 41
Chapter 4: Finding Facebook Friends..51
Chapter 5: Privacy and Safety on Facebook 67

Part II: Sharing Your Life on Facebook *83*

Chapter 6: Building Out Your Profile..85
Chapter 7: Social Stories 107
Chapter 8: Filling Facebook with Photos, Videos, and Notes..............117
Chapter 9: Keeping Up with Your Friends 141

Part III: Getting Organized *161*

Chapter 10: Creating and Joining Groups on Facebook........................163
Chapter 11: Scheduling Your Life with Facebook..................................183
Chapter 12: Creating a Page for Your Business 197

Part IV: Delving Further into Facebook *231*

Chapter 13: Facebook and the Web..233
Chapter 14: Facebook on the Go...259
Chapter 15: A Different Kind of Advertising..275

Part V: The Part of Tens *291*

Chapter 16: Ten Great Third-Party Applications....................................293
Chapter 17: Ten Ways Facebook Uniquely Impacts Lives 297
Chapter 18: Ten Questions That Leah and Carolyn Get a Lot................305
Chapter 19: Ten True Facebook Tales 313

Index *319*

Table of Contents

Introduction *1*

About Facebook For Dummies..1
Foolish Assumptions...2
Conventions Used in This Book...2
What You Don't Have to Read...3
How This Book Is Organized 3
    Part I: Getting Started with Facebook 3
    Part II: Sharing Your Life on Facebook....................4
    Part III: Getting Organized...............................4
    Part IV: Delving Further into Facebook....................4
    Part V: The Part of Tens..................................4
Icons Used in This Book 5
Where to Go from Here..5

Part 1: Getting Started with Facebook *7*

Chapter 1: The Many Faces of Facebook **9**

Figuring Out What Facebook Is Exactly 10
Discovering What You Can Do on Facebook..................................11
    Establish a Profile 11
    Connect with friends 13
    Communicate with Facebook friends........................13
    Share your words...14
    Share your pictures......................................14
    Plan events, join groups.................................15
    Facebook and the Web.....................................15
    Promote your business 16
Keeping in Mind What You Can't Do on Facebook...........................17
    You can't lie..17
    You can't be twelve 18
    You can't troll..18
    You can't upload illegal content 18
Realizing How Facebook Is Different from Other Social Sites..............19
Who Is on Facebook..19
    Students of the 'Book 21
    The School of Life 23
    Putting Facebook to work at work.........................24
    Facebook is all grown up 24
    Le Facebook International 28

Chapter 2: Adding Your Own Face to Facebook 29

Signing Up for Facebook 29
Making Facebook Revolve Around You 32
    Current city 32
    Networks 32
Setting Up Your Profile 34
    The Information Box 36
    Education and work history 36
    Profile picture 36
Trust Me: Getting Verified 37

Chapter 3: Finding Your Way Around Facebook 41

Checking Out the Blue Bar on Top 41
Discovering the Home Page 44
    News Feed 45
    Getting published 45
    Down the left 46
    Accessing applications 47
    Chat 48
    Right column, what's up? 48
    Lowest links 49

Chapter 4: Finding Facebook Friends 51

What Is a Facebook Friend? 52
    A reflection of reality 52
    A contact 52
    A privacy implication 53
    A News Feed implication 53
    A real-time implication 53
Discovering the Facebook Friend Philosophy 54
    Choose your friends wisely 54
    It's quality, not quantity 54
Finding Your Friends on Facebook 55
    If only real life had a Friend Finder 55
    Find what you're looking for: Search 61
Keeping Track: Friend List Management 64
    Creating and applying Friend Lists 64
    Spring friend–cleaning 66

Chapter 5: Privacy and Safety on Facebook 67

Seeing the Win-Win of Privacy 68
Know Your Audience 68
    Custom-made privacy 70
Know Your Privacy Options 71
    Basic Directory 72
    Sharing on Facebook 74
    Applications and Web sites 75

Block lists..76

The Application Privacy page 78

Taking Personal Responsibility for Safety.....................79

Remembering That It Takes a Village to Raise a Facebook....................80

Peeking Behind the Scenes...81

Protecting minors 81

Preventing spam and viruses 82

Part II: Sharing Your Life on Facebook........................... 83

Chapter 6: Building Out Your Profile.........................85

"Wall" You Need Is Love..86

Understanding the Publisher 87

Getting the Lowdown on Info.......................................92

Back to basics...93

Getting personal...93

Getting in touch..94

Education and work...94

Hello, Photos 94

Thinking Inside the Boxes 95

Profile picture, Action links, and Bio box 96

The Friends box 97

Application boxes 98

Profile-Building Strategies 99

Building a Profile for yourself................................99

Building a Profile for promotion 100

Sharing yourself with family, friends, and the world 101

Choosing Who Can See What 102

Know your options 102

Your Profile is in the eye of the beholder.............103

Contact information 104

Your birthday...104

Chapter 7: Social Stories 107

Going to the Wall..107

Everything but the Kitchen Sink...............................110

Just give me the Highlights................................112

Searching the World Over 113

Chapter 8: Filling Facebook with Photos, Videos, and Notes 117

Finding the Common Themes in Applications..............118

Photos and Video 118

The Photos Dashboard 119

Uploading Photos and Video..120
    Uploading photos...121
    Uploading video 123
    Recording video...125
Editing and Tagging Photos and Videos...126
    Editing and tagging photos..127
    Editing and tagging videos..130
Viewing Photos and Videos of You 131
Looking at the Profile Picture Album 132
Discovering Privacy 132
    Album and Video privacy...132
    Photos and Videos of You privacy......................................133
Notes 134
    Writing a note...135
    Formatting a Note...136
    Adding photos to a note 137
    Tagging friends in your note 138
    Importing a blog into Notes...138
    Reading, liking, and commenting
      on your friends' notes 139

Chapter 9: Keeping Up with Your Friends **141**

Just between You and Me..142
    Messages...142
    Sharing is caring..149
    Chat...152
    Anatomy of Chat 153
    Poke 155
    Requests..156
    Notifications 156
Public Displays of Affection: Comments, Publisher, and the Wall........158
    The writing's on the Wall..158
    Care to comment?..160
    Broader audience...160

Part III: Getting Organized **161**

Chapter 10: Creating and Joining Groups on Facebook **163**

Getting Going with Groups 163
    Joining a Group 164
    Anatomy of a Group...165
    Adding your two cents (or more)...169
Finding the Group for You..169
    Searching Groups...170
    Narrowing your search 170
    Checking out popular Groups..171
    Reporting offensive Groups...171

Creating Your Own Groups 172
    Step 1: Group Info 173
    Step 2: Customize.. 175
    Managing your Group 177

Chapter 11: Scheduling Your Life with Facebook 183

Getting Going with Events 183
    Anatomy of an Event 185
    Going to the after party.. 187
Finding the Event for You.. 188
    Searching Events.. 188
    Checking out popular Events 189
Creating Your Own Events 189
    Big Events 189
    Quick Events 192
    Managing your Event 194

Chapter 12: Creating a Page for Your Business 197

Pages and You... 198
    Anatomy of an Official Fan Page 198
    Community Pages 199
    Connecting and interacting with Pages 200
Why Create a Facebook Page? 201
    Pages versus Profiles versus Groups 203
    Who should create a Facebook Page?............................... 205
    Who shouldn't build a Facebook Page? 205
    Living In the Gray Netherworld between Pages and Profiles....... 206
Creating and Managing a Facebook Page 207
    Creating a Page for your business 207
    Making your Page yours.. 210
    Promoting your Page.. 222
    Engaging your fans.. 223
Know-It-All 226

Part IV: Delving Further into Facebook 231

Chapter 13: Facebook and the Web 233

Understanding What Facebook Platform Is............................. 234
Applications That Live on Facebook.. 235
    Figuring out why to use applications inside Facebook................ 236
    Getting started: Request for Permission, sir 236
    Now what? Using applications 239
    Using Facebook outside of Facebook................................ 243
    Login.. 243
    Plugin Play 245
    Instant Personalization 249

Discovering Other Applications 250
    Applications for your business 250
    Applications for your desktop 250
    Applications for your phone 250
Finding Your New Favorite Application..251
    The Applications dashboard 251
    The Games dashboard 252
    Signs of a trustworthy application 253
Managing Your Applications...253
    The Application Settings page 254
    The Application Privacy page 256
    Controlling what you see from friends.................................257

Chapter 14: Facebook on the Go **259**

Is That Facebook Mobile Web in Your Pocket . . . ?...................260
    Getting started 260
    Mobile uploads..261
    Mobile texts 262
    What's all the buzz about?...265
Using Facebook Mobile Web..266
    Facebook Mobile for the touch screen 272
    Touch screen layout..273

Chapter 15: A Different Kind of Advertising **275**

Realizing How Advertising Has Improved.......................................275
Defining Social Ads...277
    Social actions...277
    Social ads plus social actions rules......................................278
    Who uses social ads?..279
Creating a Social Ad...279
    Getting started 279
    Designing your ad 280
    Targeting your ad 281
    Figuring out campaigns and pricing.....................................284
    Reviewing your ad 286
Managing Your Social Ads...287
Spam Is Not Delicious 289

Part V: The Part of Tens... **291**

Chapter 16: Ten Great Third-Party Applications **293**

Typing Maniac...293
Marketplace...294
Music, by iLike 294
Groupcard 294
Digg...295
Graffiti 295

Carpool by Zimride 295
Visual Bookshelf 296
Lady Gaga 296
Restaurant City 296

Chapter 17: Ten Ways Facebook Uniquely Impacts Lives 297

Keeping in Touch with Summer Friends 297
Preparing to Head Off to School 298
Going on Not-So-Blind Dates 298
Meeting People in Your New City or Town 299
Reconnecting with Old Friends.. 299
Keeping Up with the 'rents 300
Keeping Up with the Kids 300
Facebooking for Food (or Jobs) 301
Goin' to the Chapel 302
Hey, Facebook Me! 303

Chapter 18: Ten Questions That Leah and Carolyn Get a Lot 305

Is My Computer Infected with a Virus?.............................. 305
Do People Know When I Look at Their Profiles? 306
I Have a Problem with My Account — Can You Help Me? ... 307
What Do I Do with Friend Requests I Don't Want to Accept? 308
What's the Difference between Facebook,
      MySpace, Twitter, and LinkedIn?................................. 309
I Keep Getting Invites for Those App Thingies —
      Should I Accept Them?... 310
How Do I Convince My Friends to Join Facebook?.............. 310
What if I Don't Want Everyone Knowing My Business? 311
I Heard Facebook Owns Everything I Put on its Site — True? 311
Does Facebook Have a Feature That Lets Me
      Lock Myself Out for a Few Hours? 312

Chapter 19: Ten True Facebook Tales 313

I'm Kelly — I'm Kelly, Too 313
One Million Voices.. 314
Facing Autism... 314
Bringing Home Baby.. 315
Twenty-Year Reunion... 315
Activism Like an Egyptian 315
Kids with Compassion 316
Virtual Support Network.. 317
From a Skinny Kid to President 317

Index 319

Introduction

*F*acebook connects you with the people you know and care about. It enables you to communicate, stay up-to-date, and keep in touch with friends and family anywhere. It facilitates your relationships online to help enhance them in person. Specifically, Facebook connects you with the *people* you know around *content* that is important to you. Whether you're the type to take photos or look at them, or write about your life, or read about your friends' lives, Facebook is designed to enable you to succeed. Maybe you like to share Web sites and news, play games, plan events, organize groups of people, or promote your business. Whatever you prefer, Facebook has you covered.

Facebook offers you control. Communication and information sharing are powerful only when you can do what you want within your comfort zone. Nearly every piece of information and means of connecting on Facebook comes with full privacy controls, allowing you to share and communicate exactly how — and with whom — you desire.

Facebook welcomes everyone: students and professionals; grandchildren (as long as they're at least age 13), parents, and grandparents; busy people; socialites; celebrities; distant friends; and roommates. No matter who you are, using Facebook can add value to your life. Results are typical.

About Facebook For Dummies

Part I of this book teaches you all the basics to get you up and running on Facebook. This information is more than enough for you to discover Facebook's value. Part II and Part III explore all the powerful ways of sharing all kinds of information with the people you care about. Part IV does a deep dive into some of the more advanced ways of using the site that can be of great additional value, depending on your needs. Finally, Part V explores the creative, diverse, touching, and even frustrating ways people have welcomed Facebook into their lives.

Here are some of the things you can do with this book:

✔ **Find out how to represent yourself online in a way that's specific to each member of your online audience.** Friends may see you one way, family another way, co-workers another, and friends of friends yet another (or not at all).

✔ **Connect and communicate with people you know.** Whether you're seeking close friends or long-lost ones, family members, business contacts, teammates, businesses, and celebrities, Facebook keeps you connected. Never say, "Goodbye" again . . . unless you want to.

✔ **Discover how a rich toolset online can help enhance your relationships offline.** Event and group organizational tools, photo-sharing, and direct and passive communication capabilities all enable you to maintain an active social life in the real world.

✔ **Bring your connections off Facebook and on to the rest of the Web.** Through Facebook Platform and Connect, you see how many services you already use can be made more powerful by using them in conjunction with your Facebook friends.

✔ **Bring your business to the consumers who can bring you success.** Productive audience engagement coupled with deeply targeted advertising can help you ensure that your message is heard.

Foolish Assumptions

In this book, we make the following assumptions:

✔ You're at least 13 years of age.

✔ You have some access to the Internet and an e-mail address.

✔ There are people in your life with whom you communicate.

✔ You can read the language in which this sentence is printed.

Conventions Used in This Book

In this book, we stick to a few conventions to help with readability. Whenever you have to type text, we show it in **bold**, so it's easy to see. Monofont text denotes an e-mail address or Web site URL. When you see an *italicized* word, look for its nearby definition. Facebook pages and features — such as the Friends box or the Privacy Overview page — are called out with capital letters. Numbered lists guide you through tasks that must be completed in order from top to bottom; bulleted lists can be read in any order you like (from top to bottom or bottom to top).

Finally, we, the authors, often state our opinions throughout this book. Though we have worked or do work for Facebook, the opinions expressed here represent only our perspective, and not that of Facebook. We are avid

Facebook users and have been since before we joined the company. While writing this book, we took off our "employee hats" and put on our "user hats" to allow us to serve as reliable tour guides and to share objectively our passion for the site.

What You Don't Have to Read

This book is written with the new Facebook user in mind. Some information pertains to readers looking to use Facebook to launch or expand a business. If you want to get on Facebook primarily to keep in touch with family and friends, feel free to skip these sections. Sprinkled throughout the book, sidebars cover many bits of extra information; these are simply added points of interest that can be skipped without detriment to your Facebook experience.

How This Book Is Organized

Facebook For Dummies, 3rd Edition, is split into five parts. You don't have to read it sequentially, and you don't even have to read all the sections in any particular chapter. We explain the most generalized functionality — that which applies to just about everyone — up front. The first chapter of each part gives you an overview of the application and functionality covered in that particular part, along with a description of the likely audience for that part. If you're unsure whether a part of this book pertains to you, try reading its first chapter; if you're unsure about a particular chapter, try reading its introduction to decide.

Topics in this book are covered mostly in the order in which most people use each particular feature. We recommend that you feel comfortable with the material in Part I before you move to Part II, and so on. As the book progresses, we dive deeper into specialized functionality that may be relevant only to certain audiences.

Don't forget about the Table of Contents and the Index; you can use these sections to quickly find the information you need. Here's what you find in each part.

Part 1: Getting Started with Facebook

Chapter 1 introduces you to Facebook and gives you an overview of the most popular and useful ways different types of people incorporate Facebook into their lives. In the few chapters that follow, we help you get your profile set up and orient you to the site so you can always find your way around. Finally, you discover all the privacy tools and safety tips you need to take full control of your own Facebook experience; when each individual feels safe, the entire Facebook community benefits.

Part II: Sharing Your Life on Facebook

When you're familiar with the basics, Part II helps you create an honest, interactive online presence, linking you with all the people you know in the Facebook community, a community that is getting larger every day. We introduce some of the most popular uses of Facebook, including Photos, and explain how you can tailor the system to meet your specific needs.

Part III: Getting Organized

Part III covers how Facebook can help you stay connected and close to the people you know. We explain the differences between private and public communication, and active and passive interactions, all of which fulfill different needs in different social situations. In this part, you discover how people also keep connected and in touch using Facebook Groups and Events.

Part IV: Delving Further into Facebook

Along with providing value for people in their personal lives, Facebook can also help businesses connect with their customers in specialized ways. Whether in the Facebook Platform or in Facebook's spam-free ad system, your business's message can reach consumers in an engaging and uniquely targeted way.

Part V: The Part of Tens

The final section of this book gives fun-to-read and easy-to-digest views on the creative ways people use Facebook. We highlight ten very different applications other companies have integrated into the Facebook environment, including one that helps people raise money for nonprofit causes. Next, you get the answers to ten of the questions these authors hear most often about how to use Facebook. Ten real-world scenarios provide you a perspective on the value of integrating Facebook with your lifestyle. Finally, we share ten truly amazing tales of Facebook.

Icons Used in This Book

What's a *For Dummies* book without icons pointing you in the direction of great information that's sure to help you along your way? In this section, we briefly describe each icon we use in this book.

The Tip icon points out helpful information that is likely to improve your experience.

The Remember icon marks an interesting and useful fact — something that you may want to use later.

The Warning icon highlights lurking danger. With this icon, we're telling you to pay attention and proceed with caution.

Where to Go from Here

Whether you've been using Facebook for years or this is your first time, we recommend you start by reading Chapter 1, which sets the stage for most of what we describe in detail in the rest of this book. After reading the first chapter, you may have a better sense of which topics in this book will be more relevant to you, and you can, therefore, flip right to them. However, we recommend that *everyone* spend some quality time in Chapter 5, which covers privacy on Facebook. Facebook is an online representation of a community, so it's important that each person understand how to operate in that community to ensure a safe, fun, and functional environment for everyone.

If you're new to Facebook and looking to use it to enhance your own personal connections, we recommend reading this book from Part I straight through Part III. If you're *so* new to Facebook that you're not even sure that it's for you, you'll find your answer in Chapter 1. (We'll go ahead and ruin the surprise by telling you now that Facebook *is* for you, whoever you are.)

You may already be quite familiar with Facebook when you pick up this book. But because the site is constantly growing and changing, there is always more to know. Part IV is the section of the book that will keep you ahead of the curve.

No matter which category you fall into, it's time to get started: Let one hand flip the pages of this book, the other drive your computer mouse, and let your mind open up to a revolutionary way to enhance and experience your real-world relationships.

Part I
Getting Started with Facebook

The 5th Wave   By Rich Tennant

"These are the parts of our life that aren't on Facebook."

In this part . . .

So, we've persuaded you to read beyond the Introduction. Go team! (You can't see it, but we're high-fiving right now.) Because you started at the beginning, we assume that you have some pretty basic questions, such as

What is Facebook?

Am I too old for Facebook?

How do I use Facebook effectively?

I know I want to use Facebook, but how do I get started?

These are all great questions for starting a journey into the 'book. In this part, we answer all these and more. We start with the bigger picture of who's using Facebook and how, and then we move into the nitty-gritty of signing up, creating your Profile, and finding a few friends. Additionally, we show you how to navigate around the site and protect your information.

Chapter 1

The Many Faces of Facebook

In This Chapter

▶ Discovering Facebook

▶ Knowing what you can and can't do on Facebook

▶ Finding out how Facebook is different from other social sites

▶ Seeing how different people use Facebook . . . differently

*I*magine trying to get from New York to California via some way other than riding an airplane, or baking a pie (pecan, please) without an oven, or getting to the seventieth floor without riding an elevator. Certainly there are ways to achieve those tasks, but without the right tools, they may take longer, come out less-than-perfect, and *really* make you sweat.

Like an airplane, an oven, or an elevator, Facebook is a tool that can make life's *To-Do*s fun and easy. Facebook enables you to manage, maintain, and enhance your social connections. Think about how you accomplish these tasks:

✔ Getting the phone number of an old friend

✔ Finding out what your friends are up to today

✔ Making a contact in a city you're moving to or at an office where you're applying for a job

✔ Planning an event, tracking the guest list, and updating everyone when the time changes

✔ Garnering support for a cause

✔ Getting recommendations for movies, books, and restaurants

✔ Showing off the pictures from your latest vacation

✔ Telling your friends and family about your recent successes, showing them your photos, or letting them know you're thinking of them

✔ Remembering everyone's birthday

The preceding list is merely a sampling of life's tricky tasks that Facebook can help you accomplish more easily and enjoyably. The list could go on, but we need to leave *some* space in the book to tell you how to solve these problems.

Facebook facilitates and improves all your social relationships — we realize that's a big claim. Almost as big as the claims about the blender that can prepare a seven course meal in six minutes, the pill that can give you the abs of Chuck Norris and the legs of Tina Turner, or the six easy steps that can make you a millionaire. However, Facebook is a little different than these in at least three ways. First, we won't claim it's so easy your Chihuahua can do it. Getting set up and familiar with Facebook does take a little work (which you know or you wouldn't be starting out on this 360-page journey). Second, Facebook costs only three low payments of $0, but if you aren't totally satisfied, you can be fully refunded. Finally, unlike the blender or the pill, Facebook *will* actually change your life, make it better, more fun, easier, and, did we mention . . . more fun?

Figuring Out What Facebook Is Exactly

Think about the people you interacted with throughout the past day. In the morning, you may have gone to get the paper and chatted with the neighbor. You may have asked your kids what time they'd be home and negotiated with your partner about whose turn it is to cook dinner. Perhaps you spent the day interacting with co-workers, taking time out for lunch with a friend who's in town for business. In the evening, you may have shot off an e-mail to an old college roommate, called your mom (it's her birthday after all), and made plans with the gang to get together this weekend. At the end of the day, you unwound in front of your favorite newscaster telling you about the various politicians, athletes, businessmen, and celebrities whose lives may (or may not) interest you. Every day, you interact with so many different people in unique ways. You exchange information: "Did you catch the news this morning?" You enjoy another's company: "Who's up for a good joke?" You enrich lives: "I made you something at school today." Throughout your day, most of the decisions you make and actions you take are thanks to, or on behalf of, someone you know.

That's a one-foot view of the world in which you're the center. Pan the camera back a ways (farther . . . farther . . . even farther), and you see that each person you interact with — family, friends, the newspaper delivery guy, the lunch lady, your favorite musician, and even the people who are writing this book — are at the center of their own realities. So is each person *they* know. The connections between every single person in the world intertwine, interplay, and interlock to form *the social graph*. Bold claim: This living, throbbing, shifting, growing web of human relationships is one of life's most awesome and powerful concepts.

The power of the social graph refers to how information travels quickly and (somewhat) reliably among folks who are connected with one another. Facebook's function is to make the social graph accessible — that is, to help people keep track of and reach the people they know and help individuals leverage the power of the graph by enabling them to communicate and exchange information with anyone or everyone they trust.

Another powerful aspect of the social graph on Facebook is that it builds and maintains itself. Each member helps define his or her place in the graph. When you sign up for Facebook, you start by finding the Profiles of the people you know and establishing your virtual connection to them. As a Facebook user, it's in your best interest to keep your portion of the graph mapped as accurately as possible — form a complete set of connections to the people you know. Facebook can become your single access point for the people you know, so it becomes more useful when you can confidently find exactly who you're looking for. Because of how Facebook is built, you are not the only one responsible for connecting with everyone you know (imagine the longest game of Hide and Seek *ever*). After you make a few connections, mutual friends are automatically made aware of your presence on the site, and they seek *you* out to establish a connection. ***Remember:*** It's also in their best interest to keep their contact list up-to-date.

Discovering What You Can Do on Facebook

Now that you know that Facebook is a means by which you can connect with people who matter to you, your next question may be, "How?" It's a good question — such a good question that we spend almost the rest of this book answering it. But, first, an overview.

Establish a Profile

When you sign up for Facebook, one of the first things you do is establish your *Profile*. A Profile on Facebook is a social résumé — a page about you that you keep up-to-date with all the information you want people to know.

Facebook understands that if you were handing out résumés in the real world, you'd probably give different documents to different people. Your social résumé may have your phone number, your favorite quotes, and pictures from that crazy night in you-know-where with you-know-who. Your résumé for a potential employer would probably share your education and employment history. Your résumé for your family may include your personal address as well as show off your recent vacation photos and news about your life's changes.

You show different slices of your life and personality to different people, and a Facebook Profile, shown in Figure 1-1, allows you (no, *encourages* you) to do the same. To this end, your Profile is set up with all kinds of privacy controls to specify *who* you want to see *which* information. Many people find great value in adding to their Profile just about every piece of information they can and then unveiling each particular piece cautiously. The safest rule here is to share on your Profile any piece of information you'd share with someone in real life. The corollary applies, too: Don't share on your Profile any information that you wouldn't share with someone in real life. We provide more detail about the Profile in Chapter 2. For now, think of it like a personal Web page with privacy controls for particular pieces of information. This page accurately reflects you so that you hand the right social résumé to the right person.

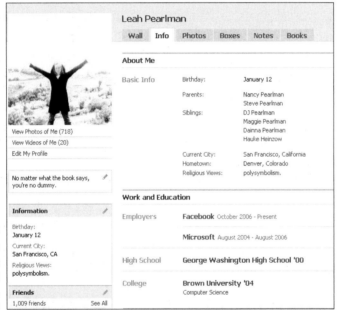

Figure 1-1:
Leah's
Facebook
Profile.

The motivations for establishing a Profile on Facebook are twofold. First, a Profile helps the people who know you in real life find and connect with you on Facebook. Each individual is actively (or actively trying) to keep track of the people she knows. If your name is something relatively common, such as James Brown or Maria Gonzales, it's difficult for people to find you without additional identifiers. Information about you, such as your hometown, your education history, or your photos, helps people find the right James or Maria.

The second (and way cooler) reason to establish an accurate Profile is the work it saves you. Keeping your Profile detailed and relevant means that your friends and family can always get the latest information about where you live, who you know, and what you're up to. You no longer have to read your phone number to someone while he fumbles to find a pen. Just tell him, "It's on Facebook." If a cousin wants to send you a birthday present, he doesn't have to ruin the surprise by asking you for your address. When your Profile is up-to-date, conversations that used to start with the open-ended, "How have you been?" can skip straight to the good stuff: "I saw your pictures from Hawaii last week. *Please* tell me how you ended up wearing those coconuts."

Connect with friends

After you join Facebook, start seeing its value by tracking down some people you know. Facebook offers the following tools to help you:

- ✔ **Facebook Friend Finder:** Allows you to scan the e-mail addresses in your e-mail address book to find whether those people are already on Facebook. Selectively choose among those with whom you'd like to connect.

- ✔ **Suggestions:** Will show you the names and pictures of people you likely know or celebrities whose news you'd like to follow. These people are selected for you based on various signals like where you live or work or how many friends you have in common.

- ✔ **Search:** Helps you find the people who are most likely already using Facebook.

After you establish a few connections, use those connections to find other people you know by searching through their connections for familiar names. We explain how to find people you know on Facebook in Chapter 4.

Communicate with Facebook friends

As Facebook grows, it becomes more likely that anyone with whom you're trying to communicate can be reached. These days it's a fairly safe assumption that you'll be able to find that person you just met at a dinner party, an old professor from college, or the childhood friend you've been meaning to catch up with. Digging up a person's contact information could require calls to mutual friends, a trip to the white pages (provided you know enough about that person to identify the right contact information), or an e-mail sent to a potentially outdated e-mail address. You may have different methods of reaching people depending on how you met the person, or what limited information you have about him or her.

Facebook streamlines finding and contacting people in a reliable forum. If the person you're reaching out to is active on Facebook, no matter where she lives or how many times she's changed her e-mail address, you can reach one another.

Share your words

You have something to say. We can just tell by the look on your face. Maybe you're proud of the home team, maybe you're excited for Friday, or maybe you can't believe what you saw on the way to work this morning. All day long, things are happening to all of us that make us just want to turn to our friends and say, "You know what? . . . That's what." Facebook gives you the stage and an eager audience. In Chapter 6, we explain how you can make short or long posts about the things happening around you, and how they're distributed to your friends in an easy, nonintrusive way.

Share your pictures

Since the invention of the modern-day camera, people have been all too eager to yell, "Cheese!" Photographs can make great tour guides on trips down memory lane, but only if we actually remember to develop, upload, or scrapbook them. Many memories fade away when the smiling faces are stuffed into an old shoe box, remain on undeveloped rolls of film, or are forgotten in some folder on a hard drive.

Facebook offers three great incentives for uploading, organizing, and editing your photos:

- ✔ **Facebook provides one easy-to-access location for all your photos.** Directing any interested person to your Facebook Profile is easier than e-mailing pictures individually, sending a complicated link to a photo site, or waiting until the family reunion to show off the my-how-the-kids-have-grown pics.

- ✔ **Every photo you upload can be linked to the Profiles of the people in the photo.** For example, you upload pictures of you and your sister and link them to her Profile. Whenever someone visits her Profile, he sees those pictures; he doesn't even have to know you. This is great because it introduces a longevity to photos that they've never had before. As long as people are visiting your sister's Profile, they can see those pictures. Photo albums no longer have to be something people look at right after the event, and maybe then again years later.

- ✔ **Facebook gives you the power to control exactly who has access to your photos.** Every time you upload a photo or create a new photo album on Facebook, you can decide whether you want everyone on

Facebook to see it, just your friends, or even just a subset of your friends based on your comfort level. You may choose to show your wedding photos to all your friends, but perhaps only some friends see the honeymoon. This control enables you to tailor your audience to those friends who might be most interested. All your friends might enjoy your baby photos, but maybe only your co-workers will care about photos from the recent company party.

Plan events, join groups

Just about anything you do with other people is easier on Facebook . . . except cuddling. Facebook isn't meant to be a replacement for face time; it's meant to facilitate interactions when face time isn't possible or to facilitate the planning of face time. Two of the greatest tools for this are Facebook Events and Facebook Groups.

Groups are basically Web pages people can subscribe to, or *join.* One group may be intimate, such as five best friends who plan several activities together. Another group could be practical, for example, PTA Members of Denver Schools. Some groups garner support, such as AIDS Awareness. Others exist for solidarity; for example, the When I Was Your Age, Pluto Was a Planet Group allows people to come together in the name of some common interest or goal. Depending on the particular group's settings, members may upload photos or videos, invite other people to the group, receive messages, and check on news and updates.

Events are similar to groups, with the addition of being time-based. Rather than joining, users RSVP to events, which allows the event organizers to plan accordingly and allows attendees to receive event reminders. Facebook Events are often used for something as small as a lunch date or something as big as a march on Washington, D.C. Sometimes events are notional rather than physical. For example, someone could create an event for Ride Your Bike to Work Day and hope the invitation spreads far and wide (through friends and friends of friends) to promote awareness. At Facebook headquarters, Events are used to plan company meetings, happy hours, ski trips, and more. Read more about Facebook Groups and Facebook Events in Chapter 10.

Facebook and the Web

Facebook Photos, Groups, and Events are only a small sampling of how you can use Facebook to connect with the people you know. In Chapter 13, we explain in detail Facebook and the Web. In short, Facebook is a service that helps you maintain connections with your friends, but any company can build the tools — Web sites, or *applications* — that allow sharing. Photos, Groups, and Events are tools that are built on top of the Facebook Platform; they are the means by which people can share information through their social connections.

Examples of Web sites and applications that have been built by other companies include tools to help you edit your photos, create slideshows, play games with friends across the globe, divvy bills among people who live or hang out together, and exchange information about good movies, music, books, and restaurants. After you get a little more comfortable with the Facebook basics, you can try some of the thousands of applications and Web sites that allow you to interact with your Facebook friends through their services.

Promote your business

Say, you have something to sell — that fancy blender, maybe. How do you get people's attention? You don't go to a deserted parking lot and yell, "Hey! Buy my blender!" do you? Of course not. You go to where the people are, and the people are on Facebook. Although anybody can (and should) use Facebook to connect with their friends and family, more and more people are using it to connect with their patrons, fans, or supporters. In addition to their personal Profiles, people create additional Profiles to promote their bands, businesses, brands, products, services, or themselves, in the case of celebrities or politicians. These special kinds of profiles on Facebook are called Pages with a capital P. Pages are similar to user Profiles in that they're a page on Facebook meant to

✔ Represent a specific real-world entity

✔ Consist of truthful, necessary information required to engage with that entity

Pages differ from user Profiles in that the relationships are essentially one way. We may have a relationship to Starbucks, but Starbucks doesn't really have a specific relationship with us, which leads to a number of differences in the functionality of Pages. We discuss the details of those differences and explain the benefits of promoting your business on Facebook in Chapter 15.

Chapter 15 discusses how you advertise your business without, or in addition to, establishing a Page on Facebook. Because Facebook users enter detailed information about themselves (and their actions on Facebook reveal even more about the kinds of people they are), Facebook can offer a compelling advertising platform by allowing advertisers to reach a targeted audience based on who people are and what they like.

Facebook also offers another kind of targeting, which is *social targeting*. For many kinds of commercial goods, we're often more likely to buy something if we know people who've already had a positive experience with the particular good or the company selling it. When Facebook shows someone an ad, it lets that person know whether any of their friends had an experience with that product, service, or business. In fact, if that person has a friend who interacted with an ad, that person is more likely to see that same ad than someone with friends who haven't interacted with that ad. This type of targeted advertising is a win-win for business owners and consumers because business owners don't have to waste money or dilute their message on people who don't care about their product, and users are more likely to see ads for products that actually interest them — or, at the very least, tell them something about their friends' consumer habits.

Keeping in Mind What You Can't Do on Facebook

Facebook is meant to represent real people and real associations; it's also meant to be safe. Many of the rules of participation on Facebook exist to uphold those two goals.

Note: There are things you can't do on Facebook other than what we list here. For example, you can't message multiple people unless you're friends with all of them; you can't join the school network of a school you didn't attend (or a workplace network of a company you don't work for); and you can't spin straw into gold. These rules may change how you use Facebook, but probably won't change *whether* you use it. We separate the four rules in this section because, if any are a problem for you, you probably won't get to the rest of the book.

You can't lie

Okay, you can, but you shouldn't, especially not about your basic information. Lying about your identity is a violation of the Facebook Terms of Use and grounds for Profile deactivation. In other words, thank you, bye-bye. Although many people try, Facebook doesn't let anyone sign up with an obviously fake name like Marilyn Manson or Fakey McFakerson. Those who do make it past the name checks will likely find their account tracked down and deactivated.

Some fake accounts survive on Facebook undetected for a very long time because the Facebook user operations team goes after people who are breaking serious and safety-compromising offenses first. So, if you're considering setting up a fake Profile to test our claim, you're probably better off just going outside to play. Take a Frisbee.

You can't be twelve

Or younger. Seriously. Facebook takes very seriously the U.S. law that prohibits minors under the age of 13 from creating an online Profile for themselves. This rule is in place for the safety of minors, and it's a particular safety rule that Facebook takes extremely seriously. If you or someone you know on Facebook is under 13, deactivate (or make them deactivate) the account now. If you're reported to the Facebook user operations team, your account is deleted instantly, and Facebook (and Carolyn and Leah as well) will be very unhappy. Facebook is vigilant about keeping minors off the site, so if you're under 13, be aware that the people you hang out with won't be on Facebook either. If you happen to be older than 13 and looking for people under 13, check out the next section for what else you can't do.

You can't troll

We can't stress this enough, and putting it in bold definitely isn't enough stress. Maybe we should add underline, italic, and all caps. Let's try.

YOU CAN'T TROLL.

Facebook is about real people and real connections. It's one thing to message a mutual friend or the occasional stranger whose Profile implies being open to meeting new people if the two of you have matching interests. However, the moment the people you contact have a problem with you sending unsolicited messages, your account is flagged; if the behavior continues, your account is deactivated.

Imagine going to a coffee shop and introducing yourself to each and every person while they try to mind their cup of joe. That is how we view the sending of unsolicited messages on Facebook, and the user operations team will make like an angry barista and kick you to the coffee shop curb.

You can't upload illegal content

Respecting United States law is something Facebook has to do regardless of its own position on pornography (where minors can see it), copyrighted material, hate speech, depictions of crimes, and other offensive content.

However, doing so is also in line with Facebook's value of being a safe, happy place for all people (older than the age of 12). Don't confuse this with censorship; Facebook is all about freedom of speech and self-expression, but the moment that compromises anyone's safety or breaks any law, disciplinary action is taken.

Realizing How Facebook Is Different from Other Social Sites

Several social sites besides Facebook try to help people connect. Some of the most popular sites are Twitter, MySpace, Friendster, Orkut, LinkedIn, Windows Live Spaces, Bebo, Meebo, Match.com, and QQ.

In some cases, these sites have slightly different goals than Facebook. LinkedIn, for example, is a tool for connecting with people specifically for career networking. MySpace initially started out as a way for small, local bands to gain popularity outside of the politically-complicated music industry by creating a space for people to connect with others who had similar tastes in music. Match.com is a social networking site specifically geared toward people looking to date. Alternatively, other sites have the same goals as Facebook; they just have different strategies. MySpace gives users complete customization over the look and feel of their Profile, whereas Facebook maintains a pretty consistent design and expects users to differentiate their Profiles by uploading unique content. On the other extreme, Twitter allows its members to share only very short bits of text to achieve super-simple and consistent information sharing, whereas Facebook allows more flexibility with respect to sharing photos, videos, and more. That's not to say one model is better than another; different models may appeal to different people.

Who Is on Facebook

Originally, Facebook was created as a way for students at a particular college or university to find and connect with each another. In fact, when Facebook launched, only those people with a verified college e-mail address were permitted to sign up.

After the success of the university-only model, Facebook opened its doors to high school students in the United States as well. High school students don't have e-mail addresses to verify which high school they attend; therefore, Facebook has a fairly complicated system that relies on students verifying one another before gaining access to a particular high school network.

Facebook took off in high schools with such momentum that Facebook next opened its doors to workplace networks. Workplace networks followed the same model as the college networks — in order to join, you had to sign up with a verified e-mail address, in this case, from a particular corporation. Therefore, workplace networks existed only for the companies big enough to offer its employees e-mail addresses, such as Microsoft, Apple, Amazon, and others.

Finally, in the fall of 2004, rather than opening any more doors, Facebook just knocked down its walls. Today, anyone with any e-mail address is welcome to join the Facebook party.

People can still limit the visibility of any part of their Profiles, or they can open up parts of their Profiles to anyone. Now that Facebook is used by more than 500 million people, the name of the game is control and choice. You can share as much or as little with as many or as few people as you so desire. Put under lock and key the parts of your Profile you *don't* want to share with everyone. Chapter 5 goes into much greater detail on how to protect yourself and your information.

Here are two reasons Facebook made the leap from *verified networks* (those in which you must offer some kind of proof of identity, such as an e-mail address, in order to join) to enabling people to share with everyone:

- **Facebook was offering a tremendous amount of utility to the people who had access to it.** Before opening to the general public, about 85 percent of registered users were logging in at least once per month, and 75 percent of those people were logging in daily. Numbers like that proved Facebook creators were onto something special and that other people — in addition to students and employees of large corporations — could gain value from access to Facebook.

- **Facebook is better when lots of different people are active on Facebook.** This reason for allowing any and everyone on Facebook is a little less obvious, so we offer this example as an explanation:

   A University of Colorado alumnus wants to throw himself a birthday party. At college, he used Facebook to plan his events and manage his guest lists, but now some of his friends are older and were out of college before Facebook became popular. Creating the event on Facebook could lead to an incomplete guest list. If he chooses not to use Facebook, he may end up using a less efficient means of communicating, such as e-mail, which requires that he dig up the e-mail address of everyone he wants to invite and then manage all the RSVPs as they flood his inbox. He may also decide that it's not worth the hassle and invite only people who are on Facebook. Facebook actually allows him to create an event and generate special invites to those not on the site, but he still has to locate those friend's e-mail addresses and enter them on Facebook.

Facebook has great tools for organizing people, information, and communication. Their utility, however, depends on you being able to reach your friends with them. The more contacts you have on Facebook, the more useful each of these tools becomes.

Significant to the utility of the social graph is its reliability. Having a single source to find and interact with friends, mutual acquaintances, family, or others with shared interests and beliefs would be one of the greatest solutions to many of life's most complicated tasks. Managing our relationships with everyone we know or want to know is the service Facebook is trying to provide. To anyone for whom Facebook has become the primary source for information and interaction, the moment someone in particular isn't represented on Facebook, the whole service becomes less powerful because its reliability for finding whomever you're looking for is reduced. To that end, welcoming everyone onto Facebook was a way to make the service more valuable to those already using it.

A majority of Facebook users are not, nor have ever been, part of a school network, and most of Facebook's growth is in demographics other than high school or college. In the following sections, we talk about how people in different demographics use Facebook. Note that these cases aren't exclusive to the particular category they're listed under; people in workplace networks may use many of the same features and functionality as students, and international users clearly span all three of the demographics. These sections simply emphasize the general trends in particular demographics and highlight some of the differences among them.

Students of the 'Book

Students live in a somewhat unique environment in that the shared affiliation to the same school implies a level of trust. This trust allows students to create Profiles for themselves, and if they choose, share their information only with other students at their school (and people they manually verify). Because of the close quarters and accountability of their peers, students are perhaps the group most open about the information they exchange on Facebook. As long as students are safe about the information they choose to share (see Chapter 5), this abundance of information flow is actually a very good thing that can make their lives and relationships extremely rich.

Students use Facebook for all kinds of fun and practical things:

- ✓ **Getting information:** Students can easily connect with others who live in their dorm or take the same classes. Connecting with peers can be great for (approved) collaboration on class work, finding out when homework is due, or borrowing a book for research.

✔ **Planning events:** A big source of student engagement is event planning. Say, Tau Phi Beta wants to plan an event. The fraternity's officers can create the Event page on Facebook, and with a few clicks of a few buttons, invite everyone they want to. They can specify whether the invite should go only to those initially invited — say, a Tau Phi Beta brothers–only dinner — or whether anyone can be invited (a must for a giant frat party — er, *fundraiser*). This is just one example, but events are rampant across universities. Every club, dorm room, sports team, and group of friends organizes their events on Facebook.

✔ **Tagging photos:** The Photos feature is one of the most popular on Facebook. Students regularly engage in a lot of memorable activities, such as dances, games, and rallies. Generally, a large number of students and a nearly-as-large number of cameras attend these events. We hear many students confess that in the time it takes them to hop a shuttle or stumble to their dorm room, someone has already uploaded photos from the event to Facebook. No sooner does a student experience a magical moment than she gets to remember it.

One of the fancy aspects of Facebook Photos is that each photo can be tagged with links to the Profiles of the people in the photo. All the photos a particular person is tagged in are aggregated into one album, so when you look at a person's Profile, you see all the photos he's ever been tagged in. After a big night on campus, students can see all the pictures their friends took or go straight to all the photos of them. Narcissistic maybe, but also human.

✔ **Keeping up with friends from home:** Sometimes college can feel like its own little universe, especially for those who travel far from home to attend. By establishing friend connections with those friends they *don't* see every day, they can more easily stay in touch. When they upload photos from the University Gala, friends from home can send a message to say, "Nice dress!" or "Who's the boy?" An RSVP to an event, such as the National Championship Dinner, informs friends from back home of their friend's recent success. And, even though students often get caught up in the action of campus life, sometimes they'll hear a song or read a passage that reminds them of a friend back home. Rather than digging for the e-mail address or finding time to call, they can just use Facebook to drop their friend a *thinking of you* Wall post, Poke, or message. (Find out more about these options in Chapter 9.)

✔ **Flirting and gossip:** We should've stuck this bullet point first because it's probably the biggest piece of the time-spent-on-Facebook pie. Mmmm, Facebook pie. Throughout this book, you read about messaging, poking, chatting, and gifting, which are all ways that students virtually bat their eyelashes at one another — and avoid doing their homework.

Everyone has the ability on their Profile to inform people who they're looking to meet (women, men, or both) and for what purpose (relationship, dating, friendship, and so on). Those already in a relationship can link to their significant other for the world to see. Provocative *Wall posts* (one friend can write a public message on a friend's *Wall*), intriguing photo uploads, and changing relationship statuses are all sources of juicy gossip without which high school or college just wouldn't be the same.

The School of Life

Chronologically speaking, there's only a small difference between someone nearing the end of their school career (whether that be high school, college, or graduate school) and someone starting life after school. But these two phases share a few other similarities. During school, most people have a set crowd of folks they interact with. They're very familiar with the city or town they live in and the daily routine (class, sports, studying) they've been doing for years. After school, things can change. Many folks move to new cities, start new jobs, and meet new people. Their groups of friends start to disperse (geographically and emotionally), and creating environments for social interaction requires more effort when people cut out lunch time, study hall, or Friday nights at the student center. Because Facebook is all about nurturing relationships, when the nature of people's relationships change, their usage of Facebook changes as well. After school, people find different kinds of utility from their social graph:

✔ **Moving to a new city:** Landing in a new city with all your worldly belongings and an upside-down map can be hugely intimidating. Having some open arms or at least numbers to call when you arrive can greatly ease the transition. Although you may already know some people who live in your new city, Facebook can help connect with all the old friends and acquaintances you either forgot live there or have moved there since you last heard from them.

   When Leah first moved to the Bay area, she filtered her Friend List to everyone in the San Francisco and Silicon Valley networks. The final list probably contained four times as many people as she remembered living in the area. She sent messages announcing her imminent arrival and then connected with her various contacts to get settled into an apartment, meet other people, and find doctors, bike routes, Frisbee leagues, and restaurants. Even if you don't have friends or acquaintances in your new city, someone you know probably does. Your friends can give you names of people to look up when you arrive — use Facebook to do that.

✔ **Getting a job:** Recently, more and more people began using Facebook as a tool for managing their careers as well as their social lives. If you're looking at a particular company, find people who already work there to get the inside scoop or to land an interview. If you're thinking about moving into a particular industry, browse your friends by past jobs and interests to find someone to connect with.

✓ **Finding activity partners:** Many folks would agree that it's harder to meet people after they leave school. Facebook is a great tool for meeting new friends with similar interests, activity partners, or even potential love interests. You can browse Profiles of people in your network based on various kinds of information, such as age, political views, and work history. Plenty of online sites offer these kinds of services, but Facebook works particularly well because the connection you make is often based on mutual acquaintances, making them less awkward, better informed, and safer.

Putting Facebook to work at work

Facebook is still finding its footing within the workplace networks. Therefore, it's tricky to generalize how people in workplace networks use Facebook because it really depends on the particular workplace. However, here are some uses we've heard about anecdotally:

✓ Getting to know co-workers and putting names to faces.

✓ Hosting events specific to the company. Facebook uses Events to plan company parties and host happy hours.

✓ Using Groups for people in the company with similar interests or needs, such as athletic endeavors, carpool requirements, or artistic interests.

✓ Having a business presence on Facebook. Advertising on Facebook is one way to use Facebook at work. Additionally, when companies work together, sometimes their employees become fans of one another's businesses on Facebook to show support.

✓ Posting and sharing stories about the company relevant to the business.

Facebook is all grown up

Facebook isn't just for students. Anything you've heard to the contrary is dated information. Like we mention before, the fastest growing group of Facebook users is the group for whom school is a distant memory. Many of these folks find the same value in Facebook as people in other demographics; however, they also use it for some different kinds of interactions.

Keeping in touch with family

These days, families are often spread far and wide across state or country lines. Children go to college, parents travel for work, grandparents move to Florida. These distances make it hard for families to interact in any more significant way than gathering together once per year to share some turkey and pie (pecan, preferably). Facebook offers a place where families can virtually meet and interact. Parents can upload photos of the kids for everyone to see, grandparents can write notes about what everyone is up to, and college students can gather support for a cause, plan a graduation party, or show off their class schedule — great information for family members who may have a hard time extracting the information in other ways.

We often hear parents and older family members say they feel being on Facebook may infringe on their kid's social life. If you fit this description, we have a few comments for you:

- ✔ **You may be right that your kids want you nowhere near their social lives.** If that's the case, and you respect that, don't connect with them on Facebook. Exist within your social graph on Facebook, and let them exist within theirs — you never have to interact with one another whatsoever. Not joining Facebook because your kids are using it is like not eating ice cream because your kids eat ice cream. Sure, you *can* go for ice cream together (or be connected on Facebook), but you certainly don't have to. Don't deprive yourself of the sweet creamy deliciousness just because your kid may be offended that you have similar taste in desserts.

- ✔ **You may be wrong that your kids don't want you on Facebook.** Depending on your kids' age and personality, they may actually prefer that you join Facebook. Some kids, especially the college-aged or twenty-somethings, are very busy and active. It can be hard for them to remember to call home, let alone call the grandparents, aunts, and uncles. Even when they do, they may leave out interesting information about their lives simply because they forget (this hypothetical is coming from personal experience). These relationships can be much stronger when everyone is on Facebook. Relatives can always see the latest news or photos even when they've been out of touch for some time; they can also connect in a lightweight way in between longer phone conversations. (See Chapter 9 on communicating through Facebook.)

- ✔ **Kids are *really* good at using Facebook.** If you are connected to your children on Facebook and they want to upload something they don't want you to see, they know exactly which privacy controls to put in place so that you don't see it. It may be easy for them to connect with you and share only the information they want to and hide the information they (and you) may be better off not sharing. Whether this concern is a relevant one to you, we recommend sitting down with your kids (sometime after the birds-and-bees conversation but before the how-to-pay taxes conversation) and figuring out how to happily cohabitate on Facebook.

Facebook reunion

Thanks to life's curve balls, whoever your friends are at any given time may not be the people in your life at another. People you consider to be most important in your life fade over the years so that even trying to recall a last name causes you pause. The primary reason for this lapse is a legitimate one: There are only so many hours in a day. While we make new, close friends, others drift away because it's impossible to maintain many intense relationships. Facebook is an extremely powerful tool; however, it hasn't yet found a way to extend the number of hours in a day, so it can't exactly fix the problem of growing apart. Facebook can, however, lessen the finality and inevitability of the distance.

Assuming Facebook achieves the longevity and reach it's striving for, those who have started using Facebook at a young age (13 is the minimum) will, at an old age, actually have a lead on every single person they've ever been friends with. This extremely powerful concept actually alters how people keep and maintain human relationships. Thirty years after you last speak to someone, you may have a funny memory, something important to share, or just genuine curiosity about that person's whereabouts. If you keep her on your Facebook Friend List, it doesn't matter how many times you both move, change your phone numbers, or get married and change your name, you can still get in touch with each another. If that concept scares you, Facebook also has the tools to explicitly sever connections with people you'd rather didn't find you.

Because Facebook is less than seven years old (and because you're reading this book), you probably don't have your entire social history mapped out. Some may find it a daunting task to create connections with everyone they've ever known, which we don't recommend. Instead, build your graph as you need to or as opportunity presents. Perhaps you want to upload a photo taken from your high school graduation to tag various classmates. Search for them on Facebook, form the friend connection, and then tag them. Maybe you're thinking about opening a restaurant, and you'd like to contact a friend from college who was headed into the restaurant business after graduation. Perhaps you never told your true feelings to the one who got away — your unicorn. For all these reasons, you may find your cursor in the Facebook Search box.

Frequently, we receive reports from adopted children who connect with their biological parents, or estranged siblings who find each other on Facebook. Carolyn once heard from her sixth-grade bully, who found her on Facebook to apologize for how he terrorized her back then.

Organizing groups

Unlike students, adults don't often have the luxury of participating in lots of events organized by other people. Instead, they organize their book clubs and cooking groups or gather to watch sporting events and have dinner parties. Facebook Groups can add value to all these events. Creating a group on Facebook for your book club makes it easy for someone to update everyone each week about times, dates, locations, who should bring what, and what everyone should read before attending. People can join and leave groups as they see fit, so you never have to worry about notifying those who've moved or are no longer interested in your group.

For one-time gatherings, such as a Super Bowl party, Facebook Events offers a great solution. All you have to do is fill out the guest list and event description — the rest takes care of itself. For the three days prior to the event, everyone receives a reminder on their Facebook Home pages, so they have no excuse for not showing (unless someone invited them to a better party). If you want to ensure your guest list is accurate or that people don't forget, message everyone who RSVP'd (attending or tentative, that is) or who hasn't replied. After the event is over, upload photos or leave funny comments and quotes on the event's Wall. Your Super Bowl party is forever immortalized online — and everyone who RSVP'd has total access.

The birth of the 'Book

In the old days, say, seven or eight years ago, most college freshmen would receive a thinly bound book containing the names and faces of everyone in their matriculating class. These *face books* were useful for matching names to the students seen around campus or for pointing out particular people to friends. There were several problems with these face books. If someone didn't send his picture in, they were incomplete. They were outdated by junior year because many people looked drastically different, and the book didn't reflect the students who had transferred in or who were from any other class. Finally, they had little information about each person.

In February 2004, Mark Zuckerberg, a sophomore at Harvard, launched an online "book" to which people could upload their photos and personal information; a service which solved many of these problems. Within a month, more than half the Harvard undergraduates had created their own Profiles. Zuckerberg was then joined by others, including Dustin Moskovitz

and Chris Hughes, to help expand the site into other schools. Your very own author, Carolyn Abram, was the first non-Harvard student to receive an account. During the summer of the same year, Zuckerberg, Moskovitz, and another partner, Andrew McCollum, moved the company to Palo Alto, California, where the site and the company kept growing. By December 2004, the site had grown to one million college students. Every time Facebook opened to a new demographic — high school, then work users, then everyone — the rate at which people joined the site continued to increase. At the end of 2006, the site had more than 10 million users; 2007 closed out with more than 50 million active users (*active users* are defined as unique accounts that accessed the site in the last 30 days). By the end of 2009, Facebook had reached well over a quarter of a billion users and 1,000 employees. At the time of this book's publication, that final count has more than doubled, passing 500 million active users logging in each month.

Le Facebook International

Facebook was launched in universities in the United States, and then it spread to U.S. high schools. As a result, it wasn't until the fall of 2006 (when Facebook opened to everyone) that Facebook started making a showing in any other country. When Facebook finally ventured into Canada and the United Kingdom, it took off fast, like Vin Diesel fast. Many people speculate that the reason for Facebook's insta-popularity in these countries, more so than in the United States, came from the fact that citizens in Canada and the U.K. (and, randomly, Norway) didn't have the same preconception that U.S. citizens had: that Facebook was only meant for students. People in the United States had heard the buzz about Facebook for two years when it was only for students. This stigma used to be a significant hurdle for Facebook's growth in older U.S. demographics. However, during the last couple years, the fastest growing demographic of U.S. Facebook users has been in the over-35 age group, and the notion that Facebook is only for the kiddies is becoming a distant part of Facebook history.

The next major leap for Facebook's growth came at the start of 2008, when it was clear that many people on Facebook wanted to be connecting with people who spoke other languages. Facebook is more valuable for each person when more of their friends use the site. Facebook's strictly English interface was keeping many people from connecting with people they knew. So Facebook launched the Facebook Translation Application. This allows any bilingual (English + Other) user of Facebook to volunteer to help translate Facebook into other languages. Volunteers are shown various English text on the site, and they can either offer a translation or vote on translations that other people have suggested.

When a suggested translation receives enough votes, that translation becomes the text that other people using the site in that second language see. People can sign up for the site and change their language setting to Spanish. Rather than seeing all the English text, they see all the text that the Spanish speaking volunteers have suggested and approved. In this way, Facebook has been translated into 100 languages in just more than two years.

Chapter 2

Adding Your Own Face to Facebook

In This Chapter

▶ Signing up and getting started

▶ Joining a network

▶ Creating your Profile

*I*n Chapter 1, we cover why you want to join Facebook. In this chapter, we actually get you signed up and ready to go on Facebook. Keep a couple of things in mind when you sign up. First, Facebook gets exponentially more useful and more fun when you start adding friends. Without friends, it can feel kind of dull. Second, your friends may take a few days to respond to your friend requests, so be patient. Even if your first time on Facebook isn't as exciting as you hope, be sure to come back and try again over the following weeks. Third, you can have only one account on Facebook. Facebook links accounts to e-mail addresses, and your e-mail address can be linked to only one account. This system enforces a world where people are who they say they are on Facebook.

Signing Up for Facebook

Officially, all you need to join Facebook is a valid e-mail address. When we say *valid,* we just mean that you need to be able to easily access the messages in that account because you're e-mailed a registration confirmation. Figure 2-1 shows the sign-up page. As you can see, you need to fill out a few things:

✔ **Full Name:** Facebook is a place based on real identity. It's not a place for fake names or aliases. Numerous privacy settings are in place to protect your information (see Chapter 5), so use your full real name to sign up.

✔ **E-mail:** You need to enter your valid e-mail address here. If you want to join a school or work network automatically, use your school or work e-mail.

✔ **Password:** Like with all passwords, using a combination of letters and numbers is a good idea for your Facebook password. It's probably not a good idea to use the same password for every site you join, so we recommend using something unique for Facebook.

✔ **Gender (I am):** Facebook uses your gender information to construct sentences about you on the site. Especially in other languages, it's weird to see sentences like "Jennifer added a photo of themself." If you want to hide your gender, or don't want to associate with either gender, you'll be able to do so after you sign up.

✔ **Date of Birth:** Enter your date of birth. You can hide this information on your Profile.

✔ **Security Check (not shown):** The security check on Facebook is in the form of a CAPTCHA. A CAPTCHA is that funky-looking word-in-a-box. Computers can't read CAPTCHAs, but humans can. Asking you to solve a CAPTCHA is Facebook's way of keeping out robots who want to spam you, while still letting you sign up. You see the CAPTCHA after filling out your information and clicking Sign Up.

Sign Up
It's free and anyone can join

First Name:
Last Name:
Your Email:
New Password:
I am: Select Sex: ⬍
Birthday: Month: ⬍   Day: ⬍   Year: ⬍
Why do I need to provide this?
Sign Up

Create a Page for a celebrity, band or business.

Figure 2-1:
Enter infor-
mation here
to create a
Facebook
account.

After you've filled out this information and agreed to the Terms of Service and Privacy Policy, click Sign Up. You'll be able to start using Facebook, but you won't yet be confirmed. *Confirmation* is Facebook's way of trying to make sure you are really you, and that the e-mail address you used to sign up is really yours. You receive a confirmation e-mail; click the link in that e-mail to make sure you are confirmed. When you log in to Facebook for the first time, Facebook takes you through a series of steps to help you get started and find your friends. These steps focus on entering information that helps you find friends, either immediately or later on. For example, these steps ask you to use the Friend Finder, which we cover in Chapter 4. The Friend Finder checks your e-mail address book and matches e-mails to Facebook accounts, so you can immediately send friend requests to people you know.

The set-up wizard has a tendency to change depending on what kind of e-mail address you join with and whether a friend invited you to use Facebook. Therefore, instead of going through every possibility for what Facebook may look like when you first log in, we suggest you read the "Making Facebook Revolve Around You" section, as well as the "Education and work history" section, later in this chapter. These concepts definitely come into play as you are prompted for information in the set-up process.

Am I too old for Facebook?

No. Most emphatically, no. This is a common misconception, mainly because Facebook was originally exclusive to college students. Facebook's origins, even its name, are rooted in college campuses, but its utility and nature aren't limited to being useful to only college students.

Everyone has networks of friends and people with whom they interact on a day-to-day basis. Young or old, in college or working, this is true. Facebook tries to map these real-world connections to make it easier for people to share information with their friends.

If you're reading this section and thinking maybe you're just too old for Facebook, you're wrong. More and more people in older age demographics are signing up for Facebook every day to keep in touch with old friends, share photos, create events, and connect with local organizations. Almost everything we discuss in the book is non-age-specific.

Obviously, how people use the site can be very different at different ages, but you will discover these nuances when you use Facebook more and more. Generally, you should feel confident that you and your friends can connect and use Facebook in a meaningful way.

There are more than 500 million people using Facebook, and that number isn't made up of "a bunch of kids." Rather, it's a bunch of people from every age group, every country, and every walk of life.

Making Facebook Revolve Around You

For this section, try imagining Facebook as a map in a car navigation system. Except, instead of mapping out only the streets of your neighborhood, Facebook layers on top of that the Profiles of your friends, the photos they've uploaded, and the coffee shops that are their favorites. Facebook is your own digital map of your life. Back in that navigation system, it's hard to figure out where to turn unless your car is right at the center, and the map shifts and reformats as you move through it. Adding your location — whether through your current city or networks — ensures that Facebook is keeping you in the center of the picture.

Current city

At some point in the first few days, you will be asked — and we certainly encourage you to — to identify your current city. Adding a current city helps centralize search results around you so that if you search for pizza, you'll get local results before you get some pizza place in Italy. That's just a tease — for more details on searching, see Chapter 11.

Adding your current city also helps people around you find and connect with you through Search. If you want to add it right now, you can do so from your Profile page. Look for the pencil icon next to the word Edit in the About Me portion of your Info tab. Clicking it takes you to a form where you can enter your Current City (in addition to other information).

Networks

The word *network* can be a bit overused around Facebook from time to time. After all, isn't Facebook a giant network? Aren't your friends, with whom you have direct connections, a network? What about if you're using Facebook for business networking? When getting started on Facebook, *network* refers to a group of people with a real-world connection but who may not actually know each other.

Each of the three types of networks has a real-world counterpart. High school networks and college networks mirror high school and college campuses; workplace networks mirror companies and businesses. Similar to your current city, joining a network re-centers the site around you and your location.

Unlike your current city, however, networks aren't for everyone. When you're deciding to join a network, keep in mind these limitations:

✔ **You cannot join a high school network unless you're actually in high school.** High school networks cannot, for security reasons, accommodate high school alums or even teachers.

✔ **You can join college and workplace networks only with authenticated e-mail addresses.** If you've already graduated from college but want the capability to see classmates, request an alumni e-mail address from your alma mater. Without it, you won't be able to join that school's network.

If you aren't in high school, and if you don't have an "authenticated" e-mail address, you can skip on over to "Setting Up Your Profile." Otherwise, read on to learn more about how you can and why you should join a network.

To join your most relevant networks, look for the link to the Account Settings page in the Account menu (at the top of any page). Click the Networks tab, and enter the network you would like to join. Figure 2-2 shows the options you see if you haven't yet joined any networks.

Figure 2-2:
Look no
farther than
this page
to find a
network to
join.

Networks are nice because if you have some to join, they can be quite useful, but people who don't have any don't really miss out. For example, you can use network privacy to keep something shared only with people you work with. So let's say that Carolyn and Leah both work at Company Q and have joined its corresponding network on Facebook. However, (and this is really sad) they haven't yet added each other as friends. Carolyn may take photos at the company picnic, and publish them to her "Friends and Networks." That way, Leah can see Carolyn's photos despite them not being friends. This is just one example of how privacy can work; for more details about controlling privacy on Facebook, check out Chapter 5.

This privacy setting doesn't just apply to photos, but to all sorts of information. Because you can give the people around you a little more access, and you can get a little more access, joining a network makes connecting and sharing even easier.

To join your workplace or school network(s), you need an e-mail address from your company or school.

Setting Up Your Profile

You're probably thinking, "Didn't I set up my Profile when I joined?" The answer to that is, not quite. Your account is what you already created; however, your *Profile* — what people can see about you — is probably still blank. We talk more about the bigger picture of Profiles and what they mean for you in Chapter 6. For now, just say that setting up your Profile is important so that when you start to find friends and friends start to find you, they can identify who you are, and that you really are you. The main pieces we cover here help people figure out who you are.

But what does your Profile actually consist of? You can check out your current Profile by clicking the Profile link, in the big blue bar on top of any page. Your Profile is made up of *boxes* and *tabs*. You see *boxes* — literally small rectangles each containing a type of information — running down the left side of your Profile. You see *tabs* — similar to the tabs that emerge from file folders — running across the top of the page. Together, the information contained in these boxes and tabs tells your story.

To get you set up on your Profile, we focus on the Info tab. The Info tab contains mostly text fields. Go to the Info tab of your Profile. To fill out your Info tab, click any of the links to edit your Profile. This takes you to the Edit Profile page, which is broken up into various sections based on information categories. Figure 2-3 shows the page for editing Basic Information; you can select any of the other sections to edit that information, as well. (For example, in the far-left pane, you see Profile Picture, Relationships, Likes and Interests, Education and Work, and Contact Information.)

As you edit this information, you may wonder who can see it. By default, everyone can see the sections we're diving into right now. Sensitive stuff like your contact information is available only to your confirmed friends by default. You can restrict both of these settings further by using your privacy settings, if you choose (see Chapter 5).

Look for the little pencil icon you see next to Edit Information all over Facebook. It often appears when your mouse is hovering over something as well. Wherever you see it, you'll be able to change or edit the content it marks.

In the rest of the chapter, we detail a few fields you should fill out early on. Here, we briefly describe the types of fields contained within each section (and we get into more depth with a lot of these in Chapter 6):

 ✔ **Basic Information:** Basic Information contains a variety of fields that you may want to share with people. This information includes things ranging from your political and religious views to the kind of relationship you're looking for. None of these fields are required, but they are meant to encourage you to share some biographical details that help people understand who you are.

✔ **Profile picture:** This section provides you with an easy way to upload a Profile picture — we talk more about the importance of Profile pictures a little later in this chapter.

✔ **Relationships:** This section can be filled out so that you can link your Profile to that of your spouse or significant other, and to your parents and siblings. People refer to this sort of linking as being *Facebook Official.*

✔ **Likes and Interests:** Likes and Interests includes a lot of fields for what basically amounts to your favorites — favorite books, music, movies, and so on. When you enter these items, you automatically link to Facebook Pages representing them. We'll talk more about how this works in Chapter 6.

✔ **Education and Work:** We spend a lot more time on this in the following section. It's pretty self-explanatory; this section allows you to share where you went (or go) to school and the various places you've worked.

✔ **Contact Information:** Facebook has an amazing ability to be a one-stop address book. Because of the ability to restrict visibility, you can share your phone number, address, e-mail addresses, and screen names easily. We'll talk more about how to restrict privacy on these things in Chapter 5.

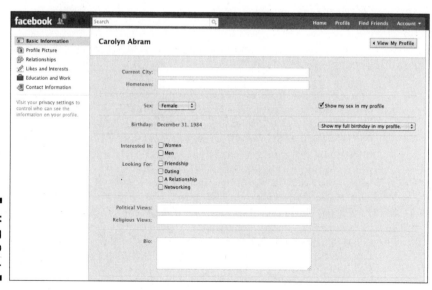

Figure 2-3:
Updating your Info tab.

The Information Box

Here's where it can get a bit confusing: the *Information Box,* which appears below your Profile picture on your Profile, displays a variety of Information culled from your *Info Tab,* which we went over in the preceding section. This box is intended to be an "at-a-glance" window into you. Once you fill out your Info tab, you can choose which ones appear in this box by clicking on the pencil icon in its header. We recommend keeping *at least* your hometown because that's a really common way old friends use to make sure that it's really Susan from gym class. If you want to keep other fields visible, that's great, too. All the fields help you tell your friends about you and what matters to you.

Education and work history

Entering your education and work history usually helps people identify how they know you when you request a friend or send someone a message. For example, if you meet someone at a conference or social function, the ability to remind them, "Remember me, the one with the cool job writing *For Dummies* books?" is built right into your Profile. Additionally, if someone performs a search for a certain class year from your school, you appear in the search results, and old friends can get in touch with you.

Profile picture

Your Profile picture is another way that people can identify you, especially if you have a common name. If your Profile picture features a light blue silhouette, you can change it by rolling your mouse over it and clicking the Change Picture link that appears. A few considerations about Profile pictures that fit into the larger idea of a Profile are covered in Chapter 6. For now, keep these points in mind when choosing a Profile picture:

✔ **Make a good first impression.** Your Profile picture is one of the first ways people interact with your Profile and how you choose to represent yourself. Most people pick pictures that are more or less flattering, or that represent what's important to them. Sometimes, Profile pictures include other people — friends or significant others. Other times, the location matters. If the first photo you see of someone is at the beach versus at a party or sitting at his desk, you may draw different conclusions about that person. What picture represents you?

✔ **Consider who will see your Profile picture.** By default, your Profile picture appears in search results that are visible to all of Facebook and can even be made available to the larger Internet population. So, generally, people who search for your name can see that picture. Make sure it's something you're comfortable with everyone seeing.

✔ **Remember that you're not stuck with it.** After we put all this pressure on you to represent yourself and let people identify you, keep in mind that you can easily change your Profile picture at any time. Is it the dead of winter and that photo of you on the beach last summer is just too depressing to look at? No problem; simply edit your Profile picture.

Trust Me: Getting Verified

As we say over and over, Facebook is a Web site for real identity and real people. To protect this fact, Facebook has systems in place to detect any fake Profiles. Fake Profiles may be jokes (for example, someone creating a Profile for her dog), or they may be *spammers* (robots creating accounts to send thousands of fake friend requests). Regardless, they're not allowed on the site.

You, however, aren't fake or a spammer; how does Facebook know that? Facebook figures that out by verifying you. Now, you may start out verified, or it may take a little while. To figure out whether you still need to get verified, look at these questions:

✔ **Did you join with an *authenticated* e-mail address?** *Authenticated* e-mail addresses are ones that not just anyone can get. For example, Google provides e-mail addresses to its employees that end with a specific domain (in their case, @google.com). You can't have that address unless you work for Google. Most colleges and workplaces have authenticated e-mail addresses. If you joined with one of these, you were automatically verified.

✔ **Do you have an authenticated e-mail address that you didn't join with?** Joining a network with your authenticated e-mail address also serves to verify you. (Refer to Figure 2-2 to see how you join an authenticated workplace or school network.)

✔ **Do you not have an authenticated e-mail address?** You will need to get verified as you use the site. To do that, keep reading this section.

Without an authenticated e-mail address, Facebook unfortunately has to assume the worst about you. You may send spam or inappropriate content to people on Facebook. It's suspicious and paranoid. But it wants to trust you, so it's going to start testing you.

Remember the CAPTCHA you filled out when you joined? Until Facebook trusts you, you will continue to see these when you interact with other people on Facebook. Through your normal use of the site, eventually Facebook will believe you are not, in fact, malicious, and it will stop showing you CAPTCHAs wherever you turn. You can forgo having to solve many of these by instead being verified through your mobile phone. In order to do this, your mobile phone needs to be able to receive text messages (also known as SMS messages). If you don't have a mobile phone, or it doesn't have this capability, don't worry — you'll still get verified as you start using Facebook.

To get verified via mobile, follow these steps:

1. **Search for someone and click Add to Friends.**

   A pop-up appears that double-checks that you want to add this person as a friend.

2. **Click Send Request.**

   A security check will appear in the form of a CAPTCHA, shown in Figure 2-4.

3. **Click the Verify Your Account link (located beneath the CAPTCHA).**

   A new Confirm Your Phone pop-up appears, as shown in Figure 2-5.

4. **Select your country and enter your mobile phone number.**

5. **Check your mobile phone for a text message that contains a code.**

6. **Enter the code into the Code field in the Confirm Your Phone pop-up.**

7. **Click Confirm.**

Figure 2-4: Still seeing a CAPTCHA like this? End the madness with mobile verification.

Confirm Your Phone

Facebook uses security tests to ensure that the people on the site are real. Having a mobile phone helps us establish your identity. Please verify your account by confirming your phone here. We'll text you a confirmation code.

Please select your country code (e.g. '1' for US/Canada) and enter your mobile number without any special characters.

Country Code: United States (+1)

Phone Number: 1231241235

Confirm

[Learn More]

Figure 2-5: Confirm your phone to prove you're real.

Facebook won't send you any other mobile messages unless you choose to opt into Facebook Mobile. (For more information about Facebook Mobile, see Chapter 14.)

If you're already verified, you won't see a CAPTCHA. You may not be able to use mobile verification if your phone can't receive text messages, but don't worry, you'll still get verified eventually just by being a normal user of the site.

Chapter 3

Finding Your Way Around Facebook

In This Chapter

▶ Navigating Facebook

▶ Looking around after logging in

▶ Reading about friends on the Home page

▶ Finding out about what's new, now, and next in the right column

*I*magine a universe with you at the center. Cool, huh? This is how you can think of the page you see each time you log in to Facebook. The Facebook Home page is entirely oriented toward you and *your* friends. The main column tells you what your friends have been up to recently, and the right column shows key pieces of information, such as what events are coming up, people with whom you haven't yet connected, and the most interesting content your friends have been adding. Even the ads in the right column are targeted specifically to you and your interests. Navigation bars line the top and bottom of this page and every other page on the site. These ensure that you can always find your way back to a page you recognize, no matter where you end up.

In this chapter, we explain everything you see on this Home page when you log in, and how you can use this page to get around the rest of the site.

Checking Out the Blue Bar on Top

Leah and Carolyn both happen to spend a lot of time in coffee shops working alongside writers, students, businesspeople, and hobbyists — all drinking steamy beverages and manning laptops. We can always tell at a glance when someone is browsing Facebook by the big blue bar across the top of the page. The blue bar is home to many of the important navigational links on Facebook. Once you can adequately navigate the blue bar, you might as well kick off your shoes and put up your feet because you'll undoubtedly be feeling right at home on Facebook. Figure 3-1 shows the blue bar links from left to right.

Figure 3-1:
The blue bar
at the top:
link by link.

Here's what you need to know about each one:

- ✔ **Facebook logo:** The Facebook logo on the left of the blue bar serves two purposes. First, it reminds you what Web site you're using. Second, no matter where you are on Facebook, if you click this icon, you're back at the Facebook Home page.

- ✔ **Friend requests:** Next to the Facebook logo is an icon of two people, intended to depict friends. Clicking this icon takes you to any pending friend requests you may have. This icon also lets you access the various methods for finding friends. Whenever you receive brand new friend requests, a little red number totaling the number of new requests shows up on top of this icon. When you view the new requests, whether or not you respond to them, the red flag goes away.

- ✔ **Messages:** An icon depicting two speech bubbles lets you access your message Inbox. Clicking it shows you snippets from your five most recent messages, as well as links if you want to send a new message or go to your Inbox. As with the friend requests, a little red flag appears to show you how many new messages you have. When you click that flag, you'll see the new messages, and the flag will clear.

- ✔ **Notifications:** When someone on Facebook has done something to you or your Profile, you are notified by a red flag on top of the next icon — the globe. Maybe the person has tagged you in a photo, written on your Wall or the Wall of a group you are in, given you a virtual gift, or commented after you on a post. Click the globe to see the five most recent notifications, as well as a link to the rest.

- ✔ **Search:** In Chapter 7, we go into all kinds of detail about Search on Facebook. The short version is that you can use Facebook search to find people, groups, events, and applications on Facebook. As you start typing a search topic, a list of items begins to autocomplete. If you see the person or item you're looking for, scroll down or use your mouse to select it. Pressing Enter automatically takes you to the top item in the list. You can also use Search to see what your friends or anyone in the world is publishing about a particular topic. You can find your long-lost elementary school friend, a gaming application, what people are saying about the recent election, what they think of a product you're thinking of buying, or even the up-to-the-minute score of a sports event.

People sometimes try queries that the Search box isn't designed to handle. Searching for elements of Facebook itself, such as Account or Privacy, for example, doesn't give you what you're looking for. A better way to discover or navigate to a particular feature of the site is to click Help Center under the Account link on the right side of the blue bar.

✔ **Home:** This link works just like the Facebook logo. Wherever you are on the site, clicking it brings you back to the screen you see when you log in.

✔ **Profile:** Next to the Home link is a link to your own Facebook Profile. You can also get to your Profile by clicking your own name or photo, wherever you see them on the site. (See Chapter 2 for more on Profiles.)

✔ **Account:** This link gives you access to most of the administrative actions you can take on Facebook. We spell these out here:

- *Your Picture and Name:* One of the many ways to get to your Profile.

- *Edit friends:* Lets you manage your existing Facebook connections or find more people with whom you may want to connect. When you first land on the Friends page, you see all the same friend-finding tools you saw during sign-up (Chapter 2). Clicking the tabs down the left side of the Friends page shows all your friends; if you've organized your friends into different lists, you see those lists here, along with the tools to edit them. We explain the Friends page in much more detail in Chapter 4.

- *Manage Pages:* Likely you will not see this link if you're just getting started. If you find yourself using Facebook to promote something with the Pages feature (described in Chapter 12), however, this is where you'll find access to the Pages you administer.

- *Account Settings:* Enables you to change your name, your e-mail address or password, your mobile information (which allows you to access the site from a mobile phone), or the language you want to use on the site. This is also where you go to deactivate your account.

- *Privacy Settings:* Enables you to set the visibility of the information in your Profile (see Chapter 5).

- *Application Settings:* Allows you to adjust various privacy and setting configurations on a per-application basis. You can also make choices about which pieces of information from your Profile you want to share with applications. The various applications use this information to personalize your experience on their sites (see Chapter 13).

- *Credits Balance:* Takes you to a settings tab where you can see how many credits you have purchased for playing games or buying gifts. Here you can also enter and edit your credit card information and set your preferred currency.

- *Help Center:* Takes you to all sorts of tools for finding out how to use the site, how to stay safe on Facebook, and where to send your suggestions about how the site may be improved.

Many Facebook applications are written by external developers (not by Facebook). If you're having trouble using one of these applications, the Facebook Help page offers methods for contacting the developers directly.

- *Logout:* Ends your Facebook session. If you share your computer with others, always be sure to log out to ensure that another person can't access your Facebook account.

Another way to log out of Facebook is to end your browser session. However, if you have the Remember Me option selected, you won't ever be logged out until you explicitly click Logout. Remember Me keeps you logged in despite closing the browser; therefore, we recommend using the Remember Me option only on a computer not shared with others.

Discovering the Home Page

The Home page is what you see when you first log in to Facebook. It's comprised of three columns of information, described in the following sections.

Note: Before you have your first friend, the Home page looks very different than it does after you start making connections. Because the sign-up flow described in Chapter 2 guides you through finding your first friends, everything that follows in this section assumes that you've connected to at least one person on Facebook. If you haven't yet connected, flip ahead to Chapter 4 to see how to find and connect with people you know, but don't forget to flip back because this chapter is a juicy one.

News Feed

Imagine if your morning paper, news show, or radio program included an additional section that featured articles solely about the specific people you know. That's what News Feed (in the center column of the Home page) is. As long as the people you know are active on Facebook, you can stay up-to-date with their lives via your Facebook home page. A friend may post photos from his recent birthday party, another may write a Note about her new job, and several others may RSVP to a wine-tasting party. These may all show up as stories in your Facebook News Feed. A News Feed bonus: You can often use it to stay up-to-date on current events just by seeing what your friends are talking about. In this morning's News Feed, Leah found out the latest news on the World Cup, which concerts were playing on the upcoming weekend, and that fighting in Thailand seems to have calmed. We're not recommending that you rely on Facebook for all your current event news, but sometimes it can be a decent proxy.

At the top of your News Feed, you see two links: Top News and Most Recent. Most Recent shows you every story every friend publishes. When you have a lot of friends, this can be overwhelming — you might miss some important pieces. Top News features only the most popular stories from among your friends. We talk more about Top News in Chapter 7.

Getting published

Hey, reader: *What's on your mind?* Don't answer us here; we can't hear you. Answer us at the top of your Home page, in the box that asks this very question. This box, called the Publisher, sits just under News Feed in the center of your Home page and works just like the Publisher box on your Profile. Any time you have something you want to share, whether it's a quick update about what you're doing, where you are, or where you're going, right now, or in life, you can share it through the Publisher.

Anything you post in the Publisher shows up on your Profile for those you allow to see it. In Chapter 5, we go into great detail about how you can set the privacy on each piece of content you post to Facebook. Although many people may be able to see your Profile, they may see different things depending on how you set the privacy on the items you post. In addition to showing up on your Profile, the items you post may show up in the streams of the people who can see these items. If you create a status telling all your friends to "Remember to vote on November 4!," it will get published into all their streams. Whether they see it depends on their stream-reading habits. If you post a story to everyone in your family except your grandmother, saying "Remember to wish grandma a happy birthday!," every one of your family members — and only your family members — sees this story in his or her own stream.

Down the left

The left side of the Home page houses many more of the key navigational links you use to go deeper into Facebook. Additionally, the left column shows which friends are currently online and using Facebook and gives you access to start a real-time conversation by using Facebook Chat. The following list explains each link you see on the left side of the Home page:

- ✔ **<Your Name>/Edit My Profile:** Clicking your own name always takes you to your own Profile. Some people find the Profile link more intuitive; but for people who use a shared computer, it's reassuring to see your name up there in the blue bar to quickly verify you're logged in to the proper account. Clicking Edit My Profile is just a shortcut to filling out the information that will show up there.

  Remember that after clicking either of these links or any others that navigate you away from the Home page, you can always get back by clicking the Facebook logo in the upper-left corner or the Home link in the upper-right corner.

- ✔ **News Feed:** Clicking this link resets your home page so you see exactly what you see upon logging in: the News Feed of your friends' activities. News Feed remembers whether you were last looking at Top News or Most Recent and retains that state.

- ✔ **Messages:** Anyone on Facebook can send you a message unless you change the messaging privacy settings. This link is one way to retrieve those messages. The number of new or unread messages you have in your Inbox is shown in parentheses next to the Messages link. When you click Messages, two additional options show up beneath the link. These let you navigate to Updates (messages sent by the Pages of which you're a fan) and to your Sent messages.

- ✔ **Events:** You use the Events application to organize real-life events with guest lists, reminders, and a space to add relevant comments and photos. Click Events to see three additional options: Friends' Events, Birthdays, and Past Events (see Chapter 11).

- ✔ **Photos:** Use this application to browse your friends' recent photos, view photos in which you're tagged, and upload your own photos. For more details on the Photos application, see Chapter 8. Click Photos to see four additional options. The Video option shows videos you or your friends have uploaded or been tagged in, as well as giving you access to add more videos. You can also see Recent Albums your friends have posted and Mobile Uploads specifically to see what friends are doing on the go. Finally, My Uploads takes you to your personal albums.

✔ **Friends:** Clicking this link shows a list of your friends sorted by those who have been most active recently on Facebook. After clicking Friends, you'll see a few additional options, such as one to Find Friends you haven't yet connected with on Facebook. You can also see only the most recent Status Updates from friends. If you've created Friend Lists, which we cover in Chapter 4, you'll see these lists below the Friends link after you click Friends. Clicking a Friend List filters your News Feed down to show only the stories from the friends in that list. Only the first few Friend Lists will show up, but you can click the More link to access the rest.

Accessing applications

In Chapter 1, we introduce the term *application* as it's defined on Facebook. *Applications* are the services that leverage the core Facebook elements, including Profile information, Friends, and the Inbox. These enable you to engage in more specific and sometimes niche activities. Click the Applications menu in the left column to see the applications you already have, the applications your friends are using, and some of the more popular applications in the Facebook community.

When you join Facebook, a few default applications are added to your account and are listed below the Applications link in the left column. You'll see some of the following by default; for the rest, click the More link.

✔ **Games:** Click this app to go to a dashboard of the most popular games being played among the Facebook community and your friends.

✔ **Groups:** Any user can create a Facebook Group for any reason. Groups are intended to bring people together (virtually) around common causes or interests. The Groups bookmark takes you to a page for viewing groups recently joined by your friends, groups to which you belong that have recently been updated, or generally popular groups that you can browse (see Chapter 10).

✔ **Notes:** Known to techy-types as a blogging tool, the Notes application offers users a blank page for sharing thoughts, anecdotes, tirades, dia-tribes, and more. The Notes link, located beneath More on the Applications menu, gives you quick access to Notes you've written, and to those recently written by and about your friends (see Chapter 8).

✔ **Links:** This application lets you highlight interesting content from the Web or Facebook and then provides a forum for discussion. Clicking Links takes you to a list of items recently posted by your friends, as well as your own links and other popular links (see Chapter 6).

If you've been using Facebook for a while, you may see a different set of applications than the ones we list here, which may have something to do with what you've used recently or what you've added to or removed from your Profile. The applications described here are simply the defaults you have upon signing up, but ultimately you have complete control over which applications you add to your Facebook experience (see Chapter 13).

Each time you start using a new application on Facebook, a bookmark for that application shows up in the Application menu. You can remove a bookmark to any application you've used by clicking the "x" that appears next to the new bookmark.

Chat

The Facebook Chat feature lets you see which friends are online at the same time you are and enables you to send quick messages back and forth with any of those people. Similar products are AOL Instant Messenger (AIM), Windows Live, or Yahoo! Messenger. In the left column of the Home page, you can see a list of friends who are currently online and may be available to chat with you. (Theoretically, of course. You never know when a friend's boss is looking over her shoulder.) A green dot next to a name means that person has been using Facebook in the last 10 minutes. The crescent moon means the person has Facebook open but hasn't clicked anything for a while; she may have gone to lunch. If there are more friends online than fit in the left column, you can click the See All link to open the rest of your Chat list from the bottom right of the screen. Note that you can always access your online friends from any page on Facebook using the Chat menu in the bottom right (see Chapter 9).

Right column, what's up?

On the right side of the Home page, next to the News Feed, you find a somewhat random smorgasbord of what's new, what's now, and what's coming up next on Facebook:

- **Events:** Reminders about all Events to which you're invited show in this column for three days prior to the start of the Event — unless you RSVP as Not Attending. Click See All to see all the Events to which you've been invited. After Events, see all the friends who have birthdays coming up in the next three days. You won't see birthday reminders for those friends who have chosen in their Profiles to hide their birthday information.

- **Suggested Pages, People, and More:** Going out and finding all the people you know on Facebook would be a lot of work. Same goes for the Pages you like or other things on Facebook you might be interested in viewing. In this space, you'll see rotating suggestions that might interest you, and the headline of this section will rotate to match. You'll see people, celebrities, and bands that Facebook believes you may know or like. These suggestions are calculated using a number of factors, the most important of which being how many mutual friends you have with the suggested person, or how many of your friends are fans of the suggested brand or celebrity. If you see someone you recognize, click on her photo to add that person as a friend. Like the Requests box, this box may not appear if Facebook doesn't have recommendations for you at this time.

✔ **Sponsored:** Facebook doesn't grow on trees, you know. Nor was it brought into this world hanging from the beak of a magical stork. Facebook is built from pure manual labor (where manual labor equals a lot of typing) and a whole lot of computers storing all the information you and your friends add to the site each day. Labor and technology — these things cost. The ads that appear in this section fund the entire system.

✔ **Requests:** Someone on Facebook wanting you to confirm that you two are friends is an example of a request. The request contains links to accept or ignore the friend's request. Another example is an invitation to an Event to which you should RSVP. When any request is pending, a link to it appears at the top of the right column on your Home Page. If nothing appears there, you have no unanswered requests.

✔ **Pokes:** Read about a Poke in Chapter 9. Just know for now that if you receive a Poke, you find out about it on the Home page.

✔ **Get Connected:** This section doesn't particularly fall into the new, now, or next theme, but if getting someone you care about to join Facebook would improve your Facebook experience, you have easy access to invite them. Click Find Your Friends to search Facebook for the people you're friends with in real life, but have not yet connected with. Click the Invite link to start inviting people to Join Facebook so you can communicate with them. Track Your Invites is a way to see how convincing you've been at getting your friends to join, and clicking Facebook on the Go launches you into the world of Facebook Mobile, keeping you connected to your friends wherever you are (see Chapter 14).

Lowest links

In blue type at the very bottom of every Facebook page, you see a set of links collectively called the *Footer*. The Footer is the catch-all for important information about Facebook the social network, Facebook for business, Facebook the company, and the Facebook policies. Here is a description of each link:

✔ *<Language>:* The first link on the left of the footer shows the name of the language in which you're seeing the rest of Facebook written — English, for example. Click the name of the language to see a drop-down with all the languages in which Facebook is available.

✔ **About:** Takes you to the About Facebook page where you can read about key features of Facebook, see the latest headlines from the Facebook Blog, discover the newest Facebook features, and see links to recent articles written about Facebook.

✔ **Advertising:** Explores Facebook's primary promotional offerings: Facebook Ads, Pages, Share, and Connect (see Chapters 12, 13 and 15 for more about these advertising solutions).

✔ **Developers:** Most of the applications you can add to your Facebook Profile are written by developers who don't work at Facebook. If you're interested in creating a new Facebook application, this is your link.

✔ **Careers:** Wanna work for Facebook? Click this link to find out what jobs are available and all about the working environment.

✔ **Privacy:** Details the Facebook Privacy Policy, which states

Facebook's Privacy Policy is designed to help you understand how we collect and use the personal information you decide to share, and help you make informed decisions when using Facebook.

✔ **Terms:** Although this link may see the least traffic of all the links on the site, it's one of the most important. Facebook is eerily adept at catching users who break the Terms of Use in any damaging way. For the sake of those who use the site in a respectful way, Facebook takes violations of the Terms of Use seriously. The use of fake birthdays, fake names, pornographic or copyrighted content, and spam-like behavior are all grounds for disabling an account.

✔ **Help Center:** The Help page gives you all sorts of tools for finding out how to use the site, how to stay safe on Facebook, and where to send your suggestions about how the site may be improved.

Chapter 4

Finding Facebook Friends

In This Chapter

▶ Understanding what *friending* someone means

▶ Finding friends on Facebook in various ways

▶ Organizing and controlling your Friend List

*H*undreds of sayings abound about friendship and friends. We looked up a bunch of them online, and we boiled them down into one catch-all adage: Friends, good; no friends, bad. This is true in life, and it's also true on Facebook. Without your friends on Facebook, you find yourself at some point looking at a blank screen and asking, "Okay, now what?" With friends, you find yourself at some point looking at photos of a high school reunion and asking, "Oh, dear. How did that last hour go by so quickly?"

Most of Facebook's functionality is built around the premise that you have a certain amount of information that you want your friends to see (and maybe some information that you don't want *all* your friends to see, but we get to that later). So, if you don't have friends who are seeing your Profile, what's the point in creating one? Messages aren't that useful unless you send them to someone. Photos are made to be viewed, but if the access is limited to friends, well, you need to find some friends.

On Facebook, all friendships are *reciprocal,* which means if you add someone as a friend, they have to confirm the friendship before it appears on both Profiles. If someone adds you as a friend, you can choose between Confirm and Ignore. If you confirm the friend, congrats: You have a new friend! And if you ignore the friend, the other person won't really find out.

Now that we made you feel as though you're the last kid picked for the team in middle-school dodge ball, we're also here to tell you to have no fear because there are many ways to find your friends on Facebook. If your friends haven't joined Facebook, invite them to join and get them to be your friends on Facebook as well as in real life.

What Is a Facebook Friend?

Good question. In many ways, a *Facebook friend* is the same as a real-life friend (although, to quote many people we know, "You're not real friends unless you're Facebook friends"). However, subtle differences exist among your real-life friends and your Facebook friends: There are a few Facebook-specific things about friendship that you should know.

A reflection of reality

The first and foremost definition of Facebook friends is that they're just friends. These are the people you hang out with, keep in touch with, care about, and want to publicly acknowledge as a friend. These aren't people you met on Facebook; rather they're the people you call on the phone, stop and catch up with if you cross paths at the grocery, or invite over for parties, dinners, and general social gatherings.

In real life, there are lots of shades of friendships. Think of the differences between acquaintances, a friend from work, an activity buddy, an "ex-significant other but we're still friendly," and a BFF (best friend forever). In real life, these designations are always shifting — say, when you start calling up an activity buddy for advice, or it turns out that you and your significant other really can't be just friends. On Facebook, though, all these nuanced relationships are still your friends.

There are ways to account for these different relationships using Friend Lists, which we discuss later in this chapter. For the most part, though, all friendships are created equal on Facebook. When people see your Friend List, they see a big list that can be sorted only by networks, not your personal designations of *best friends* and *too awkward to say no*.

A contact

A Facebook friend is also a contact, meaning that you are giving all your Facebook friends a way to get in touch with you. In many cases (depending on privacy settings and what information you choose to share), you are also giving your friends access to other info, such as your phone number, address, and e-mail address.

In return, your friends become your contacts: You can always contact them through Facebook, in addition to having access to their phone numbers, addresses, and e-mail addresses.

A privacy implication

One important thing to remember when you send and confirm friend requests is that friends likely get access to your Profile. You can limit the visibility of most things on your Profile to a subset of friends, but most people have all of their Profile visible to all of their friends, if not more people. If your Profile is set up this way, accepting a friend request means you're granting that person access to anything to which you've given all your friends access.

That may sound a bit scary, but it's similar to the access we give friends in real life. The only difference is that in real life, this process happens gradually, as opposed to at the click of a button. At some point, a person you know becomes someone you enjoy spending time with, care about, and are willing to listen to. This sort of friendship intimacy is akin to the intimacy of letting someone see your Profile. In addition to that, it's a way to acknowledge to the world, "Hey! This is someone I care about."

A News Feed implication

News Feed is a constantly updating list of stories about all the actions your friends take on Facebook, as well as a few stories about actions your friends take on other sites. Think of News Feed as a personalized cable news show. Instead of reporting on everything happening around the world, it reports on everything happening around *your* world. News Feed stories may be something like "Blake wrote on Will's Wall" or "Eric was tagged in a video." All these stories link to relevant content about your friends.

When you add people as friends, the stories they post will automatically begin showing up in your News Feed. Right away, you can start to see their statuses, what sorts of photos they upload, and so on. However, if you're less interested in that person (say it's someone you just met at work and you don't care much what she's up to on a day-to-day basis), or you find you're not interested in her posts, you can always hide her posts from News Feed later, which we cover in Chapter 7.

A real-time implication

Not only may you want to know what someone is up to in general, but you may want to know what certain people are up to *the moment* they are up to it. If you have a mobile phone, you can be notified in real-time about what your most favorite friends are doing as often as they choose to let you know.

When you add someone as a friend (or later, when you go to her Profile and look at the links beneath her picture), you can choose to subscribe to her updates via SMS. This means that, after you set up your phone on Facebook Mobile (described in Chapter 14), each time she publishes something to her Profile, you get a text message containing the status update. This feature should be reserved for your absolute favorite, best, most wonderful people in the whole world, who generally update their Profiles with interesting relevant content (otherwise, you may start resenting the buzz of your phone).

You may want to know what your daughter, your spouse, your best friend, or maybe your close co-worker, is up to in real time. Subscribing to someone's status can be a neat way to discover that you're in the same physical location as someone or to be able to answer a time-sensitive question, such as "Who wants to go get dinner with me?"

If you ever change your mind about receiving real-time updates, head over to that person's Profile, and click Unsubscribe from SMS updates beneath the Profile picture.

Discovering the Facebook Friend Philosophy

You may hear different reports on the rules for Facebook. You may hear that it's rude to ignore a friend request. Pay no attention to these ugly rumors. The truth about Facebook Friend etiquette is here.

Choose your friends wisely

Generally, you send friend requests to and confirm friend requests from only people you actually know. If you don't know them — *random friend requests* — click Ignore. For all the reasons enumerated in the preceding section — your privacy, News Feed, and reflection of reality — don't declare friendship unless some kind of relationship actually exists. Remember the lecture you got about choosing good friends when you were in high school? It's every bit as true now. Accept a friend request that you shouldn't, and the next thing you know, you're fleeing for the border on the back of a motorcycle belonging to some guy who insists his name is Harley. Trust us: It will happen exactly like that.

It's quality, not quantity

Another common misperception about Facebook is that it's all about the race to get the most friends. This is very, very wrong. Between the News Feed and privacy implications of friendship, aim to keep your Friend List to the people you actually care about. Now, the number of people you care about — including the people you care about the most and those you care about least — may be large or small. The average number of friends that a person has on Facebook is around 120. Does a person with 120 friends care about them all equally? Probably not. Does this mean that person is shallow? No. It means that this person is keeping up with and keeping track of all the friends who have come and gone through a lifetime. Changing jobs, schools, and locations also comes with new friends, but that doesn't displace the fact that you care about friends from your past.

Should you aim to have 120 friends? No. Carolyn's mom has a great Facebook experience with fewer than 30 friends. With that number, she still can share her photos with her friends, play games with people she knows, and have a pretty active News Feed. Aim to have all the people you care about on your Friend List. Maybe that's a big number, or maybe it's a small number; the part that counts is that you want to see them in the list, smiling back at you.

Finding Your Friends on Facebook

Now that we've impressed upon you how important friends are, you may be feeling a bit lonely. How do you get to the people you want to be your friends? Facebook is big, and if you're looking for your friend John, you may need to provide some more detail. Facebook has a couple of tools that show you people you may know and want as your friend, as well as a normal search-by-name functionality for finding specific people.

If only real life had a Friend Finder

Friend Finder is a tool that matches e-mail addresses from your e-mail address book to people's Profiles on Facebook. Because each e-mail address can be associated with only one Facebook account, you can count on your matches finding the right people whom you already know through e-mail.

With your permission, Friend Finder also invites those people who don't have a Facebook account that matches the e-mail in your address book to join Facebook. If they join based on an invite you send, they will find a friend request from you when they join.

To use Friend Finder, you need to give Facebook your e-mail address and e-mail password. Facebook doesn't store this information: It just uses it to retrieve your contacts list that one time.

Chances are that you came across Friend Finder when you first set up your account. The following steps make several assumptions, namely, that you use Web-based e-mail (Hotmail, Gmail, Yahoo! Mail, and so on), that you haven't used Friend Finder recently, and that the address book for the e-mail has a bunch of your friends in it. We cover other options, such as a client-based address book or using an Instant Messenger Buddy List later in this chapter. Here's how to use Friend Finder:

1. **From the Account menu in the big blue bar across the top, choose Edit Friends.**

2. **Choose Find Friends from the tabs on the left.**

   Figure 4-1 shows the Friend Finder. Below it, you may also see Friend Suggestions, which we cover later in this chapter.

Figure 4-1:
An unfilled
Friend
Finder.

> **Find People You Email**
> Searching your email account is the fastest way to find your friends on Facebook.
>
> Your Email: thefemale@gmail.com
>
> Email Password:
>
> [Find Friends]
>
> 🔒 Facebook will not store your password. Learn More.

3. **Enter your e-mail address into the Your Email field.**

4. **Enter your e-mail password (not your Facebook password) into the Email Password box and then click Find Friends.**

These instructions are meant for first time users of the Friend Finder. If you've used it before, or if you're currently logged into your webmail client, you may see some fields pre-filled or additional pop-up prompts asking you for your permission to send information to Facebook. Don't worry if it doesn't match the figures here at the beginning.

If Facebook finds any matches with the e-mails in your address book, you see a page that looks similar to Figure 4-2. (If it doesn't find any friends, go to Step 6.) These people are the ones Facebook thinks you may know. Anyone you select is sent a friend request from you. You can use the Select All link at the top if you'd rather not spend your afternoon checking off little boxes.

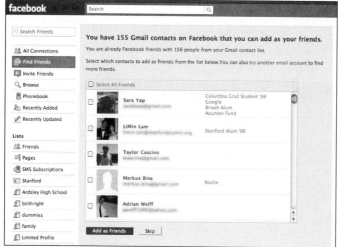

Figure 4-2:
The friend
selector
portion
of Friend
Finder.

5. Decide whether to

- *Add everyone as a friend.* Click Add as Friends.

- *Not friend anyone.* Click Skip.

- *Add many people as a friend.* First click the Select All Friends option at the top of the screen. Then deselect the check boxes to the left of the specific names that you don't want to be friends with. After you deselect all the people you don't want, click Add as Friends.

- *Add a few people as friend.* Check the box to the left of the name of anyone you want to add as a friend. When you've selected everyone you'd like to invite, click Add as Friends.

After you click either Add as Friends or Skip, you land on the Invite portion of Friend Finder. It should look something like Figure 4-3. These e-mails are those that have no matches on Facebook.

6. (Optional) Invite people to join Facebook and become your friend.

Similar to adding friends, you can

- *Invite all these contacts.* Click Invite to Join.

- *Invite none of these contacts.* Click Skip.

- *Invite many of these contacts by deselecting the ones you don't want to invite.* Use the check boxes to the left of their e-mail addresses and then click Invite to Join.

• *Invite some of these contacts to join.* Deselect the Select All/None check box at the top. Then reselect the ones you want to add by using the check boxes to the left of their e-mails and clicking Invite to Join.

Figure 4-3:
The Invite portion of Friend Finder.

After taking all these steps, we hope you manage to send a few friend requests. Your friends need to confirm your requests before you officially become friends on Facebook, so you may not be able to see your friends' Profiles until that confirmation happens.

If the whole experience yielded nothing — no friends you wanted to add, no contacts you wanted to invite — you have a few options. You can go through these steps again with a different e-mail address. You should probably use the one that you use for personal e-mail (from where you e-mail your friends and family). If that's not the problem, you have more ways to use Friend Finder.

Import an address book

If you're someone who uses a *desktop e-mail client* — a program on your local computer that manages your e-mail (like Microsoft Outlook, or Entourage) — create a file of your contacts and import it so that Facebook can check it for friend matches. The way to create your contact file depends on which e-mail client you use. Here's how to get the right instructions:

1. **Go to the Find Friends page (by selecting Edit Friends from the Account menu and then clicking the Find Friends tab on the left).**

2. **Select Upload a Contact File, a blue link to the right of Find People You Email.**

   This first asks you to choose a contact file to upload. If you don't know where to find your contact file, click the How to Create a Contact File link just above the upload field. This expands a window that looks similar to Figure 4-4.

Figure 4-4: Importing a contact file.

3. **If you already have a contact file created, import it here.**

   Next, you're taken through Steps 4–5 in the preceding section.

   Also, if you're on a PC, you may have an option to Automatically Import your Microsoft Outlook Address Book, by choosing that option.

4. **If you haven't created a contact file already, click the How to Create a Contact File link and follow the instructions; then import the file and follow Steps 4–5 in the preceding section.**

Instant messaging Friend Finder

This option works for you only if you use Windows Live Messenger, AIM (AOL Instant Messenger), ICQ Chat, or Skype as an instant messenger (IM) client for chatting with your friends. The biggest difference among these and the previous steps in the Friend Finder is that all invitations you send this way are delivered via instant message. Thus, instead of your friends receiving an e-mail asking them to join, they get an instant message from Facebook Bot. Again, follow these steps:

1. **Go to the Find Friends page (by selecting Edit Friends from the Account menu and then clicking the Find Friends tab on the left).**

2. **Scroll to the bottom right. Under Find People You IM, click Import AIM Buddy List or Import Windows Live Contacts (whichever you use).**

   The page expands as shown in Figure 4-5.

Figure 4-5:
The AIM
Friend
Finder.

Find People You IM

Enter your AIM Screen Name and password to import your buddy list, or import your Windows Live Messenger contacts.

Screen Name:
AIM Password:

Find Friends

Facebook will not store your password. Learn More.

3. **Enter your screen name and password and click Find Friends.**

4. **Follow Steps 4–5, as in the preceding sections, for the regular Friend Finder.**

If none of these methods yields any results for you, don't worry; you'll find friends in other ways, and you can still use the site.

Suggestions

After you have a friend or two, Facebook can start making pretty good guesses about others who may be your friends. Facebook primarily does this by looking at people with whom you have friends or networks in common. In the Suggestions box, shown in Figure 4-6, you see a list of people Facebook thinks you may know and, therefore, may want as friends. In this list, if you see the name of someone you know, simply add her as a friend by clicking the aptly named Add as Friend link beneath the person's name. If you're not sure, you can click on a name or Profile picture to gather more evidence from the Profile about if and how you know that person. Then you can decide whether to add that person as a friend.

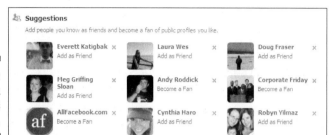

Figure 4-6:
Facebook
suggests
friends.

If you're sure you don't know someone, or if you do know someone, but are sure you don't want that person as your Facebook friend, click the X next to her name and picture, and she will stop appearing in your Suggestions list. As you add or remove people from suggestions, more will pop up to take their place. This fun can last for hours, so make sure you have time and a comfortable chair before you decide to start going suggestions-crazy.

You'll also see a smattering of suggestions on your home page every day when you log in. Finding friends is an ongoing thing, so don't feel like you must go through every single friend finder option in one day. Pay attention to the right side of your home page, and your friend list will expand pretty quickly.

Find what you're looking for: Search

Friend Finder is a great way to build your Friend List quickly without a lot of work. After you build it a bit, though, what if you find other people who may want to be your friends? Facebook Search has a few different methods that let you search for groups of people you may know. Facebook Search also offers you the capability to seek out certain friends by name.

Classmate Search

Classmate Search takes the information from people's Profiles to create a big, searchable list. Classmate Search lets you easily find your friends from high school, college, graduate school, and so on. Ever wonder what that awkward kid from the dining hall wound up doing? Look no further.

To get to Classmate Search:

1. **Select Edit Friends from the Account menu in the big blue bar and then click the Find Friends tab on the left.**

2. **Scroll to the bottom and select the links that read either Find Former High School Classmates or Find Current or Past University Classmates.**

   These take you to the Classmate/Coworker search page, as shown in Figure 4-7.

Search By Name or E-mail

Person's Name or E-mail:

[Search by Name or E-mail]

Classmate Search

School Name: Class Year: ▼

Person's Name: (optional)

[Search for Classmates]

Search by Company

Company:

Person's Name: (optional)

[Search for Coworkers]

Figure 4-7:
Classmate
and
Coworker
Search.

If you've already entered your education information to your Profile, instead of Find Classmates links, you may see a link specific to searching people from the schools you've listed. Clicking these links takes you straight to searching within these schools/graduating years, but you can always search for people from other schools by clicking More Search Options in the upper-right corner of the resulting page.

3. **Enter your high school or college, as well as the relevant graduating year.**

The graduation year is important in getting the results filtered down to the people you actually know. If you just search for *Brown,* you'd get thousands of results, which is too many to sift through looking for those few people you knew once upon a time. Limiting it to a certain graduation year makes it easier to find more people who you actually know.

4. **Click Search for Classmates.**

Check to see whether you know anyone in the search results.

Coworker Search

Coworker Search is based on information that people enter into their Profiles about their work history. Generally, people enter the company they work for (and companies they used to work for) and the dates they've worked there.

Coworker Search lets you search for people who work at the same places you do (or did). Depending on the size of the place where you work and how many of your co-workers have joined Facebook, this sort of search may yield entirely too many people or not enough. But keep your fingers crossed, Goldilocks: It may turn out to be just right. To account for the "too many" problem, search for specific names at specific companies, if you wish. It may be easier to search for "John" at Microsoft, rather than anyone at Microsoft. If you don't find people you expect, it doesn't necessarily mean they're not on Facebook. It may just mean they didn't list the relevant information in their Profiles, so you may have to try and track them down by name through normal search.

To get to Coworker Search, follow these steps:

1. **Select Edit Friends from the Account menu in the big blue bar and then click the Find Friends tab on the left. Scroll to the bottom and select the Find Current or Past Coworkers link.**

   This brings you to the Search by Company page, as shown in Figure 4-7.

   If you've already entered work information to your Profile, instead of a Find Current or past co-workers link, you may see a link specific to searching people from the places you've listed. Clicking these links takes you straight to searching within these companies, but you can always search for people from other companies by clicking More Search Options at the upper-right of the resulting page.

2. **In the Company field, start typing the name of the company you want to search.**

   The Company field tries to autocomplete what you're typing.

3. **(Optional) If you want, enter a specific person you're looking for.**

4. **Click Search Coworkers.**

   Voilà! A list appears of people who listed that company in their Profiles.

Quick-Search

In directing you to Classmate Search and Coworker Search, we keep bypassing the convenient-sounding Quick-Search box. The Quick-Search box is (more or less) what it sounds like. You enter a name of someone you want to find on Facebook, press Enter, and very quickly get a list of search results.

If Friend Finder hasn't yielded any results and you're looking for more friends, try thinking of some people you know who are on Facebook. Enter their full name into the Quick-Search box and see whether that finds them. Read results, lather, rinse, repeat.

Keeping Track: Friend List Management

After you do all this work finding and adding your friends, at some point, you may get a little overwhelmed and yell, "Stop the madness!" at your computer. This may freak out your computer, so here are some ways to spare your computer's feelings and keep your Friend List under control.

Creating and applying Friend Lists

Friend Lists (capital L) are subsets of your giant list of friends (lowercase l). Confused yet? Friend Lists are a way of organizing your friends into lists to make your Facebook experience even easier and more personalized to you and your types of friends. Organizing your friends into Friend Lists allows you to

- ✔ Share different types of information with different sets of friends. For example, your best friends may get to see your party photos, and your family may get to see your wedding photos. Using Friend Lists for privacy is discussed in Chapter 5.

- ✔ See different information from different friends. You can filter your News Feed down to specific Friend Lists. Some people make Friend Lists for the different places they've lived, so their friends in Seattle are in one list, San Francisco another list, and Denver another list. Then, when reading their News Feeds, they see first what's going on in Seattle, then SF, then Denver.

- ✔ Communicate with the same groups of people. Friend Lists can be used in the Inbox. Say that you always invite the same group of people to go biking. Add them all to a Friend List, and then you can simply message the list rather than typing their names each time. To send a message to a Friend List, simply type the name of the list in the To line, where you normally type a name.

- ✔ In Chapter 9, we discuss using Friend Lists in Chat so that you can show yourself as online or offline to different groups of people, or easily scan for certain types of friends currently online, such as social friends if you're looking for a dinner date, or carpool friends if you need a ride.

The options for how you create Friend Lists are virtually limitless. You can have 1,500 friends on each list, each friend can be on more than one list, and you can make up to 100 Friend Lists. Your lists can be for silly things (Girls' Night Out Girls), real-world needs (Family), or general bucketing (co-workers).

To create a Friend List, follow these steps:

1. **Go to the Friends page by clicking Edit Friends from the Account menu in the blue bar at the top.**

   Most people land on the All Connections tab. If you don't, simply click the All Connections tab on the left side of the page.

2. **Click the Create New List button (at the upper-left of the screen).**

3. **In the window that opens, name your list.**

   Maybe something like *Dummies* for the Dummies Team (see Figure 4-8).

Figure 4-8:
Creating a
Friend List.

4. **Input the names of the people who belong on this list and then press Enter.**

   When you see the picture of the person you're looking for pop up, click it or keep typing until there is only one person left, at which point that person is automatically selected.

5. **Click Create List.**

   Now, wherever Friend Lists appear on Facebook, including where you set privacy, News Feed, Chat, the Inbox, and the Friends page, you have access to the new list you just created.

   You can always edit the name or membership of a list later by selecting the list name from the tab on the left of the Friends page (beneath the Lists heading) and then clicking the Edit List button at the top of the page. From there, you can change the name or delete or add members. Also, whenever viewing friends on the Friends page, you can add them to lists by selecting the Add to List drop-down menu to the right of their names and checking the list to which you'd like to add them.

Friend Lists are private, so even if the list you're messaging is known in your mind as *Annoying Co-Workers,* all that your annoying co-workers see is a list of names.

Spring friend–cleaning

Every now and then, no amount of Friend Lists can hide the fact that you just have too many friends you don't care about anymore. This isn't your fault; after all, you can't help being popular. If they are cluttering your Facebook Experience, though, it's time to do a little *friend pruning.*

No, friend pruning doesn't mean waiting for your friends to shrivel in the sun. Instead, go to your huge master Friend List and start working your way through all your friends. The rules that apply for friend pruning are similar to the rules for spring-cleaning: If you haven't used it in a year, you can probably throw it out. If you haven't even thought about a friend in a few years, or if you can't remember why you accepted a friend request in the first place, it's okay to remove that person as a friend. When you're looking at your friends on the Friends page, you see a small X to the right of that person's listing. Just click the X to remove your friend, and that friend is gone.

Don't worry — your friends are never told that they've lost a coveted place on your Friend List. Chances are that if you had no contact over several months, they won't notice, either. You merely disappear from his Friend List (and he from yours), and both move on happily with your lives.

Chapter 5

Privacy and Safety on Facebook

In This Chapter

▶ Navigating the many privacy options on Facebook

▶ Protecting yourself online and on Facebook

▶ Deciding what to share and when

*U*nfortunately, a lot of horror stories are out there about the Internet, especially about social networking sites. Many of them involve teenagers and predators, some of them involve identity theft, and others involve far less salacious (but no less real) problems, such as spamming and computer viruses. The bad news is that these things are out there. The good news is that Facebook has some of the most granular privacy controls on the Internet, enabling you to share real information comfortably on Facebook.

Facebook has created a trusted environment that provides three major assets:

✔ **In general, people create real accounts for themselves, and people are who they say they are on Facebook.** This means that the community enforces a standard of reality. When people ask you to view their webcasts or click some mysterious link, those actions are reported by the community and the offenders are removed from Facebook. This also means that it's usually easy to tell a real person from a fake one and that you can make informed choices about whom you interact with online.

✔ **Facebook provides granular privacy controls that are built into every piece of information you create on the site.** We discuss how these work in depth in this chapter. Before we get to that, however, we talk a bit about privacy in general and how Facebook approaches it.

✔ **Facebook makes it easy for you to see your own Profile as other specific people see it.** This means you can easily verify that you're sharing the information you want to share with the right set of people.

Seeing the Win-Win of Privacy

Would you display your phone number on a public billboard? Probably not. Would you write it down for your friends to hold on to? Probably yes. What Facebook has learned is that the more we control our information, the more likely we are to share it. If we feel confident that our phone number will be seen only by those people we want to see it, then we'll probably post it on Facebook. The win-win of privacy is that the more we share, the better it is for information flow among us and our friends. So, when we each share more information, our friends share more information. As individuals, we win in that our information is shown to the specific people we want to see it, and not to the people we don't. Our friends win because they can have access to more information about us. If our friends see us sharing, and decide to do the same, we win again because we have access to more information about our friends. And then, well, the cycle keeps building.

Keeping this in mind, using your privacy options wisely is the best way to share the right information with the right people. Using your privacy options wisely is also the best way to keep your information away from the wrong people. With this control, Facebook becomes a place where you can share very personal things — not just in a "my phone number is private" way, but also in a "see photos of my new niece" way. Because of the privacy controls, Facebook is a place for you to truly share your life the same way you do in the real world.

Know Your Audience

Before we go too deep on where all the privacy controls live for each piece of information, we are first going to explain how Facebook encourages you to think about your audience. Once you have made decisions about which set of friends you want to see which types of content, then you can speed through the privacy options, making quick decisions for each item.

For most pieces of information, you have four or five options for the audience to which you want to make a piece of content visible, along with a "custom" option.

- **Everyone:** By setting the visibility of something you post or list to Everyone, you're saying that you don't care who, on the entire Internet, knows this information about you. Many people list their favorite bands, and, just as they'd shout this information from the treetops, they set the visibility to Everyone. This is a totally reasonable setting for innocuous pieces of information. A restaurant recommendation in your status could have an Everyone setting. There are many types of information which we, and Facebook, would *not* recommend you share with everyone. Read on . . .

✔ **Friends of Friends:** By setting the visibility of some information to Friends of Friends, you're saying that the only people who can see that information are your friends and their friends. This might seems like a pseudo-safe setting for sensitive information. In real life, there's a pretty legit level of trust borne out of sharing mutual friends. Facebook, how- ever, while striving to mimic real-world relationships, isn't quite there yet, and the truth is that many of your friends may have "friends" on Facebook they can't actually vouch for in real life. Setting the visibility of your information to Friends of Friends, as far as your authors are concerned, is pretty similar to opening it up to just about anyone. The real difference between the Friends of Friends and Everyone settings is that Web sites and applications won't have access to your information if you've guarded it under Friends of Friends. So feel free to use this set- ting for information you want to hide from, say, Google, but that you don't mind Joe Schmo seeing.

✔ **Network privacy:** In Chapter 2, we talk a little bit about joining a net- work and how that is a way of affiliating yourself with other people who have something in common with you, such as attending the same school or working for the same company. When you join a network, you're usu- ally saying, "I choose to trust people who have this thing in common with me to see more information about me." It is often the case that many students are perfectly comfortable sharing their phone numbers with other students, but they wouldn't want just anyone in the world to see their phone numbers. The same may be true of people who share a work network.

Facebook takes Network-level privacy pretty seriously. It's difficult for anyone who doesn't legitimately belong in a school or work network to join one, so many people find the Friends and Network privacy option the ideal balance between sharing information with their friends as well as a wider audience. The people in your network may not be friends yet, but they may be a pretty trustworthy bunch. If you trust your co- workers or your classmates in addition to your friends, you may choose to share the typically more private information, such as your e-mail address, physical address, or phone number. Many students share their dorm room phone numbers with their entire school, making it easier for classmates to contact one another for questions, for example. Facebook employees are wary about sharing their personal numbers to a wide audience, in case a stranger uses them instead of going through Customer Support channels. However, employees are perfectly willing to share their phone numbers with the entire Facebook company network because it makes our jobs much easier.

✔ **Friends Only:** Any information for which you set visibility to "Friends" will be accessible only by your confirmed Facebook friends. If you trust your friends, this is a reasonably safe setting for most of your infor- mation. If you feel uncomfortable sharing your information with your "friends," we suggest you rethink who is on your friends list before you rethink what information you share.

Custom-made privacy

All relationships in real life are not created equal. You share different stories with your family than you do with your co-workers. The photos you show your closest friends may not be the same ones you put up on the refrigerator. For that reason, the *Custom* privacy option allows you to both include and exclude individuals or groups of friends from being able to see parts of your Profile and your content. Find the Custom option for any piece of content by clicking the little lock wherever you see it, and selecting the last option on the menu that appears, Custom (edit). The Custom Privacy dialog box pops up and enables you to configure the audience of your photo, or note, or address, in many different ways:

- **Limit the visibility of a piece of content to all your friends plus a subset of your networks.** Leah shares her contact information with her friends and the Facebook network because she knows most of her co-workers. She does not share her contact information with the Brown network (where she went to school) because she doesn't want her information in the hands of that many strangers. Open the Custom Privacy dialog box and select Only Friends, along with whichever specific networks you'd like to share. (*Note:* This is relevant only if you are in more than one network.)

- **Target a piece of information to just one network.** Leah uses two e-mail addresses — one for work and one for her personal life. She has both listed on her Profile, but she's set the visibility of her work e-mail address to the Facebook network, and the visibility of her personal e-mail address to her friends. To show a piece of information to a network but not your friends, again you'll use the Custom option. Click Custom from a privacy drop-down menu, and then click the These People drop-down menu. There you will see an option for Only Me. Select that along with the network with which you'd like to share.

- **Limit the visibility of information to a subset of your friends.** In Chapter 4, we give you all the details for making Friend Lists, groups of friends who have something in common. These lists can be used in conjunction with privacy to show a particular list something you don't want other people to see, or you don't think other people care about. Say that you're having a housewarming party and want all your local friends to know about it, but don't want to bother friends who don't live nearby. You can mention your party on your Profile and limit the visibility to your list of friends who live in your city (assuming you've made such a list; if you haven't, you can make one now by reviewing the steps in Chapter 4.). To do so, select Specific People from the Custom Privacy dialog box and then enter the name of the Friend List(s) you want to invite.

✔ **Restrict certain people from seeing your content.** Conversely, sometimes you have information you're comfortable sharing with the majority of your friends but that you don't want certain people knowing about.
Many people keep a list of friends called "Limited" or "Acquaintances"
that consists of all the people they've met, but aren't quite comfortable
inviting into their homes, for example. After creating such a list, you can
announce your housewarming party on your Profile and then set the visibility of the announcement to All Friends. Then, in the Hide This From
box at the bottom, type the name of the list you'd like to exclude. You
can also exclude someone by name. In Figure 5-1 you can see the space
at the bottom of the Custom Privacy dialog box where you can hide content from specific friends. This is a great feature when you're trying to
plan a prank or a surprise party.

Custom Privacy

✓ **Make this visible to**

These people: Friends Only ▼

And these networks: ☑ Facebook

☐ Brown

Only friends and the Facebook network can see this.

✗ **Hide this from**

These people:

☐ Make this my default setting   **Save Setting**   Cancel

Figure 5-1:
The Custom
Privacy
dialog box.

Anyone in a Friend List that is excluded from seeing something — whether it's
a photo album on your Wall or your Profile — will never be able to see that
content. If someone is on two lists, one of which can see something and one of
which is excluded from seeing it, that person won't be able to see it. In order
to verify that you've set your privacy correctly for a particular friend, navigate
to the Privacy Settings under Account, where you will see a link to view settings in the first paragraph under Basic Directory Information. From there you
can click Preview my Profile in the upper right to view your Profile as a specific friend sees it. Type the friend's name in the box and press Enter in order
to verify that she sees your Profile the way you intended her to see it.

Know Your Privacy Options

As we mentioned, Facebook prioritizes giving you control over all of the
information you want to share. This is an absolutely fantastic principle, but it
does have a downside — Facebook privacy controls are abundant and take a

while to learn and use. The good news is that all the privacy settings default to a level of openness with which most people are comfortable. If you have particular taste in your sharing, or sensitivity to sharing types of content, however, then you'll want to read this chapter thoroughly, and make sure you feel comfortable with the material here before you start listing any personal information on Facebook.

Everything there is to know about Privacy on Facebook can be learned in one place. In the blue bar on top — click the Account drop-down box in the upper-right corner, and then select Privacy Settings.

On the resulting page, you'll see five separate sections. The first four (Basic Directory Information, Sharing on Facebook, Applications and Websites, and Block Lists) are what you'll need to understand all about Privacy on Facebook. The fifth, Controlling How you Share, is basically a guide to using the other four.

After reading this chapter, you'll be well equipped to use Facebook Privacy. However, you'll find that as you become a more advanced user, different privacy settings may become more or less relevant. Also, some people keep things tightly locked down at first, but as they see the usefulness of different types of sharing, they'll start opening up. This means that as your relationship to your privacy settings change, you may want a quick refresher on how it all works. When that happens, we'd obviously love it if you come back to this book and this chapter, but perhaps much more convenient will be to go to the Controlling Your Information section of the Privacy Settings page for a brief recap of everything covered here.

Basic Directory

Certain information is visible to everyone because it's essential to helping people find and connect with you on Facebook. This information includes your name, Profile picture, your gender, and networks. The name and picture are what help your friends find and connect with you. Without requiring visible Profile pictures, looking for people with common names would be a very frustrating task as you would have no way to distinguish which John Smith is the one you know. It's also really nice that, when looking at a friend's Wall or at the RSVP list for an Event, you see the faces of the people writing or attending. Without the faces showing, it would look a little bit like attending a part in which everyone is wearing a paper bag over his or her head.

The reason for keeping gender public is a little less obvious — it's born out of the fact that in the English language, there is just no great way to refer to someone without using gendered pronouns. Facebook used to allow people to hide their gender, which resulted in silly looking sentences like, "Add them as a friend" or "Write on his or her wall."

Finally, Networks is always public because its primary use is to see who else is in your network before you join it and then use that network setting to gate your privacy.

These are only a few of the many fields that Facebook encourages people to fill out in order to help their friends find and connect with them. The rest of the fields are as follows:

- ✔ **Search:** The Search setting determines whether people can find you on the site. If you don't allow people to find you, you'll likely be responsible for finding and connecting with people yourself.

- ✔ **Send Me Friend Requests:** This setting determines who can request your friendship through the site. The recommended setting here is Everyone because, especially as you're getting started, many people you know may come across your Profile and send you a request. As you build up a lot of friends, you may consider dropping the setting to Friends of Friends so that total strangers don't ask you to be a friend.

- ✔ **Send Me Messages:** This setting determines who can send you a message through Facebook. The recommended setting here is Everyone, but Leah prefers to keep her setting to Friends of Friends because this keeps total strangers from reaching out to her ("You work at Facebook!?? Will you deactivate my ex-boyfriend's account!??").

- ✔ **See My Friend List:** Depending on what kinds of friends you have and how comfortable you are with them knowing about each other, seeing your Friend List is one of the best ways for your real friends with whom you've not yet connected on Facebook to be able to find you. We (strongly) recommend setting this option to Everyone.

- ✔ **See My Work and Education Info:** Where you've worked and gone to school is often key information in helping people know whether they know you. People with whom you went to college may search for your school by name, for example, and if you have this information listed and public, they'll be able to find you. You may consider this a good or bad thing depending on your college experience. If you've proactively kept in touch with everyone you care about, then by all means, keep the visibility of this information restricted. If you're curious who might be trying to track you down, share it with the world.

- ✔ **See My Current City and Home Town:** Search results are partially ranked by location. If you've listed that you live in San Francisco and I live in San Francisco, then when I search for your name, I will see your Profile listed closer to the top than someone who lives halfway around the world. Like the rest of the Basic Directory Information, share this information if you want to help people find and connect.

✔ **See My Interest and Other Pages:** Interest and Other Pages refers to the interests you've listed on your Profile, such as bands, foods, movies, and more. It also refers to the Facebook Pages that you've liked (more on Pages in Chapter 12). This information is probably more interesting to the people with whom you're already Facebook friends, so feel free to restrict the visibility with minimal consequence, if that makes you more comfortable.

You may be wondering what people can really see about you. Remember that you can check this out at any time by clicking Preview My Profile at the top of the Basic Directory Information section. Keep in mind that people can always see certain information about you: your name, your Profile picture, your current city, any networks you belong to, pages you're a fan of, your Friend List, and your gender.

Sharing on Facebook

The Sharing section of the privacy page has three different bundles of information. To be honest, the distinction between the bundles isn't that important because for each item in each bundle, you get to choose a specific privacy setting. To help with readability of the page and to offer additional clarity about what each setting means, the Sharing page within privacy settings is really broken into three categories:

✔ **Things I share:** Posts by Me refers to anything you write in the publisher at the top of News Feed or your profile. Of course, you know you can set a different privacy option for each post, so this setting refers to the default. Family, Relationships, Interested In, and Looking For, Bio and Favorite Quotes, Web site, Religious and Political views, Birthday, Photo album privacy — these are all things you add to your profile through Edit My Profile.

✔ **Things others share:** Photos and Videos I'm Tagged In, Can Comment on Posts, Friends Can Post on My Wall, Can See Wall Posts by Friends. What these settings all have in common is that someone else adds content that ends up on your wall. When someone tags you in a photo, it ends up on your wall. When you share a photo and someone comments, that comment ends up on your wall. This group of privacy settings lets you choose who can leave content on your wall, and who can see that content.

✔ **Contact Information:** The Contact Information section lets you control who can see the various pieces of contact info you may have added to your Profile — such as phone number or e-mail address. Additionally, you can control who has the ability to send you a message or add you as a friend. Remember, friends can always send you a message, so the lowest setting for both of these is Friends of Friends.

Wherever you can set the privacy of a piece of information on Facebook, you see a small gray lock icon. Clicking it allows you to choose one of the audience options from the drop-down menu: either Everyone, Friends and Networks (if you're a member of a network), or Friends. Choosing Custom (as shown in Figure 5-2) lets you get specific about who can see your content. We talk about this a little later.

Figure 5-2: Privacy controls for sharing on Facebook.

Applications and Web sites

Much of the richness of Facebook is the way you can take your Facebook Identity and your friend relationships to other places on the Internet without having to re-create any relationships or reenter any information into a new Web site. If you review a restaurant on Yelp.com, for example, your Facebook friends will see that when they visit Yelp.com. We cover this in much more detail in Chapter 13, so feel free to flip ahead if your curiosity is piqued. For the purpose of this chapter, we're simply going to explain the control you have over your information when using other Web sites in conjunction with Facebook.

On The Applications and Websites Privacy page shown in Figure 5-3, you'll find five settings:

✔ **What You're Using:** This section may be empty if you're new to Facebook. This section lists all the Web sites and applications with which you've linked your Facebook Profile. If at any time you don't feel comfortable with the way a site is using your information, simply delete the site from this list; just click the Remove link, and from the dialog box that appears, select which site you no longer want to have access to your Profile and click Remove.

✔ **Game and Application Activity:** Application dashboards are the landing pages for games and activities that you can access through the quick links on the left side of your home page. The games dashboard shows a list of popular games, who's playing, and how they are doing. This setting allows you to keep your name from showing up in those stats. Other applications have dashboards, too.

✔ **Info Accessible Through Your Friends:** When your friends use other Web sites and applications in conjunction with Facebook, it may be useful to their experience to see their friends' (that is, your) information. An example of this is a birthday calendar application which may alert them when a friend's birthday is on the horizon. In this section, you can say which of your information your friends can allow sites to access. If you want your friends to be able to use a birthday reminder Web site to remember your birthday, you may want to allow them to give your birthday to the sites they trust. If you never want any application having access to some of your information, the notes you write, for example, then uncheck that box and your friends will not be able to import that information into their applications.

✔ **Instant Personalization:** The shortest possible summary of Instant Personalization is that Facebook has made some deals with highly trusted partner Web sites to give them quick access to the information that you have already allowed to be public. These Web sites can then use that information to show you a personalized experience whenever you use them. We go into great detail on Instant Personalization in Chapter 13 — not to mention the detailed summary of Instant Personalization when you click this link from the privacy page. Rather than explain it again here, we'll simply say that this is where you go to turn Instant Personalization off — not that it's enabled by default.

✔ **Public Search:** This refers to a limited view of your Profile that anyone can see if he searches for your name in an external search engine, such as Google. Your Public Search Listing shows a portion of the content you've made available to everyone.

Block lists

Blocking someone on Facebook is more or less the digital equivalent to some combination of a restraining order and a witness protection program. For the most part, if you add someone to your Block list, he can't see any traces of you on Facebook. You won't show up in his News Feed; if he looks at a photo in which you're tagged, he may see you in the photo (that's unavoidable), but he won't see that your name has been tagged. When you write on other people's Walls, that will be hidden from him. A few key things to remember about blocking:

✔ It's almost entirely reciprocal. If you block someone, then he is just as invisible to you as you are to him. So you can't access his Profile, nor will you see anything about him anywhere on the site. The only difference is that if you block the relationship, you're the only one who can unblock it. This fact actually leads to an interesting fact about blocking. You might think that one person (let's call him Pedro) blocks another person (call her Lucy) because Pedro doesn't want Lucy to see what he's up to. When in fact Pedro is quite likely to block Lucy because he doesn't want to see anything about her anymore; maybe she writes really annoying status updates; maybe they had a nasty break-up.

✔ You can only block people who are not your friends. If you go to a non-friend's Profile, you'll see an option to block the person at the bottom-left corner of his Profile. If you go to a friend's Profile, you'll have to remove that person as a friend before you can block her. If you block from the privacy page, you can enter the name or e-mail address of anyone, and you will automatically be unfriended (if you were friends), and that person will be blocked.

Figure 5-3:
Controlling the information you share with applications and Web sites.

As you get going on the site you may find out you know people who LOVE to send a ton of application invites — "Play this game! And this game! Try this! Check out this!" You might even become that person. But say that you don't turn out to be a big fan of using applications. Rather than block the overly friendly person who's sending you all those invitations, you can simply block invitations such that you can still interact with your friend in every other way, but you won't receive application invites. You can block both people and applications by going to the Privacy Settings page under Account. When you click Edit Your Lists underneath Block Lists, you'll see the options show in Figure 5-4.

Figure 5-4:
Block
people and
applications
from con-
tacting you.

Block users	Once you block someone, that person can no longer be your friend on Facebook or interact with you (except within applications and games you both use).

Name: [   ] Block This User

Email: [   ] Block This User

You haven't added anyone to your block list.

Block application invites	Once you block application invites from someone, you'll automatically ignore future application requests from that friend. To block invites from a specific friend, click the "Ignore All Invites From This Friend" link under your latest request.

Block invites from: [Type the name of a friend...   ·]

You haven't blocked invites from anyone.

The Application Privacy page

In addition to all of the privacy settings listed on the Privacy settings page, there are even more settings regarding the visibility of specific information within specific applications. Applications built on top of the Facebook Platform are sometimes built by Facebook and are sometimes built by other people. (For more information on adding applications, see Chapter 13.) The Applications section of the Privacy page controls which applications interact with your information as well as what information they're allowed to interact with. For each application, you can select a number of options that control the way in which that application shares information with your friends:

✔ **Profile:** The Profile tab of the Applications settings lets you specify which people can view the content you post in a particular application. For example, if you use the Facebook Events application, you can specify whether there's a box or tab on your Profile that shows all the events you've attended or plan to attend, and then the Privacy option lets you decide who you want to see that box or tab. Here are the steps to setting the Profile privacy for applications — Figure 5-5 shows an example:

   1. **Click the Account link at the top of the page.**

   2. **Choose Application Settings from the drop-down menu.**

   3. **Click Edit Settings next to a particular application.**

   4. **On the Profile tab of the dialog box that appears, you can set the privacy level of the box and/or tab (if you have one) for that application using the Privacy drop-down menu list.**

✔ **Additional Permission:** You also are in control of which of your own information applications or other Web sites you use in conjunction with Facebook, and how those sites can contact you or publish content on your behalf. Use Steps 1 through 3 in the preceding set of steps and then select the Additional Permissions tab of the Edit Settings box. Different Web sites and applications will have different options, but generally speaking, this is where you go to change permissions on whether an application can publish stories to your Wall while you're using it, and others.

Figure 5-5:
Setting
application
privacy
prefer-
ences.

Though you can restrict most of your information from applications, remember that applications can always access your name, Profile picture, and gender.

Taking Personal Responsibility for Safety

No one wants anything bad to happen to you as a result of something you do on Facebook. Facebook doesn't want that. You don't want that. We, your authors, don't want that either. We are trying, right now, to keep it from happening by telling you about these options and explaining how they work. Facebook tries to keep bad things from happening by giving you all these privacy options in the first place. You're the third piece of the pie, or the puzzle, or whatever. In order to ensure your own safety on Facebook, you have to make an effort to be smart and safe online.

So what *is* your part? Your part is to be aware of what you're putting online and on Facebook by asking yourself a few questions:

Is what I'm putting on Facebook legal or illegal?

Would I be embarrassed by someone in particular finding this information?

> Will the audience with whom I'm sharing this information use it in a way I trust?

You need to be the one to choose whether displaying any given piece of information on Facebook is risky. If it's risky, you need to be the one to figure out the correct privacy settings for showing this information to the people you choose to see it — and not to the people you don't.

Your part is equivalent to the part you play in your everyday life to keep yourself safe: You know which alleys not to walk down at night, when to buckle your seatbelt, when to lock the front door, and when to toss the moldy bread before making a sandwich. Add these to your list:

> I use my Facebook privacy settings wisely.

> I am careful about what information I expose to lots of people.

Remembering That It Takes a Village to Raise a Facebook

Another way in which you (and every member of Facebook) contribute to keeping Facebook a safe, clean place is in the reports that you submit about spam, harassment, inappropriate content, and fake Profiles. Facebook assumes that your friends aren't putting up bad stuff, but when you're looking at content of people you're not directly connected to, you should see a little Report link beneath it. This is true for Photos, Profiles, Groups, Links, Applications, Pages — more. When you click one of these links, you see the Report page. Figure 5-6 shows an example of someone reporting an inappropriate photo. (Photo not pictured, for obvious reasons — sorry.)

Figure 5-6:
Reporting inappropriate content.

Report a Picture

You are about to report a violation of the Statement of Rights and Responsibilities. **All reports are strictly confidential.**

We will **NOT** remove photos just because they're unflattering.

Reason:
(required)

Choose one...
Choose one...
Nudity or pornography
Drug use
Excessive Gore or violent content
Attacks individual or group

Is this your intellectual [

Submit   Cancel

The various Report options that you see may vary, depending on what you're reporting (a message as opposed to a photo, for example). These reports are submitted to the Facebook User Operations team. The team then investigates, taking down inappropriate photos, disabling fake accounts, and generally striving to keep Facebook clean, safe, and inoffensive.

When you see content that you don't like — for example, an offensive group name or a vulgar Profile — don't hesitate to report it. With the entire Facebook population working to keep Facebook free of badness, you wind up with a pretty awesome community.

After you report something, Facebook's User Operations team evaluates it in terms of violating Facebook's Terms of Use. This means that pornography gets taken down, fake Profiles are disabled, and people who send spam get a warning. However, sometimes something that you report may be offensive to you but doesn't violate the Terms of Use and, therefore, will remain on Facebook. Due to privacy restrictions, User Operations may not always notify you about actions taken as a result of your support, but rest assured that the team handles every report.

Peeking Behind the Scenes

Facebook's part in keeping everyone safe includes a lot of manpower and technology power. The manpower involves responding to the reports that you and the rest of Facebook submit, as well as proactively going into Facebook and getting rid of content that violates the Terms of Use.

The technology power that we talk about is kept vague on purpose. We hope that you never think twice about the things that are happening behind the scenes to protect you from harassment, spam, and pornography. Moreover, we hope that you're never harassed or spammed, or *porned* — the unofficial verb form meaning "being assaulted by accidentally seeing unwanted porn" — but just so you know that Facebook is actively thinking about user safety and privacy, we talk about a few of the general areas where Facebook does a lot of preventive work.

Protecting minors

Again, we keep this section purposefully vague to avoid becoming *Gaming Facebook's Systems For Dummies*. In general, we want you to note that people under the age of 18 have special visibility and privacy rules applied to them. For example, users under the age of 18 don't have Public Search Listings created for them. Public Search Listings enable people to be found in outside search engines, such as Google. Facebook decided never to expose minors in this way. Would anything bad have happened if Facebook had decided otherwise? Probably not, but better to be safe than sorry.

Other proprietary systems are in place that are alerted if a person is interacting with the Profiles of minors in ways they shouldn't, as well as systems that get alerted when someone targets an ad to minors. Again, with reference to the personal responsibility part, as a teenager (or as the parent of a teenager), you are responsible for understanding privacy and safe behavior on Facebook. Facebook tries to prevent whatever it can, but at the end of the day, you have to be a partner in that prevention.

You must be at least 13 years old to join Facebook. No one younger than that can have an account without violating the Terms of Use.

Preventing spam and viruses

Ah, spam, that delicious little can of . . . something once meat-like? Male-enhancement medications? Prescription drugs delivered to your door? "Please sir, send me $, and I promise to return $$$." Everyone can agree that spam is the bane of the Internet, all too often sliming its way through the cracks into e-mail and Web sites — and always trying to slime its way into Facebook as well, sometimes in the form of messages to you, or Wall posts, or groups of events masking as something it's not to capture your precious attention.

The spam reports that you provide are incredibly helpful. Facebook also has a bunch of systems that keep track of the sort of behavior that spammers tend to do. If you haven't read this yet, hop to Chapter 2 for the scoop on CAPTCHAs, the first line of defense against spammers creating multiple dummy accounts (the bad kind of dummy) that can be used to harass people with unwanted ads. The spam systems also keep track of those who message people too quickly, friend too many people, post a similar link in too many places, and other such behaviors that tend to reek of spam. If you end up really taking to this Facebook thing, at some point you may get hit with a warning to slow down your poking or your messaging. Don't take it too personally, and just follow the instructions in the warning — this is the spam system at work.

Part II
Sharing Your Life on Facebook

"I know Facebook is great and you want to be a part of it. But you're my mom - you <u>can't</u> be my 'friend.'"

In this part . . .

One thing you hear repeatedly in this book is this idea of sharing. Facebook is about sharing your real life with the people you care about. This part focuses on giving you knowledge of the tools you use to share yourself on Facebook, and the tools you use to share in the lives of your friends.

Between your personal Profile and the applications that you choose to use, there are hundreds of ways to connect to family and friends — both old and new.

Chapter 6

Building Out Your Profile

In This Chapter
▶ Sharing with your friends through your Profile
▶ Navigating the Profile
▶ Protecting your Profile privacy

*Y*our Facebook Profile is more than just a bunch of information — it's an ongoing, ever-evolving story about you. Did you ever have to respond to a writing prompt that asked you to write page 73 of your 248-page autobiography? Your Profile page is the page you are working on right now, except your autobiography is a complete multimedia presentation, pulling together your words, your photos, your friends' thoughts, and postings. All of those things together tell the reader both who you are and what's important to you. Your Facebook Profile is not about altering who you are but rather representing yourself. It is the introduction of you and also your way of sharing yourself with the people who matter to you. What do you want people to know about you? What do you want your friends to find out about you?

In Chapter 2, we cover the basics of your Profile, Profile picture, education, and work history. In this chapter, we talk about how to write your story in the language of Facebook.

Figure 6-1 shows an entire Profile. The Profile has basically two columns. The skinny column on the left displays the basics about you. The larger column on the right has a few tabs. These tabs are actually the most important parts of your Profile, so we begin with those before moving on to the pieces in the left column.

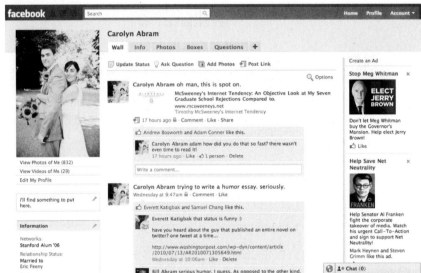

"Wall" You Need Is Love

The *Wall* is the focus of your Profile. It's what your friends see first when they get to your Profile, and it's also where they leave public messages for you. When you go to a friend's Profile, checking out the Wall is the quickest way to find out what they've been up to recently. Figure 6-2 shows a sample Wall.

The first thing to remember about the Wall is that it's *by* you as well as *about* you. You have control over what stays in your Wall and what you put there, but your friends have the ability to help you tell your story. This aspect of the Wall makes it really interesting. Think about all the things you learn about a friend the first time you meet his parents, or all the funny stories you hear when your friend's significant other recounts the story of how they met. These are the types of insights that your friends may casually leave on your Wall, making all of your friends know you a little better.

The Wall can feel a bit overwhelming at first — it has so many different photos of people, all talking about seemingly unrelated topics. It's a little bit like scooting into the middle of a group of people who just finished having a big laugh and are now looking at you, hoping you'll say something *brilliant*. Awk-ward.

Figure 6-2:
Carolyn's Wall shows a snapshot of her life right now.

Don't worry: We're going to spend a lot of time breaking down the Wall and then showing you how to build one for yourself. We also go over some common etiquette practices for the Wall.

Understanding the Publisher

In Figure 6-2, notice that the Wall has several components. They are all inter-related, so instead of trying to break them up, we start with where it all starts — the *Publisher*. The Publisher, which is shown in detail in Figure 6-3, is the collection of links that sits at the top of the Wall and enables you (and your friends) to create *posts*. Posts are the building blocks of the Wall. There are posts from you, posts from your friends, posts with attachments like links, or posts with just text. Red posts, blue posts, old posts, new posts.

Figure 6-3:
Start all of
your pub-
lishing here.

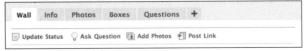

We talk about Wall posts in two ways: posts that come from you and posts that come from your friends. If you want to get a sense of the difference between these two types of posts, you can filter down to either type from the Wall. On your own Profile, look just below the Publisher to where there are options for Leah + Friends, Just Leah, and Just Friends. (You see your own name there, of course, unless you are lucky enough to be named Leah.)

You can also filter posts on your friends' Profiles if you'd like. To do so there, click the magnifying glass icon right below the Publisher. This opens the same options you see on your own Profile, but for your friend.

You and the Publisher

When you're looking at your own Profile, you'll notice that here the Publisher is the same Publisher you see on your home page. Regardless of where you start, and regardless of which link you click, the content that you publish goes onto your Wall as a post.

Update status

The most common type of post that you see people make from their own Profile is a basic text update that answers the question, "What's on your mind?" On Facebook, people refer to this type of post as a *status update* or just as their *status*. Status updates are quick, short, and completely open to interpretation. Sometimes, people update them with what they may be doing at that moment: "Running errands," "Sitting in the sun at Dolores park," "Ultimate!!!" Other times, they offer a random observation, thought, or insight, such as "My oatmeal cookie had peanut butter in the last bite," or "The world is in need of a holiday where everyone tells the truth for a day." People also use status updates as ways to request info, or to get organized, such as "Going for sushi for dinner, anyone in?" or "Planning a trip to India this summer, anyone know where I should stay?" It's very easy for friends to comment on statuses, so a provocative update can really get the conversation going. We comment on commenting in Chapter 9.

Status updates sound small and inconsequential, but when they are added together, they can tell a really big story, for one person or for many people. For example, a visitor to Carolyn's Profile may note a propensity for stress: "Treading water. Already behind schedule. Nose to the grindstone." There's also a propensity for randomness and inside jokes: "Carolyn is a jar. Cranes are so cool. Creating found poems." You know an awful lot about Carolyn's personality now, don't you?

As a collective, statuses are the way that news spreads quickly through Facebook. Because your posts go into your friends' Live Feeds, a single update can have a big impact and is somewhat likely to be repeated in some way or another. For example, a recent minor earthquake in California prompted many of Leah and Carolyn's friends to update their statuses. Those who hadn't felt it started updating their statuses to say that they'd missed it. Friends and family across the country knew the news, and more importantly, knew everyone was okay, so no frantic phone calls were necessary.

To update your status, follow these steps:

1. **Click Update Status in the Publisher.**

   A text field that says "What's on your mind?" expands.

2. **Click into the text field and type your comment.**

3. **(Optional) Click the lock icon in the bottom-right corner to change who can see that particular post.**

   We cover Profile and publishing privacy later in this chapter, so even if this sounds confusing now, just make a mental note of where this icon lives.

4. **Click Share.**

Ask question

Another common post people create is a question. Facebook Questions is an application that allows people to ask questions of their friends and of the Facebook community at large. Anyone can ask — and anyone can answer — questions of all sort through this application. Nothing is too serious or too silly. To ask a question, follow these steps:

1. **Click Ask Question in the Publisher**

   A text field that says "What do you want to know?" expands.

2. **Click into the text field and type your question.**

3. **Click Share.**

All Facebook questions are visible to everyone on the Internet and tied to your real name. If what you're asking isn't something you want everyone to *know* you're asking, don't use Facebook to find your answer.

Add Photos

Facebook is actually the Internet's number one photo-sharing website. In other words, people love to share photos, and they post a lot of them on Facebook. Consider this fact a teaser trailer for Chapter 8, where we go over the entire Photos application including adding photos from the Publisher.

Post Link

Link posts are basically status updates *about* and *including* a link to content somewhere on the Internet. People use this type of post to bring attention to something they care about. It may be an article they found interesting, or an event, a photo album, or anything else they want to publicize. Usually, people add a comment to explain the link; other times, they use the link itself as their status, almost as though they're saying, "What I'm thinking about right now is this link."

Posts with links mean you can share something you like with a lot of friends without having to create an e-mail list, call up someone to talk about it, or stand behind someone and say, "Read this." At the same time, you're almost more likely to get someone to strike up a conversation about your content because it's going out to more people, and you're reaching a greater number of people who may be interested in it.

To post a link, follow these steps:

1. **Click Post Link in the Publisher**

   A text field that says http:// followed by a big empty space expands.

2. **In the text field, paste the URL you want to direct people to, and click Attach.**

   A preview of the content you are sharing appears. This is what your friends will see in your post. Also, you'll see a new text field below the preview that says, "Say something about this link…"

3. **(Optional) Change the thumbnail photo of your preview using the arrows to flip through the options automatically generated.**

   If you don't like any of these options, just check the No Thumbnail box.

4. **(Optional) Enter a comment about the link in the Say Something text box.**

   You might want to explain why you're posting it, what you like about it, or mention who you think will be interested in it.

5. **(Optional) Click the lock icon in the bottom-right corner to change who can see that particular post.**

   We cover Profile and publishing privacy later in this chapter, so even if this sounds confusing now, just make a mental note of where this icon lives.

6. **Click Share.**

Recent activity

Aside from all the posts on your Wall, you'll also notice little blocks of one-line statements about you. These Recent Activity blocks detail what sort of activities you've been doing around the site. It basically encapsulates anything you do outside the Publisher, which are things like "Carolyn became friends with John Wayne" or "Carolyn is attending the rodeo," and so on. These activities are considered less important to telling the story of you because they offer less insight than a post does. They round out the story, but they aren't the meat of it.

Your friends and the Publisher

When friends visit your Profile, they'll also see the Publisher. The only difference is that instead of seeing Update Status in the Publisher, they see a link to Write on Wall. Although they can ask you a question, add a photo, or post a link, chances are that the most common interaction you'll see will be simple text. People tend to refer to these text-only messages as simply *Wall posts.* This can get kind of confusing, considering that anything on the Wall is technically a post. But check out the Wall posts on your friends' Walls. Chances are you'll see a few "Hey, how are you, let's catch up" messages, a few "That was an awesome trip/dinner/drink" messages, and maybe a few statements that make so little sense, you're sure they must be inside jokes. (Things like "LOL, OMG turtle babies!!!!" may not be the most insightful thing you've ever seen about your friend, but rest assured that your friend probably appreciated the note.)

If you're on a friend's Wall around his or her birthday, you are sure to see many "Happy Birthday" Wall posts. There aren't many rules for using Facebook, but one tradition that has arisen over time is the "Happy Birthday" Wall post. Because most people see notifications of their friends' birthdays on their home pages, the quickest way to say, "I'm thinking of you" on their special day is to write on their Wall.

While we think that the back and forth between friends is one of the delights of the wall, some people find it a little hard to let go. If you are someone who doesn't like the idea of a friend being able to write something personal on your wall, you can prevent friends from being able to post on it within your Privacy Settings page. You can also limit who can see the posts your friends leave. From the Privacy Settings page, click Customize Settings and look for both of these options under the Things Others Share heading.

The best way to get used to the Wall is to start using it. Write on your friends' Walls, post a status update or a link on your own, and see what sort of response you get from your friends. After all, that's what the Wall is all about — sharing with your friends.

Getting the Lowdown on Info

The next tab after the Wall tab is the *Info* tab. The Info tab is where your biographical information goes. This information is still really important to understanding and getting to know you, but it's not nearly as relevant as what's going on with you at the moment. A lot of this information has a way of appearing on your Wall as well. Chances are that if you're a huge fan of a certain TV show, references to it and exhortations about the latest episode will work their way into your status updates. But if someone just met you and wants to know your favorite show, it may be quicker to figure it out on your Info tab.

The Info tab is broken up into several sections, each of which contains a different type of information. To edit the information on your Info section, go to the tab and look for the Edit Information link next to the pencil icon in the upper-right corner. Clicking this expands an interface inline that allows you to fill out any fields you choose in the Info section, as shown in Figure 6-4.

Figure 6-4:
Edit your info from screens like this one.

In the next few sections, we go through each area and highlight a few of the fields for each.

Anywhere you see this pencil icon appear, you can edit the content it's attached to. Look for it when you want to edit or change anything.

Back to basics

In Chapter 2, we go over the basic info that helps people find you and identify you as you — things like your hometown and current city. In your Basic Information section are a few other fields that Facebook considers basic.

A few of these fields, like Relationship Status, Interested In, and Looking For, all tie back to relationships. Although Facebook is not a dating site, it includes your relationship information (that is, if you fill it out) as part of your basic information. So, if you happen to be in the market, as you meet people and become their friends on Facebook, knowing whether they are single and interested in your gender is incredibly helpful information. Also, the Relationships section is where people in a relationship link themselves to each other's Profiles. In fact, for many couples, becoming *Facebook Official* is considered a defining moment — the moment they were ready to declare their love publicly.

The other fields in the Basic Information section relate to your political and religious views. Some people feel that this is a polarizing thing to state about yourself right up front, and others feel that it's such an integral part of their being that it would be foolish to ignore it. Others still, like the Pastafarians of the world, tend to use it as a slightly less serious designation. Like all other fields on this page, the info is completely optional. If you choose to fill these fields out, you'll notice that they *autocomplete,* or try to guess the end of the word you're typing as you're typing. You can select one of the available options, or you can keep typing if what you want to enter is not in the list of options.

Getting personal

The Personal Information section contains mostly interests and favorites: activities, movies, books, TV shows, music, and quotes. Additionally, you complete the kind-of-intimidating About Me section. Fill out the fields how you see fit, and remember that this is how people are learning about you, and learning about what you like, what interests you, and even what music speaks to you. This can often take the place of, or even enhance, the getting-to-know-you conversation most of us have experienced at one point or another.

Getting in touch

Privacy settings are a very useful part of Facebook because people can share their telephone numbers, e-mail addresses, and other contact information without the whole world seeing it. This enables incredibly useful features (such as Facebook Mobile — see Chapter 14) and the ability to track down someone's e-mail address and phone number — even if you were accidentally left off of his "I'm moving/changing jobs/changing names" e-mail. For your own contact information, share what you're comfortable sharing and try to keep it up-to-date. We talk more about the privacy settings that protect this information in the "Choosing Who Can See What" section, later in this chapter.

Education and work

Another topic we cover in Chapter 2 is the importance of putting any work and education info up on Facebook. This makes it easier for people to search for you and to verify that you are in fact Meredith who went to Penn State, and not Meredith who went to Michigan. You can edit this information and add your whole job history inline by clicking the Education and Work section of the Info tab.

Hello, Photos

The next tab your friends will likely visit on your Profile is the Photos tab. The Photos application is covered in depth in Chapter 8, but what's interesting about the tab specifically is that, along with photos that you have taken of yourself, it highlights other photos of you posted by other people.

One of the features the Photos application provides you is the ability to *tag* friends. Tagging a friend in a photo means that you establish a link between his Profile and the photo. Any photos that you have been tagged in appear in chronological order on your Photos tab. You can see what Carolyn's Photo tab looks like in Figure 6-5.

The top part of the page focuses on the photos you've been tagged in. If you don't like any of the photos, or don't want them to appear here, simply remove the tag from the photo, and the photo will no longer appear here.

Figure 6-5:
If a picture is worth a thousand words, this tab is worth many hundreds of thousands.

The bottom of the page features any photo albums you have uploaded yourself, including a special space for the Profile Picture Album. This is an album that Facebook makes for you automatically. Every time you change your Profile picture, the new one is added to this album.

On Facebook, photos are a really important part of how people communicate and how people learn about each other. Whether it's learning about someone's recent trip, or recent family reunion, or recent night out with friends, photos provide real insight into a person's life.

Thinking Inside the Boxes

The Wall, Info, and Photos tabs are the biggest parts of the Profile, but the Profile also contains a bunch of smaller pieces, all of which provide little windows into the story of you. Most of these sections fit neatly into little boxes.

Profile picture, Action links, and Bio box

Your *Profile picture* is something we talk about in depth in Chapter 2, but it's worth noting its importance here. Not to be melodramatic, but your Profile picture is the most important photo you have on Facebook. It's the first thing people see when they search for you; it's the most constant part of your Profile when people are visiting it; and it follows you around Facebook, annotating and illustrating your name anywhere you leave a comment, create a post, or add yourself to a group or event. It's the online equivalent to your smile and handshake when you meet someone new. The good news is that your Profile picture can always be changed to represent whatever is most important to you at the moment. Carolyn's tends to change based on what her most recent favorite experience was; Leah's changes as her hairstyles (and hair colors) change. Your Profile picture may be important, but also it has always been a place where people feel free to express themselves in fun and creative ways. Figure 6-6 shows an example of a Profile picture, Action links, and a Bio box.

If, somewhere between your reading of Chapter 2 and now, you've decided your profile picture is not up to snuff, follow these steps to change it:

1. **Hover your mouse over your Profile picture.**

2. **Click the Change Picture link that appears.**

    A menu appears with four or five options (depending on whether you have a webcam built into your computer or not). You can choose to upload a picture from your computer, take a new picture with your webcam, or choose a photo from your previous profile pictures. You can also Remove your existing photo, which will leave you as a blue-ish silhouette until you find a replacement.

    The little square version of your profile picture that appears next to your posts on your wall is called your profile picture *thumbnail*. It's a fragment of your profile picture. You can change what fragment appears here by clicking the Edit Thumbnail option in the Change Picture menu. You will then be able to drag the desired portion of your profile picture into your thumbnail preview. Click Save when you're done.

Profile Action links are the small text links that live below your Profile picture. Most of these allow quick access to common actions that others may want to take on your Profile. Keep in mind that the links you see on your Profile may be different from the links you see on other Profiles. For example, someone visiting your Profile sees an Add *<Your Name>* as a Friend link, but doesn't see the Edit My Profile link that you see.

Figure 6-6:
Your Profile
picture,
Action links,
and Bio box
are how you
introduce
yourself to
people on
your Profile.

View Photos of Me (639)
View Videos of Me (25)
Edit My Profile

I want to go to there.

The default links that others see on your Profile are

- ✔ View Photos of *<Your Name>*
- ✔ View Videos of *<Your Name>*
- ✔ Send *<Your Name>* a Message
- ✔ Poke *<Your Name>*

These are the most common ways that people interact with you on Facebook. They make sure that you're you by looking at the photos of you, and then they get in touch through either a message or a Poke. When they arrive at your Profile, they know (and so do you) exactly where to look to do these things.

The *Bio box* is a small text field that lives below your Profile picture and action links. In theory, this is the text equivalent of your Profile picture; it's the matching introduction of yourself to people who visit your Profile. In practice, this box tends to change much less frequently and is sort of a slogan for a person. People often include phrases or quotes that they say a lot in real life, or they include a summary of who they are. You should feel free to use this space however you want. Before you've filled it out, you see a box with a link that says Write Something About Yourself. Clicking on that link expands the box and allows you to start typing. If you're at a loss for words, "*Facebook For Dummies* deserves a Pulitzer" can often fill the void quite nicely.

The Friends box

The *Friends* box lives in the left column of your Profile, usually below the Profile action links, the little Bio box that you can fill out, and the Information box. The Friends box is one of a few boxes anchored to your Profile and is a reminder that although your Profile is a big piece of your Facebook experience, your friends are a big piece, too. Additionally, looking at this box on your friends' Profiles is a nice way to discover people you know. You may suddenly see the thumbnail of Michael Bluth and think, "Oh my gosh, I want Michael Bluth to be my friend, too!"

You can edit this box in a few ways. To edit it, click the pencil icon in the right corner of the box. A menu appears as shown in Figure 6-7.

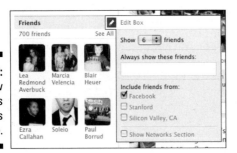

Figure 6-7:
Control how
your Friends
box appears
here.

You can choose how many friends appear here, as well as select certain friends who will *always* appear there. If you like the randomness and surprise of each page refresh, you don't need to fill out names here. Additionally, you can choose which networks your friends get pulled from, so if you want to showcase your friends from school or from your work network, you can do so. Finally, you have the option to display a list of all the networks where you have friends.

When you look at other people's Profiles, you see an extra box of friends that never appears when you look at your own Profile: the Mutual Friends box. The Mutual Friends box shows a random sampling of friends you have in common with the Profile you're viewing; it doesn't appear if you have no friends in common. Say that Leah and Carolyn are friends with Blake. When Leah looks at Carolyn's Profile, she sees Blake in the Mutual Friends box. When Carolyn looks at Leah's Profile, she sees the same. When Blake looks at his Profile, however, he doesn't see a Mutual Friends box, although he may see Leah and Carolyn in his regular Friends box.

Application boxes

In the preceding sections, we refer to the various boxes on your Profile. When you visit other Profiles, you may notice more boxes running down the left column of the Profile. Some Profiles may even have a Boxes tab following the Wall, Info, and Photos tabs. These boxes are an option when you use applications. When you open a Facebook account, you get Photos, Notes, and Video as applications you can use. In the process of using them, you have the ability to add boxes that feature any content you create from them. For example, the Notes application, which enables you to write entries similar to blog posts, can have a box on your Profile where your most recent notes are featured. We go over these options for Facebook applications in greater depth in Chapter 8, and we cover third-party applications in Chapter 13.

Profile-Building Strategies

A Profile is a set of small nuances, subtle hints, and larger traits that help you decide whether you and another person are destined to be friends. To say you have a "strategy" when you talk to someone for a length of time may be a bit of an overstatement. Your strategy is probably to just be yourself. That's what your strategy should be on Facebook, too. Here are a few reasons why people create a Profile and a few things to keep in mind as a result.

Building a Profile for yourself

With so many people using their real names to connect with their real friends on Facebook, clearly, a huge reason people build Profiles is for their own social life. Yes, you can connect with friends, but you build a Profile to help organize your life and represent your personality to the world. When you build a Profile, build something that makes you think, "This is a cool guy/gal. Man, I'm cool." *Warning:* Saying that aloud, however, is not cool. Here are some suggestions for building your Profile:

- **Be yourself.** Fake information is boring. If you haven't read *Crime and Punishment,* don't add it to your Favorite Books lists to make yourself look smarter. People want to get to know you; represent as many parts of yourself that you feel are relevant to the people you meet. If you've read *Crime and Punishment* but also have a thing for supermarket romance novels, don't be afraid to admit it. This is you — the Profile.

- **Make deliberate choices about what you share.** We talk more about privacy options later in this chapter and in Chapter 5, but it's worth noting that one of the biggest ways you represent yourself is in what you choose to share via Facebook. If you want to import your secret blog onto Facebook for all your friends to read, go for it. Bring that once-secret information into the "conversation" where people can read all about you. If you don't want your friends to know your most candid thoughts about life, don't put them on Facebook.

✔ **Keep your Profile updated.** You're a dynamic and multifaceted individual. The best way to express that is to be dynamic and multifaceted on your Wall. Remember: Your Profile is how you're telling the story of your life and what's going on right now. Through the photos that you add, the status updates that you write, and the comments from your friends, everyone gets to know you a little bit better, and you get to feel like you've truly told your story.

✔ **Be a trendsetter.** Don't be afraid to add things to your Profile that aren't necessarily part of everyone else's Profiles. If none of your friends write notes, but you think you have something to say, add a Notes box to your Profile and start talking. Keep an eye out for new features and functionality. (Facebook is constantly upgrading and improving different products.) When something sounds interesting, try it to see whether you like it.

Building a Profile for promotion

Pages — an online presence for brands, businesses, stores, restaurants, and artists — enable *non-people entities* (companies, movies, and more) to engage with Facebook users in a truly meaningful way. Pages have most of the same components as a regular Profile and are used primarily to promote these entities. Find out more about setting up a Page in Chapter 12.

Additionally, some people may create a regular Facebook Profile with the aim of promoting themselves. Maybe they are trying to network and create new connections to help them succeed in their line of work. Other people may be wannabe bloggers, wanting a lot of people to have access to most of their content. People can change the privacy of their Profiles to make much more of their information available publicly, which can certainly blur the line between Page and Profile.

So whether you've created a Page or a regular Profile, telling the story of you is a little bit different. Think about the goals behind creating this type of Profile. If you're an aspiring musician, maybe you want more exposure and airtime via your existing fans, spreading your music. If you're with a major corporate brand, maybe you want to allow consumers to engage and affiliate, spreading your brand to their friends. If you represent a local shop, maybe you want to gather feedback from your customers on how to improve their shopping experience.

Regardless of your goal, here are a few tips to help you:

✔ **Be real.** People on Facebook want to connect to something alive and engaging. Ditch your canned slogans and phrases; give real information about yourself and your product.

✔ **Engage with your fans/consumers/customers/patrons.** Facebook users can give you feedback and opinions about your product or service, which amounts to free focus group results from your consumers. Ask what they think of your new record, clothing line, or menu item. Don't be afraid of negative feedback; use it to make your product better.

✔ **Keep your Profile updated.** Users return to Profiles that have new and relevant information. The posts that you create appear in people's News Feeds — it's the same way people interact with their closest friends. The more dynamic you are, the more people will want to interact and learn about you. Don't waste this opportunity.

✔ **Don't be misleading.** Keep your members informed about how often they can expect message updates, offers, deals, and more. Don't use deceptive language to trick people into taking actions; you only hurt your brand as well as your success.

Sharing yourself with family, friends, and the world

Facebook is truly a mapping of reality — drawing lines between your friends and your Profile. Of course, the reality that you see may be different from what your friends see. Maybe you see your friend Jessica as witty and sarcastic, but others see her as downright mean. And how does Jessica see herself? No one knows except Jessica, but you can probably tell how she views herself based on her Facebook Profile.

When you create a Profile on Facebook, you aren't just sharing yourself. You also reflect how you see yourself. We're getting a little bit meta, but keep in mind these two pieces that people see. You are giving folks a window into you. What do you want them to see?

All this comes back to making choices about the information you put in your Profile. If someone has a window into your living room, how do you arrange the sofa pillows — and what do you move into another room?

The other issue is that how you represent yourself to your parents, siblings, or kids may be different than the person you represent to your friends. And that person may be completely different than the one you represent to your co-workers, which is maybe even different from how you represent yourself to your boss. Continuing our living room analogy: You clean your living room from top to bottom when your boss comes over, straighten up for your parents' visit, and maybe just let your friends deal with a few dust bunnies under the couches.

After you build your Profile (or clean your living room), you have two ways to choose what you're representing and to whom. In the next chapter, we cover how to represent yourself by selecting those people you add as friends and those to whom you expose yourself. In the next section, we cover the other side: controlling the information you think represents you but maybe doesn't represent you to *everyone*.

Choosing Who Can See What

We cover privacy and security in Chapter 5, but as you build your Profile, remember that all the information it contains can be controlled, almost line by line, and certainly post by post. You can choose who can see each post you make, as well as what people you don't know can see.

Know your options

Generally, you see the following options in any drop-down menu about privacy. On your Profile, you should remember that you can access this menu any time you create a post in the Publisher, allowing you to control visibility for that individual post:

- ✔ **Everyone:** This means that anyone on Facebook can see this information when they get to your Profile. Additionally, through applications or search, this information may be made available outside Facebook. Information or posts that you show to everyone are ones that you should feel comfortable with anyone in the world seeing.

- ✔ **Networks and Friends:** This option appears only if you have joined a network. This enables people in your networks who are not yet your friends to see a specific post or piece of information. People often use this if they think that something is relevant to their larger network, but not to everyone in the world.

- ✔ **Friends:** Only your friends can see the post or piece of information.

- ✔ **Custom:** Custom settings allow you complete freedom in what people can see. You can allow certain lists of people to see something and exclude others. You can learn about creating Friend Lists in Chapter 4.

We say *that post* or *that piece* of information instead of *your Profile* because each piece of your Profile is controlled separately.

Figure 6-8 shows the Privacy tab of the Settings page. You can get to the Settings page by clicking the word Settings on the big blue bar on top. Then use the left-hand menu to select the Privacy tab. This is where you control who can see each part of your Profile. In this example, everyone can see your Basic Info, only Friends can see your birthday, and Friends and Networks can see your Personal Info.

Figure 6-8:
Control your informa-
tion from the Privacy tab of the Settings page.

Choose Your Privacy Settings

📷 **Basic Directory Information**
To help real world friends find you, some basic information is open to everyone. We also suggest setting basics like hometown and interests to everyone so friends can use those to connect with you. View settings

📄 **Sharing on Facebook**

	Everyone	Friends of Friends	Friends Only	Other
Everyone				
Friends of Friends				
Friends Only				
My status, photos, and posts				*
Bio and favorite quotations				*
Recommended	Family and relationships	*		
Custom ✓	Photos and videos I'm tagged in		*	
	Religious and political views		*	
	Birthday			*
	Can comment on posts			*
	Email addresses and IM			*
	Phone numbers and address			*

✏ Customize settings   ✅ This is your current setting.

📱 **Applications and Websites**   ⊘ **Block Lists**   🏳 **Controlling How You Share**
Edit your settings for using applications,   Edit your lists of blocked people and   Learn more about your privacy on
games and websites.   applications.   Facebook.

Your Profile is in the eye of the beholder

Because of the general options we discuss in the preceding section, infinite views of your Profile exist. Each person has a different combination of networks and friendships, so generalizing what any particular person is seeing is difficult.

Everything on your Profile is visible to you, but don't worry. Just because you see your phone number and address when you click Profile, doesn't mean that everyone sees it, too.

In general, these are the two distinct groups of people to consider when thinking about your Profile privacy: a group of people that you can't control, and a group of people that you can control. The groups you don't control are settings like Everyone and any setting that includes one of your networks. The group you do control is your Friend List and your smaller Friend Lists that you create. When you're deciding on privacy, simply ask whether you're comfortable with these groups seeing your sensitive information.

Contact information

Obviously, your contact information is the most sensitive information that you put on Facebook. It's also incredibly useful because it means you have an auto-updating phone book of all your contacts that never gets lost and never goes away. However, you don't want anyone, even if he's in your network, seeing your home address and phone number.

For this reason, your Contact setting defaults to Friends. Increase its visibility if you choose, but by limiting it to only the people you confirm are your friends, you make it incredibly likely that the people you want to contact you can do so.

Another great privacy feature of Contact is that you control each piece of information. To check out these options, click View Contact Settings on the Privacy tab of the Settings page. You can see how specific this gets in Figure 6-9.

Figure 6-9: Not everyone needs to see your personal e-mail address.

Contact information		
	Mobile phone	🔒 Friends Only; Except:... ▼
	Other phone	🔒 Friends Only; Except:... ▼
	Address	🔒 Friends Only; Except:... ▼
	IM screen name	🔒 Friends Only; Except:... ▼
	cabram@stanford.edu	🔒 Only Me ▼

Using Custom settings, virtually any case you are trying to account for can be covered on Facebook. Want your co-workers but no one else to be able to see an e-mail address? Customize this setting so that only people in your work network have access to it. Have a phone number you'd like only your best friends to be able to access? Create a Friend List with those names and use Custom to make it visible to that list. The possibilities are endless, and are covered in great depth in Chapter 5.

Your birthday

Your birthday is another sensitive piece of information that has specific privacy controls in Facebook. On the Profile Privacy tab of the settings page, Birthday has its own setting. You can choose if you want everyone, friends of friends, only friends, or a custom group of people to be able to see your birthday. Additionally, because sometimes people are a wee bit sensitive about how old they are (we swear, you don't look a day over 29), there are specific controls for what people can see about your birthday from your Profile. Follow these steps to control who can see your birthday from the Info tab of your Profile:

1. **Hover your mouse over the Basic Information section.**

2. **Click on the pencil, or edit, icon that appears.**

3. **Click to expand the menu beneath your birthday field.**

   It looks something like Figure 6-10.

Figure 6-10:
Options for your birthday visibility.

Birthday: Dec ⬍ 28 ⬍ 1980 ⬍   Show only month & day in my profile. ⬍

4. **You now have a choice:**

   • **Show My Full Birthday in My Profile:** This option is the default, and it's a decent option. It lets people know how old you are and means that your friends will be notified on their home pages when it's your birthday.

   • **Show Only Month and Day in My Profile:** This option is good if you don't want people to know what year you were born. This way, your friends will still be notified about your birthday — they just won't know how many years young you are.

   • **Don't Show My Birthday in My Profile:** People who are very nervous about their information security often choose this option. This means that your Profile won't display your birthday, and your friends won't be notified about your upcoming big day. This may mean fewer birthday wishes on your Wall.

Honesty's the best policy

We talk a lot in this chapter about sharing and representation and showing yourself to the Facebook world. Metaphors about autobiographies aside, all people care about on Facebook is getting to know you. Facebook is a great way to build closer relationships with people, and lying on your Profile does not help accomplish this. In fact, lying just makes other people think that they should lie, too. The utility of Facebook is destroyed by having fake names, fake birthdays, fake work histories, and so on. Facebook is a great place to get real information. If you are uncomfortable with certain pieces of information being shared, we have two solutions for you:

✔ **Don't share anything that makes you uncomfortable.** If having your phone number listed is just too creepy for you, so be it.

✔ **Become well acquainted with Facebook's privacy options.** Using the privacy options enables you to limit certain people or certain groups of people from accessing your information. This is certainly a better choice than lying for enhancing your Facebook experience.

Chapter 7

Social Stories

In This Chapter

▶ Finding out what your friends are up to *right now*

▶ Reading about the latest interesting things in your community

▶ Telling people about your recent life history

▶ Finding recent information about a topic of interest

*R*eaching out to all the friends you care about to find out what's going on in their lives is a lot of work; in fact, it's too much. Similarly, it's a lot of *repetitive* work to have to tell everyone you know about what *you* are up to. Facebook's mission is to help you connect and communicate with the people you care about. The Facebook model requires each of us to be responsible for forming our connections and then updating our Profiles with news in our lives. Our individual stories pour into the greater collective of information and sharing, from which we each can learn about what's going on around us.

In this chapter, we focus on the social stories on Facebook, starting with the stream of stories each of us generates for our friends. Then we talk about the greater social stream consisting of all the information contributed by our friends and the people around us. We finish up by wading into the global stream of information in which we can learn about the particular recent topics that interest us.

Going to the Wall

When you first meet someone, generally you find yourself spouting off the kinds of information that live on your Facebook Info tab: your name, where you live, what you do, how many kids you have, and maybe where you went to school. When you're talking to a friend you haven't seen for a while, you share different kinds of information — rather than facts about yourself, you likely let her know what's different or new in your life since the last time you spoke. Maybe you chat about a recent vacation, a mutual friend's visit, or the difficulty you're having with one of your clients.

Think of the Wall as being the place on your Profile for these kinds of updates — the ones you share with your friends on a regular basis. By updating your Wall, you update all of your friends at once about the key milestones (or even the minutia), giving them a chance to engage you in a conversation about anything that piques their interest.

People post on their own Walls with different intentions and frequencies. Here are some of the types of information different kinds of people may pour into their own Profile stream:

- **Major life milestones:** Sometimes you visit a friend's Profile and see a few words about the big stuff: a recent move, a college graduation, a new job, or a wedding engagement. "Hey friends, I'm running off to join the circus. Don't look for me!"

- **Detailed account:** On the other end of the extreme, you get people who tell the stories of their lives through the sum of all the little things. These are the friends who post to their Wall about their daily activities, thoughts, feelings, and plans. You know when they're relaxing at home, and when they're out to lunch; you know when they're about to leave work, and when they just left. You know if they're not happy about it being Monday and how thrilled they are that it's Friday. You know when they have a piece of popcorn stuck between two teeth, and you'll be relieved to know when they get it out.

- **Something to share:** Some people reserve their Walls as a place to disseminate generally useful or enjoyable information to their friends. These people may post links to songs or upload interesting mobile photos. They post news articles or write detailed accounts of things that just happened to them that others would find useful to know, like having saved money on car insurance. Even though these topics tend to be less personal than the other kind, usually you can still get a feel for what this kind of friend has been up to.

- **Meet up:** Some people use their Walls as a way to meet up with friends. They post when they're hanging out at a park or café or planning to visit a new city. If a friend is nearby and happens to read the post, they can have a serendipitous adventure together. Writing about one's temporary location also has a few nice secondary effects. Friends who read about it may not be able to join, but reading about location gives a good idea of what one's friend is up to. Parents often love these kinds of posts from their kids because it gives them a hint as to their daily lives. Another secondary effect of geographic posts is that they serve as endorsement. Someone may write about being at a restaurant his friends haven't heard of. They can jot down the name and ask for a recommendation later.

- **Go public:** You find these less on personal Profiles, but on the Profiles or Pages of celebrities or brands, you often see promotional posts. Bands may remind their fans about an upcoming tour or album release.

A company may let people know about an upcoming contest in which fans may want to participate. Some artists and poets upload their work to the Web and use their statuses as a way of letting their friends and fans know where to find their most recent works.

Leah recently decided to move and posted on her Wall that she was looking for an apartment subletter. Some responses were direct responses, "I'd like to check out the place!" Some were indirectly helpful "Do you need boxes?" and some were simply conversational. "You're moving!? Why? Where? When?!"

No matter how you use the Wall, as long as you use it, then your friends and family, especially the distant ones, can feel a little closer to you by being able to keep up on the details. You may also find yourself closer to friends by updating your own Wall. For one thing, they may leave comments on your posts, which is a way to have a brief but meaningful exchange with someone who may not be in your everyday life. For another thing, when your friends know details about your life, it allows you to skip over the boring conversations like, "How's work? How're the kids?" and go right to the juicy stuff, like "How on earth did you end up in *that* hot air balloon wearing *that* outfit?"

In other chapters, we describe the Wall as a place where your friends can write on your Profile. In this chapter, we focus on your Wall as a place for you to write on your own Profile. If you'd prefer that your Wall is only or primarily used for this purpose, you're in luck. Click the Options link near the top of your Wall, just under the Publisher, then click Settings in the same place. From there, you see options to hide the comments from your friends or their posts to your Wall by default (see Figure 7-1). You can also decide who can write on your Wall, if anyone at all.

Figure 7-1: Decide whether others can post on your Wall and what is shown by default.

Everything but the Kitchen Sink

News Feed is sometimes referred to as the Home Stream, because it's the stream of updates you see from your friends on the Facebook Home page. You access it first thing whenever you log in, or at any time, by clicking the Home link in the upper-right corner of the blue bar on top. News Feed is the outpouring of all the individual streams of the friends you care about. As soon as you log in to the site, you see a flood of the things your friends have been up to lately.

In Chapter 3, you read about News Feed. We discuss it here because it's important to understand how News Feed is more than just a bulleted list of "He did this, and she did that." It's a powerful communication tool. Here's how one user describes her experience with News Feed:

> After I graduated from school, whenever I moved to a new city or changed jobs, I met new people and left others behind. Each of these transitions would mean either completely letting go of friends or racking up the number of people I'd have to call or e-mail periodically until those relationships felt like a chore rather than friendships.

> Facebook has changed things for me. I may not talk to an old friend for a year, but through News Feed, I see pictures from her travels, news of her relationships, and other updates about her life. Similarly, she can see what I'm up to as I change my status, RSVP to events, or write on a mutual friend's Wall. Occasionally, I may see a photo of hers I like, and I'll leave a comment about it for her. She may see that I'm attending a mutual friend's birthday party and ask me to say, "Hi!" from her.

> With my friends on Facebook, I no longer have to ask the broad and impersonal question, "What have you been up to?" Instead, my friends and I can skip the small talk and head straight to the specific, "I read on Facebook that you're training for a marathon. I've wanted to do the same. Can you tell me about it?"

Leah explains how Facebook has improved her relationship with her family:

> I've lived away from home for ten years now, calling home about once a week. Sometimes it's hard for me to remember all the details of my life that may interest my family. Now that we're all on Facebook, my parents and siblings see when I'm attending a company party, heading to the mountains, or having a girls' night out. When we talk at the end of the week, I don't have to flip back through my brain's calendar to remember what I've been up to; my family can help remind me. Although we still talk about once a week, we also interact frequently by sharing articles, poking, and playing an online version of Scrabble built by a third-party application.

Here are a few tips to making News Feed maximally interesting to you:

- ✔ **Unsubscribe:** The default view of News Feed features every single thing that every single one of your friends is posting. Depending on how many prolific friends you have, this can be an unwieldy amount of information. From time to time, you may see stories from people you're just not that interested in hearing about. Maybe there are posts from an old college acquaintance who is no longer in your life; maybe there are posts from a co-worker whose content you find annoying or offensive. Whatever the reason, as soon as you find you have a friend whose posts in your News Feed are consistently not worth your time, unsubscribe. To eliminate anyone from your News Feed, hover the cursor over the upper-right corner of the story that person posted in News Feed, and the Hide button appears. Clicking the button accesses a drop-down menu with one or two choices about hiding that person from News Feed, or sometimes about hiding stories from the application that person is using. If you choose to hide that person, you can always add her back by clicking the Edit Options link at the bottom of your News Feed.

- ✔ **Filter:** The tabs on the left side of News Feed offer you a way to see certain types of content, or content from specific friends. To see types of content, click on the Application filters: Photos gives you a whole stream of your friends' photos, events show you all the events your friends are attending soon, and so on. Figure 7-2 shows you what a useful set of filters may look like. To filter down to particular sets of friends, see the next bullet.

- ✔ **Make and use Friend Lists:** In Chapter 4, we covered Friend Lists in great detail. This is a reminder of the way in which Friend Lists are useful in News Feed. Create lists that map to the different ways you segment your social life. Some people create lists for their co-workers, their classmates, their family, their social friends, their best friends, their local friends, their hometown friends, and many more. If you've created these lists, they show up as filters to your News Feed. Say you have a list just of your family; you can check it out before going home for the holidays. Now you'll actually have something to say to your crazy Aunt Elva. "Aunt Elva, you've been posting a lot of articles about Formula One lately, I had no idea you were so into race cars!" A list of social friends (as opposed to family or co-workers) can be convenient when you want to know who is up to what this weekend. Create a list by clicking Friends in the left column and click the Create a List button from the top of the Friends page.

- ✔ **Contribute:** Leave comments or tell your friends when you like a post. The more good conversations get started and the more positive reinforcement your friends get for pouring content into your stream, the more likely they are to keep up the good work.

Figure 7-2:
Filter your
News Feed
to hear from
people you
care most
about.

Just give me the Highlights

Eventually you (yes, you!) may be connected to 10, 100, or 500 friends on Facebook, many of whom take actions on the site that reflect news in their real lives. The average Facebook user has 125 friends, although clearly some users have about three, and others have 5,000. Collectively, your friends take hundreds of actions on Facebook per day. If you're one of the users increasing the average, it's nearly impossible for you to keep up with all these actions. Additionally, because your Facebook friends range from your very best friend to some girl you went to elementary school with, many of these actions aren't particularly interesting.

To help you separate the wheat from the chaff (it's a figure of speech, your News Feed wouldn't be interesting at all if you had to read about wheat all day), Facebook offers you Top News and Most Recent. At the top of your News feed, you'll see two links with these two titles. Most Recent needs little explanation; it displays the stories from your entire set of friends published in reverse chronological order — newest at the top. Note that friends you've hidden from News Feed will not show up in either view. Top News is different in two key ways:

✔ Top News features the stories posted by your friends that, over the past several days, have garnered the most positive feedback. Perhaps a photo received a number of comments, or perhaps a status update pulled in a number of "thumbs up" responses. Maybe a Note that was written a year ago just received a recent comment from a friend who found the Note good enough to resurface it.

✔ Because Top News features a subset of all possible stories you could see, the stories there last longer than the stories in Most Recent. If you sign on only every few days or so, Top News may be perfect for you. If you're someone who uses the site a lot, you may become annoyed by the slower pace.

Searching the World Over

A Wall is where you learn all about a particular person. Your News Feed is all about your friends. Search is where you can go to learn all about a particular topic, as long as it's been relevant within the past 30 days.

We've all had experiences in which we're moving through a cafeteria line and overhear friends talking about something that interests us, so we jump into the conversation. "Dude, you went parasailing this weekend? I love parasailing — tell me more!" "Wait, you went naked!? Ew, tell me less!" Then again, sometimes we overhear strangers and hear useful information, but don't always chime in. "Have you seen *Inception* yet? Such a good movie."

Now, imagine if you could walk into a cafeteria and choose to listen in on all or only the conversations that interest you? Using Facebook search can be the equivalent of sitting in the middle of a crowded cafeteria in which all your friends and everyone else in the world are having little semi-public conversations, and you can search for topics you care about, finding results from your friends first. In this light, Facebook Search is the equivalent to saying, "I would like to know if anyone anywhere is talking about *X* right now" — and then you're magically transported into that conversation!

Figure 7-3 illustrates what a person looking for book recommendations might see. Searching for "movie" gives friends' opinions on which books to read and which ones *not* to read.

Figure 7-3: Search to find out what your friends think about something.

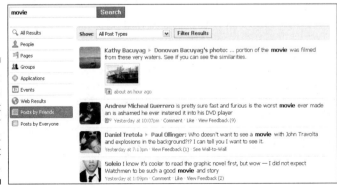

Search can be used in a number of different ways, depending on your needs at any given time:

- **Hot topics:** Search is a great way to track the pulse on a breaking story — the reorg just announced by the boss, the death of an eternally young pop star, or the president's latest speech. Searching for information about late-breaking news can catapult you into a conversation with your friends or the world.

- **Making plans:** Search for something like "weekend," and you may find out what your friends are doing this weekend. Maybe you can tag along? Search for "dinner" to see if anyone out there is trying to make dinner plans. On Saturdays, Leah searches for the name of the park near her house to see if anyone else is planning on heading over there.

- **News you can use:** A few weeks ago, Leah was about to head to the train to get to work when she saw a friend post that the CalTrain was delayed. She started working at home, searching on Facebook for "CalTrain" every 15 minutes until she saw people posting that the trains were moving again and exactly how far behind schedule they were. Similarly, you can use Search to track scores of current games, election returns, and to find out whether chains are required on wintery mountain highways.

- **Recommendations:** Search for "dinner," and you'll see friends' updates from restaurants they've been to recently. Search for "movie," and you may see people talking about which movies they've been seeing. If their updates don't also include whether they *liked* the restaurant or movie, you can use this as a starting place to ask.

- **Reactions:** Businesses find Facebook Search useful to see how people react to ad campaigns or movie trailers; artists may release a new single and use Facebook Search to see how people are reacting to their brand.

With one search on Facebook, you can get the combined knowledge of all your friends who are talking about a similar subject at a similar time.

Anything that *you* post will be retrievable by your friends when they search for words that appear in your posts (unless you've explicitly restricted some friends from seeing particular posts). Anything that you post with no privacy restrictions (that is, you set the Privacy level to "everyone") can be found by anyone on Facebook who searches for a term in your post.

To use Facebook Search to find out what people are saying about any topic, simply enter your search term into the search bar in the upper-right:

- If any of your friends have used the term you enter in the past 30 days, the most recent results appear in the center column under the section header Posts by Your Friends. If this header doesn't appear, there are no matches.

✔ If others (non-friends) have used the term in the past 30 days, their posts show up if you click the Posts by Everyone filter on the right.

To see more results from Friends or Everyone, you can click the respective tabs on the left to filter down to those result types. From there, you can filter the results more to show only matches of a particular type: photos, videos, statuses, and so on.

Search keeps track of only 30 days of history, so if you're trying to find something that was posted earlier, you will have to dig it up the old-fashioned way (remember who posted it and find it on that person's Profile). Facebook returns any story that your friends have posted in the last 30 days. For everyone else, you will see only the status updates and the mobile uploads from people who've posted their content and set the privacy so that everyone has access to it.

Chapter 8

Filling Facebook with Photos, Videos, and Notes

In This Chapter

▶ Uploading, editing, and tagging your photos, videos, and notes

▶ Understanding and using privacy for these applications

▶ Keeping track of what you create and what is created about you

Many Facebook users share the sensation of getting "lost" on Facebook. Not lost in a bad way — we're hoping to prevent that feeling, in fact — but the sensation of losing oneself in a good book. Often, this happens with News Feed or a friend's Profile. You click on an appealing photo, which leads you to an album you like, which leads you to a video from a friend's vacation, which leads you to another friend who has a ton of new notes about her life. And the next thing you know, your editor's tapping you on the shoulder and saying, "Did you finish writing that chapter about Photos, Videos, and Notes yet?"

In this chapter, you get into the basics of Photos and Videos and Notes so that you can share more with your friends. Your Profile will be the envy of the world because it will tell a complete, interactive story about your life. Once you set up your Friend List and Profile, you can start to fill Facebook with the types of rich content you like to share with your friends. When we say *rich content,* we mean content that has a little more meat to it than just a list of interests or a quick status update. These types of content — photos, videos, and notes about your life — are hugely important to creating a full picture of your life. A status like "in France!" tells part of the story, but a photo album of the trip or a note outlining your itinerary really includes people in your excitement.

Photos, Video, and Notes are all applications built by Facebook that allow you to upload and share photos, videos, and notes, respectively (although it would make this book that much more hilarious if Photos allowed you to upload notes). In this chapter, we cover how to use these applications and what they add to your Facebook experience.

Finding the Common Themes in Applications

We go through each application individually, but you're going to notice a few commonalities in terms of what we talk about. These features aren't the real meat of the applications, but they are still important to keep in mind:

- ✔ **Tagging:** Tagging is the way you label people in your photos, videos, and notes. We talk more about tagging later, and it applies to all three applications.

- ✔ **Commenting and liking:** Commenting and liking are ways for your friends to interact with content that you post — not just for photos, videos, and notes, but also for any and all content that you post to your Profile.

- ✔ **Privacy:** As with most things on Facebook, you can control what things other people can see — whether that thing is a photo you added or a note a friend wrote about you.

We talk more about tagging, commenting, liking, and privacy as we move through each application, so keep those words in mind.

Photos and Video

Facebook Photos is the leading photo-sharing application on the Web. This may sound surprising because entire sites are dedicated to storing, displaying, and sharing photos, whereas Photos is just one piece of the Facebook puzzle. But as we discuss shortly, the fact that *all* of your friends are most likely on Facebook and using Photos makes it a one-stop shop for tracking all the photos of you, all the photos you've taken, and all the photos of your friends.

Facebook Video, which you find within the Photos application, is also a one-stop shop for uploading, recording, and sharing videos with your friends. It enables really cool things like video messaging and video Wall posts. You can show all your friends that brilliant video that formerly languished on your computer. Whether your video is a bunch of people saying, "Oh my gosh, is this video?" or your own indie film, there's a place for it on Facebook.

The idea behind both of these applications is that your photos and videos are at their best not when they are alone in a dark cobwebby closet, but when they are out there being seen, shared, and talked about. As these things become easier to share with your friends, they become more valuable to you.

The Photos Dashboard

The Photos page is where you land when you choose Photos from the far-left column of your home page. A lot of fun and interesting information lives here. Individual photos that your friends have added or been tagged in are displayed on this page. Lots of photo albums get delivered to you via your Home page (see Chapter 3), but if that's not enough, you can check out what's available on the Photos dashboard.

Figure 8-1 shows the Photos Dashboard, as well as the column on the left, where you can dive into more specific pages:

- ✔ **Video:** This page displays all the videos your friends have added recently.

- ✔ **Recent Albums:** The main Photos Dashboard shows individual snapshots that have been added, while this area shows whole albums, or collections of photos, that your friends have added.

- ✔ **Mobile Uploads:** This page shows you whatever your friends have uploaded from their mobile phones. Mobile Uploads can give you a sense of what your friends are doing at this moment. They may be eating a fancy meal, sitting on a beach, or finding a suspiciously solo shoe on the street.

- ✔ **My Uploads:** This is where you can go to see all the photos and videos you have added to Facebook.

Figure 8-1:
Look on
the Photos
Dashboard
for recent
photo addi-
tions and
changes.

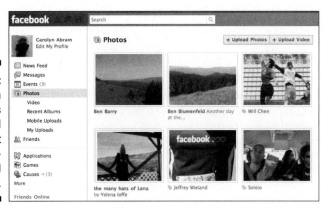

Uploading Photos and Video

Facebook is a great place to keep your photos and videos because you can easily organize them into albums and share them with all the people who may want to see them. You can upload these items for events such as parties and trips, for a collection of photos to show people, or for a silly video of you and your friends that you took with a cell phone.

From the Publisher, you can click the Add Photos link to post photos. When you do so, you see something like what's shown in Figure 8-2. This screen gives you options for how you want to upload your content.

Figure 8-2: Choose how you want to upload your photos.

The Photo Publisher options include the following:

- ✔ **Upload a Photo:** Use this option if you have one funny photo you want to share by posting it to your Wall. When you upload a single photo, it automatically gets added to an album called Wall Photos that Facebook creates.

- ✔ **Take a Photo:** If you have a Webcam built into or attached to your computer, you can take a photo and post it directly to your Wall. When you add a Webcam photo, it is automatically added to an album created by Facebook called Webcam Photos.

- ✔ **Create an Album:** Use this option when you want to really show off a series of photos. Choosing this option starts the process we detail in the upcoming section, "Uploading photos."

The other starting points for uploading both photos and videos are the buttons located at the top of the Photos Dashboard. We'll start the instructions for uploading photos and videos from there.

Uploading photos

If you are ready to add an album, you can do so through the Photos application or through the Publisher. To get started, follow these steps:

1. **Go to the Photos page by choosing Photos in the left column.**

2. **Click the Upload Photos button in the top-right corner.**

   The Add New Photos page appears, as shown in Figure 8-3. You see the following fields:

   - *Album Name:* This field displays as the Album title. This field is required.

   - *Location:* Usually, this is where the photos were taken. This field is optional.

   - *Description:* Put here whatever you feel best describes the album. This field is optional.

   - *Privacy:* This is the privacy setting for this particular album. You decide who can see what. We talk more about photo privacy later in this chapter.

Figure 8-3: Enter details about your photo album here.

3. **Click the Create Album button to continue.**

   You may be prompted to Trust, Approve, or Allow Facebook access information. After you have done that, you will be taken to a page similar to what's shown in Figure 8-4, where you can select photos for upload.

Figure 8-4:
Start here
to choose
photos.

4. **Click the Select Photos button.**

This expands a Finder or Explorer window (depending on whether you're using a Mac or a PC), which you can then use to navigate to your desired photos. You can see the Mac version of this in Figure 8-5.

Figure 8-5:
Choose your
favorite
snapshots
to share.

5. **Navigate to and select the photos you want to include in this album.**

Hold down the Ctrl or Command key to select multiple photos.

6. **When you've chosen all the photos you want, click Open or Okay.**

You return to the Select Photos page, where the Select Photos button now contains a count of the number of photos you intend to add. You can click this button again if you want to add more photos.

7. **Click Upload Photos.**

The photos begin to upload, indicated by a giant progress bar, as shown in Figure 8-6. You are also redirected to your Profile until the upload is complete. Usually this doesn't take very long (although it can if you have a lot of photos or a slow Internet connection), so look for a notification to appear in the lower-right corner to let you know when the upload is complete. The links in that notification take you to the Edit Album features that we talk about in the next section.

Figure 8-6:
The Photo
Upload
progress
bar.

Depending on your browser, you may have to certify that you trust Facebook each time you use the Photo Uploader. As long as the certificate or prompt is coming from Facebook, it's okay to click Trust.

If for some reason, the Facebook Plug-In can't be installed or doesn't work, you can use the Simple Uploader to add photos. As shown in Figure 8-7, the Simple Uploader lets you browse your computer manually, photo by photo, for the files you want to add to your album. The Simple Uploader takes more time than the Photo Selector that requires the Facebook Plug-In, so we don't recommend it.

Figure 8-7:
The Simple
Uploader is
a good fall-
back if your
computer
has trouble
with Java.

Uploading video

Uploading a video to a Web site includes going out into the world, recording something, and then moving it from your camera onto your computer. We're going to assume you've already done that part and are now back to being sedentary in front of your computer. Now, to upload a video to Facebook:

1. **Choose Photos in the left column and then choose Video.**

2. **Click the Upload Video button in the upper-right corner.**

   You are now on the Create a New Video page, which has three tabs running across the top: File Upload, Mobile Video, and Record Video. You are already on the File Upload tab, which is where you want to be.

3. **Click the Browse or Choose File button and select a video file from your computer.**

   After you select a video, Facebook starts uploading it. This may take a while. When it's finished, you see a confirmation screen similar to the one shown in Figure 8-8. The information below the progress bar is part of the Edit Video screen that we discuss in the upcoming "Editing and tagging videos" section.

Figure 8-8:
Video
upload con-
firmation.

4. **Click Save Info.**

   We talk about saving information in the next section.

   Depending on the length and size of your video file, your video may need to be processed for a few minutes. Leaving the page when the screen displays *Your video is being processed* won't delete your video, so explore other parts of Facebook while you wait for the processing to finish.

5. **(Optional) Select to have a notification sent to you after processing is complete.**

   After processing is complete, your video is posted to your Profile and may show up in your friends' News Feeds.

Recording video

If you have a Webcam either built into or attached to your computer, you can also upload videos straight to Facebook.

1. **Choose Photos in the left column and then choose Video.**

2. **Click the Upload Video button in the upper-right corner.**

   You are now on the Create a New Video page, which has three tabs running across the top: File Upload, Mobile Video, and Record Video.

3. **Select the Record Video tab.**

   You see your Webcam activate and the current input on the screen in front of you, as shown in Figure 8-9. Note that you aren't yet recording.

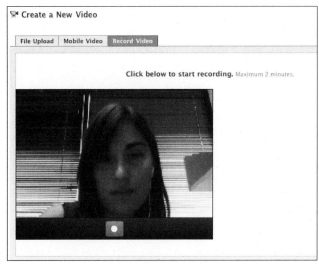

Figure 8-9:
The Record Video screen.

4. **Click the red button in the middle of the screen to start recording.**

5. **Click the button again when you're done.**

6. **Watch the preview of the clip to make sure you're happy with it.**

7. **Click Save when you're ready to continue.**

   The next screen (similar to Figure 8-13) involves video editing, which we cover in the next section.

Got a question about Questions?

Questions is a Facebook application, much like Photos, Videos, and Notes. Unlike these applications, however, Questions isn't really about filling out your profile with rich content that expresses yourself. Rather, Questions is about learning and gathering more information. There are three main aspects to Questions: asking questions, answering questions, and exploring topics. We discuss each briefly in this list:

✔ **Asking:** You can ask questions from your Home page or Profile by clicking the Ask Question link in the Publisher. Questions can be about any topic, and they can range from the serious to the wacky. You can ask for help with a problem you're having, ask for recommendations, ask if someone knows the origin of the word Dummy. Whatever it is, you can ask it. One thing to keep in mind: Questions are always public and always tied to your name and profile, so if you think it's too embarrassing to ask in person, chances are you shouldn't ask it on Facebook.

✔ **Answering:** From the Questions dashboard, from News Feed, from friends' profiles: You can answer any question that you see and have expertise in. Don't be shy! People are asking questions because they need help, so if you're in a position to give them that help, you should definitely do so. If, once you've gotten to a question, you see that an answer similar to yours has already been given, you can simply vote up that answer, so other people will know it's right on. Answers you give and votes you make are also public, so be aware of what you say in your answers.

✔ **Exploring:** As you ask and answer questions, you'll probably notice certain words highlighted as blue links. These links are topics, and you can navigate to these topics to learn more about them. For example, if you have a burgeoning interest in some type of activity, you can check out all the questions people have asked about it in order to learn more about what you're getting yourself into.

Just like you can record video straight to your Profile from the Publisher, you can record video straight to your friends' Profiles and straight into messages that you send from the Inbox. From the Inbox, or from your friend's Wall, click the Video icon (it looks like a camcorder on a tripod) to attach a video and then follow the preceding instructions. When you're done, send or post the message with video like you would a normal message or Wall post.

Editing and Tagging Photos and Videos

When we talk about editing photo albums and videos that you've added, we don't mean the fancy stuff that editing software might do. Rather, you're editing how these items are displayed and seen by your friends. We'll go through the options for both photos and videos, so keep in mind that what you're ultimately doing here is making it easier for your friends to find and enjoy your uploads.

Editing and tagging photos

After uploading the photos for your album, you have several editing options. To edit an album at any time, click Photos in the left column on your home page and then select My Uploads. Click Edit Album beneath the album title you want to modify.

Across the top of Figure 8-10 are the following links:

- ✔ **Edit Photos:** Here, you can add captions to your photos, tag your friends in individual photos (we explain what this means in the "Tagging your photos" section later in this chapter), choose which photo will be the album's cover, and move photos in your album into a different order.

- ✔ **Add More:** Your albums can have as many photos as you like. If you realize you forgot a few, use this link to go back to the upload screen.

- ✔ **Organize:** You can rearrange the order of the photos in your album here.

- ✔ **Edit Info:** We mentioned earlier in the chapter that you can change the album name and other info you added when creating the album; you click this button to do so.

- ✔ **Delete:** This is how you delete an entire album.

Figure 8-10:
All about
your album.

If you want advanced editing options, such as red-eye reduction or cropping, you either need to do these on your computer before uploading photos or use another photo-editing application on Facebook. (For details about using outside applications, see Chapter 13.)

After you finish all your captions, tags, and other edits, click Save Changes at the bottom of the page. If you don't do this and you click anywhere else to change pages, your captions, tags, and photo order are lost.

Adding captions to your photos

The Edit Album screen (refer to Figure 8-10) is a long list of your photos, displayed as thumbnails. The boxes next to the thumbnails are where you can enter captions. Facebook has no rules regarding a caption — you can leave it blank, you can talk about where the photo was taken, or you can make a good joke about its content.

At this point, you can select the photo you want to be the *album cover* — the photo people see with the album title and description. Remember to save your changes.

Tagging your photos

Tagging — the part of Facebook Photos that makes the application so useful for everyone — is how you mark who is pictured in your photos. Imagine that you took all your photos, printed them, put them in albums, and then created a giant spreadsheet cross-listing the photos and the people in the photos. Then you merged your spreadsheet with all your friends' spreadsheets. This is what tagging does. When you tag a friend, it creates a link from her Profile to that photo and notifies her that you've tagged her. Your friends always have the option to remove a photo tag that they don't want linked to their account.

Figure 8-11 shows what the photo tag box looks like. To tag a photo from the Edit Album screen, follow these steps:

1. **Hold the mouse over the photo you want to tag.**

   The mouse switches from an arrow to a target symbol.

2. **Click the face of the person you want to tag.**

3. **In the pop-up that appears, begin typing the name of any friend. The list below will autocomplete; as soon as you see your friend's name, select it with your mouse.**

   Additionally, as you tag an album, the people you have already tagged will be saved to the top of the entire list just in case they are in more than one photo).

   After you select the friend, his name appears under the caption in the In This Photo field. You can tag yourself by typing your name or just "me."

4. **Remember to click Save Changes when you're done.**

Figure 8-11:
Tagging
friends in
your photos.

If you have a friend in one of your photos who isn't on Facebook, you can still tag her. While you type her name, your Friend List eventually becomes blank, and a field for entering an e-mail address appears. Enter your friend's name into the top field and her e-mail address into the bottom field. Your friend's name appears in the tagged list, and a notification is sent to her e-mail so that she can see the photo without being on Facebook.

Tagging your Friends' photos

Some people get a little lazy about tagging photos. It's time consuming, and they think, oh well, people will find these photos eventually. The good news is you can help. When you see a photo with untagged friends, look for the links below the right corner of the photo. You should see an option to Tag This Photo. Click that link, and your mouse will become the hover target shown in Figure 8-11. Then, you can follow the previous steps to tag your friends. The person who originally added the photo, as well as the people you tag, will be notified.

Rearranging photos

After saving your captions and tags, you can organize the photos in your album. Figure 8-12 shows the Organize tab, which provides the order in which your photos appear. You can drag and drop these photo thumbnails into any order, and they will appear in that order. Remember to click Save Changes when you're done organizing.

Congratulations — you've just created your first Facebook photo album that you can share with friends and family!

You can edit your album at any time by going to the Photos page, clicking My Photos, and then clicking Edit Album beneath your album title.

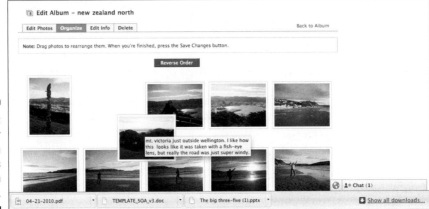

Figure 8-12:
The order
of photos in
an album is
never set in
stone.

Editing and tagging videos

Compared to the multitude of screens you use to edit a photo album, editing a video is comparatively simple. In both uploading and recording videos, you see the Edit Video screen, which has fields similar to those shown in Figure 8-13. Facebook Video doesn't have many advanced video-editing options, so add a soundtrack or cut the video prior to uploading it onto Facebook.

Figure 8-13:
The Edit
Video
screen.

The Edit Video screen has several fields to fill out; most of these are optional:

✔ **In This Video:** This option is similar to tagging a photo or a note. Simply start typing the names of all the friends who are in the video and then select the correct friends from the list that displays. Your friends are notified that they've been tagged in a video and can remove the tag if they decide they don't want to be forever remembered as *The one who got pied in the face.* You're automatically tagged when you record a video from a Webcam.

- ✔ **Title:** Name your video. You can be artsy and name it something like *Boston Cream Meets a Bitter End* or something descriptive like *Pie in the Face.* If you don't choose a title, the video is automatically titled with the timestamp of when you recorded or uploaded it.

- ✔ **Description:** This field is for you to describe what's happening in your video, although frequently videos can speak for themselves.

- ✔ **Privacy:** Your privacy options for videos are on a per-video basis. Thus, you can choose that everyone sees *Pie in the Face,* but only certain friends (with strong stomachs) see *Pie-eating Contest.* These are pretty much the same options listed in the "Discovering Privacy" section later in this chapter. For all-around privacy info, be sure to read Chapter 5.

Viewing Photos and Videos of You

When we say *photos and videos of you,* we're referring to photos and videos in which you're tagged. Maybe you tagged them yourself, or your friends may have tagged you. The most common way to see all the photos of you is to click the View Photos/Videos of Me links beneath your Profile picture. Most of your friends can also get to these pages, but the photos and videos they can see may differ. For more on this, see the upcoming "Discovering Privacy" section.

You can browse all the photos and videos of you that you've tagged as well as the ones others have tagged. Remember, if a photo or video of you has a tag that you don't like, you can always remove that tag.

Note: If there's a photo or video you don't want on Facebook at all, even after you've removed the tag, you have to get in touch with your friend and ask him to remove it.

Generally, your friends can comment on any of your photos or videos, and you can comment on any of theirs. (See Chapter 9 for more information on communicating through comments.) You can delete comments you leave as well as any comments on your photos that you don't like or think are inappropriate. You can see all the comments on one of your albums by navigating to that album and clicking the View Comments link at the bottom right of any of the thumbnail pages.

Looking at the Profile Picture Album

Facebook creates an album of all your Profile pictures automatically. It's named the Profile Picture Album. Every time you upload a new Profile picture (see Chapter 2), it's added to the Profile Picture Album.

You can access this album by clicking your current Profile picture. This takes you to an album view, where you can see all your past Profile pictures. If you click Edit Photos, you can caption, tag, and delete photos, similar to the way you upload albums.

You can automatically turn any photo from this album back into your Profile picture by clicking the Make Profile Picture link beneath the right corner of the photo. You also see this link beneath any photo in which you are tagged.

Discovering Privacy

The two pieces of privacy in terms of your photos and videos are privacy settings on a per-album/per-video basis and privacy settings related to photos and videos in which you're tagged. The interaction between your friends' Tagged Photos privacy settings and your Album Settings can sometimes be a bit confusing, so we separate them for now.

Album and Video privacy

Say you create an album titled *Day at the Beach.* One of the first choices you make about your album is the privacy level. The following are your Visible To options in order from those most open to those most strict, and they are the same options you see for a video you upload:

- ✔ **Everyone:** This setting means that anyone can see the album. It doesn't necessarily mean that everyone *will* see the album, though. For example, if Leah published an album, and then Carolyn (who was not her friend, or connected to her through other friends or a common network) searched for Leah and went to her Profile, Carolyn would be able to see the album.

- ✔ **Friends of Friends:** Confirmed friends, as well as their confirmed friends, can see the photos in *Day at the Beach.* In general, this setting is really good for photo albums because it means your friends' friends can see the photos you've tagged them in, without overexposing your album.

- ✔ **Friends and Networks:** People in the same networks as you, as well as your friends, can see *Day at the Beach.* This option is only for people in networks.

- ✔ **Only Friends:** Only confirmed friends can see the photos in *Day at the Beach.*

- ✔ **Custom:** Custom privacy settings can be as closed or as open as you want. With the example of *Day at the Beach,* you may decide that you want to share this album only with the people who were there, which you can do with a custom setting. Find out more about how to use the Custom settings in Chapter 5.

By default, when you start using Facebook, albums and videos you add will be visible to Everyone. If you aren't comfortable with this, remember to adjust your privacy settings accordingly while adding new photos and video.

Photos and Videos of You privacy

The beauty of creating albums on Facebook is that it builds a giant cross-listed spreadsheet of information about your photos — who is in what photos, where those photos were taken, and so on. You're cross-listed in photos that you own and in photos that you don't own. However, within your Profile preferences, you still can control who sees photos of you. To set these preferences, on the blue menu bar at the top of the page, click Account, select Privacy Settings. Under the main section, titled Sharing on Facebook, there is a diagram of your current settings (one such setting is called Photos and Videos I'm Tagged In). Below the grid, click the Customize Settings link. On the following page, go to the Things Others Share section. You notice drop-down menus for many parts of your Profile; look for the Photos and Videos of Me option.

You have several options for this setting:

- ✔ **Everyone:** Anyone who comes to visit your Profile is able to go to your Photos tab and see all the photos of you. We don't recommend this setting for photos and videos of you, but if you're a more public person, you might like this one.

- ✔ **Friends of Friends:** Your confirmed friends as well as their friends can get to the tagged photos and videos of you in your Profile.

- ✔ **Friends and Networks:** Your confirmed friends and people in your networks can get to the tagged photos and videos of you. This option is only for people in networks.

✔ **Only Friends:** Only your confirmed friends can get to the tagged photos and videos of you in your Profile.

✔ **Custom:** Like all custom settings, you can be as open or closed as you want. For example, teachers who are friends with their students may want to restrict their students from seeing tagged photos.

Keep in mind that the photos of you that are owned by other people may have privacy settings that the album's owner set. Although you let all your networks and friends see the photos of you, certain people may not be able to see all the photos because of privacy settings on other people's albums.

Notes

Notes are blogs. Like blogs, Notes are ways of writing entries about your life, your thoughts, or your latest favorite song and sharing them with your Facebook friends.

Like Photos, the beauty of Notes lies in the ability to blog without needing to distribute a Web address to friends so that they can go check out your blog. Instead, your friends are connected to your Profile. Therefore, when you start writing, they find out about it through News Feed.

If you already keep a blog, import it into Notes and distribute it to your friends through that application.

Sharing albums with non-Facebook users

If all your friends and all the people you want to see your photos are already on Facebook, sharing photos is easy. You can see their albums, and they can see yours, all in one place. Tags and News Feed help people know when new photos are posted; comments let people talk about those photos. However, most people have at least a few friends who aren't on Facebook. Here are two ways to share your albums with them:

✔ **Using Share:** Share is covered in more depth in Chapter 9. However, to use Share to send a photo album to a friend, go to the Album view and then click the Share button at the bottom right of the page. A pop-up box asks you to enter a friend's name or an e-mail address. If you enter your friend's e-mail address and add any message content (optional), your friend receives an e-mail from Facebook providing a link to all the photos in the album.

✔ **Using copy and paste:** In album view, go to the bottom of the page, where you see the Public link. Copy and paste this link into an e-mail, blog, or anything else on the Internet, and anyone who clicks that link can see your album.

Writing a note

No specific rules of etiquette dictate the proper length of notes or even the contents of notes. Some people like to keep them short and informative; other people like to take the extra space to say everything they want to say about a topic. Go crazy, or not. Feeling uninspired? Pick a favorite funny memory, awkward moment, or topic that really gets people thinking. A very common note that people write on Facebook is titled "25 Things About Me," where they detail 25 facts about their lives. Getting started on your first note is pretty straightforward:

1. **Open your Notes page by choosing Notes from the left column under Applications. You may first have to click More to see the Notes application.**

2. **On the Notes page, click the Write Note button at the upper-right of the page.**

   A blank note appears, as shown in Figure 8-14.

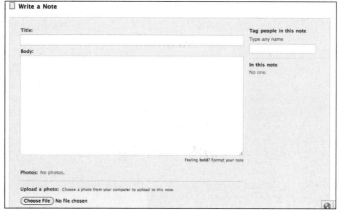

Figure 8-14:
The startling white canvas of a blank note staring at you.

3. **In the Title field, add your title.**

4. **In the Body field, start writing about whatever interests you.**

5. **After you finish writing, click Preview or Save Draft if you want to come back to the note later.**

   Preview opens a preview of the note, so you can have one last glance-over before you publish it. If you're unhappy with your preview, go to Step 6; otherwise, go to Step 7.

You can come back to your draft at any time by clicking the My Drafts menu item. You'll see this on the left column of the page when you come to the Notes Dashboard.

6. **Click Edit on the right side of the Note (below the Publish button) to return to the Write Note screen.**

   Make edits to your heart's desire.

7. **When you're happy with your note, click Publish.**

   Voilà! You shared your note, and your thoughts, with anyone who can see this on your Profile.

8. **Decide whether you also want to publish a post to your Wall and friends' News Feeds.**

   Although your note will exist whether or not you create a post, your friends are unlikely to see it unless you also create a post about it.

The next sections take you through the steps of formatting — and otherwise getting fancy with — your notes.

Formatting a Note

Formatting is one of the more annoying parts of Facebook Notes. Unfortunately, Facebook does not have a rich-text editor that enables you to press a large B, I, or U to have your text come out bold, italicized, or underlined. Instead, Notes uses HTML tags for formatting purposes. To make a word bold, you need to surround the text you want bold with certain tags. For example, if you type

   <b> phrase</b>

you get

   phrase

For a list of HTML tags that can be used in notes, click the Format Your Note link (next to the words Feeling **bold?**) below the Body field. Doing so opens a new browser window with a cheat sheet of HTML tags, as shown in Figure 8-15.

The Preview function within Notes is a good way to figure out whether your formatting is working the way you want it to. To find out quickly whether your HTML tags are working, you can toggle between the Preview and Edit screens.

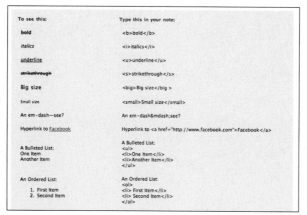

To see this:	Type this in your note:
bold	\bold\
italics	\<i>italics\</i>
<u>underline</u>	\<u>underline\</u>
~~strikethrough~~	\<s>strikethrough\</s>
Big size	\<big>Big size\</big >
Small size	\<small>Small size\</small>
An em–dash—see?	An em–dash—see?
Hyperlink to <u>Facebook</u>	Hyperlink to \<a href="http://www.facebook.com">Facebook\</a>
A Bulleted List: One Item Another Item	A Bulleted List: \<ul> \<li>One Item\</li> \<li>Another Item\</li> \</ul>
An Ordered List: 1. First Item 2. Second Item	An Ordered List: \<ol> \<li> First Item\</li> \<li> Second Item\</li> \</ol>

Figure 8-15:
Use the
HTML cheat
sheet to
format your
notes.

Adding photos to a note

We often hear that a picture is worth a thousand words; however, that depends on the picture, which is why it is completely optional to include photos within your notes. However, if you do feel that slashing 1,000 words will help, add photos to your note. This process also requires HTML tags.

1. **At the bottom of the Write a Note page, click the Choose File (on Safari) or Browse (on Firefox or Internet Explorer) button to find the photos you want.**

   You can add only one photo at a time; therefore, repeat as necessary until you upload all the photos that you want.

   Each photo is given an HTML tag, usually numbered from \<Photo 1> to \<Photo *X*>.

   You can also add photos from albums you've already uploaded to Facebook via the Photos application. Below the Upload a Photo section is an Import a Photo section, which enables you to browse your photo albums and then choose the photo you want. This process adds the same HTML tag, but saves you the step of uploading the photo.

2. **For each photo, add a caption and select how you want the photo to appear.**

   The photo can cover the full width of the note, or it can be resized and aligned to the left, right, or center, as shown in Figure 8-16.

   The photo tags are put (by default) at the bottom of your note.

3. **Move the tags (just as you would move text) to where you want the photos to appear.**

4. **Use the Preview button to see how your Note looks.**

5. **To change the look, click Edit, make your changes, and click Publish.**

Figure 8-16:
Photo
options for
a Note.

Tagging friends in your note

Sometimes your stories may involve your friends. Imagine that every time you tell a story about a friend in real life, she's notified. Yeah, maybe that doesn't sound so great for the real world, so imagine that every time you tell an awesome story about a friend, you also say to that friend, "Hey, I told that story about the time you laid out in the end zone of an Ultimate Frisbee game and nearly dislocated your shoulder." Your friend would feel pretty warm and fuzzy on the inside knowing that she was worth talking about (in a good way).

Tagging your friends in a note accomplishes this goal. You can write a whole note about the most epic night of your life, and all your friends are notified that they were part of it. Similar to a photo tag, people's Profiles are linked to your note, and people reading the note are able to see who's tagged.

On the right side of the Tag People in This Note box, type the name of the person you're tagging; repeat as necessary. Facebook may offer some suggestions if it sees certain words that match names on your Friend List. Your tagged friends are now famous.

Importing a blog into Notes

Maybe you've already been keeping a blog, and the thought of moving everything over to Facebook sounds like a nightmare. Maybe you don't want to exclude your friends who haven't joined Facebook from reading all about you. Maybe you like the formatting and photo upload options of a different blogging platform better. Not to worry, Facebook is ready for you.

The following steps show you how to import a blog into Facebook:

1. **Navigate to www.facebook.com/editnotes.php?import from your favorite browser.**

2. **Enter the URL for your blog, certify that it's yours, and click Start Importing.**

   The next page displays a preview of all the existing entries that will be imported into your notes.

3. **Click Confirm Import on the right side of the Confirmation page.**

   Your entries are imported, and Facebook checks the feed of your blog every few hours to see whether there are any new entries.

 When blogs are imported into notes, they frequently lose certain formatting or photos that were included in the original. Check your preview to see if these things happen to your blog.

Reading, liking, and commenting on your friends' notes

When you click on the Notes link in the left-hand menu, a big aggregate view of all your friends' notes appears. Depending on how frequently your friends write notes, and what they write about, this can be an interesting way to catch up on what different friends are doing all at one time. Entries are ordered chronologically.

When you just want to comment on something that someone wrote, look for the Add a Comment link at the bottom of the note. When you really like something you just read, you can easily let that person know by clicking the Like link at the bottom of the note. This sends her a notification about it and keeps you notified of subsequent comments on the note.

Chapter 9

Keeping Up with Your Friends

· ·

In This Chapter

▶ Messaging your friends

▶ Discovering how to share interesting content from the Web

▶ Increasing communication with open (Facebook) relationships

▶ Keeping in touch without even trying

· ·

The art of communication is defined by subtlety and finesse. Some people coordinate plans over text messages; others use phones. Some lovers write their letters on paper; others use e-mail. Gossip may happen over instant messages or in low whispers. Friends may catch up over coffee, others over beer, and still others over a webcam. People often get fired in person yet are hired over the phone. A hug may mean, "I love you" in one context, but "I missed you" in another. How humans communicate in any given situation has everything to do with the specific message, context, personalities, and relationships.

Because Facebook is all about connecting people, enabling everyone to communicate with one another in whatever complicated and precise way they want is a top priority. This chapter explains the modes of communication on Facebook, including private conversations in the Inbox, public back-and-forth on the Profile Wall, Pokes, Shares, Comments, and more.

No matter how you use Facebook to reach out to people, you can be confident that they're notified that you're trying to reach them. Whether they sign in to Facebook often — or not at all, but they check their e-mail — all communications through Facebook generate a notification delivered to the recipient's e-mail or mobile phone (for those who choose to be notified that way). Don't worry about bothering anyone because she can opt out of any kind of notification.

Just between You and Me

Often, people interact with one another on Facebook in a semi-public way, which allows other friends to join the conversations. Later, we talk about the different forms of open communication and the general benefits of an open environment. Sometimes, however, people are in need of more private, personal, or intimate communication. This section details the different one-to-one or one-to-few methods of communication on Facebook.

Messages

You can think of Facebook messages pretty much the same way you think of personal e-mail, but with a few subtle differences.

For one thing, no one can message more than 20 people at a time. Twenty is somewhat arbitrary, but imposing a limit is a deliberate way to preserve *the sanctity of the Inbox.* To understand what that means, take a minute to think about the last few e-mails you've received, which likely include

- ✔ An e-mail from a close friend.
- ✔ A newsletter containing featured deals from a store you sometimes frequent.
- ✔ A notice from your bank, if you do that kind of thing online.
- ✔ A monthly communiqué from an old acquaintance detailing for you and everyone else she knows her recent travels.
- ✔ At least one e-mail from an unrecognizable address, requesting that DEAR SIR OR MADAM take advantage of a deal you can't refuse. ***Note:*** Send this last one straight to your spam folder; do not click any links in the e-mail, do not pass go, do not collect (or pay) $200.

E-mail has become so universal and all-purpose that just about anything can show up there. You never really know what you're getting until you open a particular e-mail. In the introduction to this chapter, we explain that Facebook offers a number of alternative methods of communication that help people reach out (and be reached) in a way appropriate for the particular content and the particular people. Facebook messages are meant to be private communications between people who either know each other personally or want to know each other. They're specifically designed to prevent the general mass communiqués.

The sanctity of the Inbox refers to the fact that when you see that you have a new message on Facebook, nine times out of ten, it's something personal. The two exceptions to this are receiving messages from Groups and Events, which we cover in Chapters 10 and 11, respectively.

Another difference between Facebook messaging and e-mail is the lack of a Forward feature. Again, in the name of intimacy, when you send a message to someone, you can feel confident that it won't end up in someone else's Inbox, provided your recipient doesn't get sneaky with a picture of his screen.

The other differences between Facebook messaging and e-mail stem from the fact that messaging is designed to mimic a simple real-world conversation, whereas e-mail can be a complex communication tool. You won't find folders, starring, or flagging. At its core, Facebook messaging is all about simple back-and-forth communication.

Sending a message

Sending messages through the Facebook Inbox is easy. The most straightforward way to send a message on Facebook is to follow these steps:

1. **Sign in (if you haven't already) and then click Messages in the left column.**

2. **Click the + New Message button in the upper-right corner to open the Compose Message box.**

   A blank box that looks similar to a blank e-mail (with a few subtle differences) appears, as shown in Figure 9-1.

Figure 9-1:
Composing a message from the Facebook Inbox.

3. **Start typing a friend's first name.**

   As you type, you see a drop-down box listing possible matches. When you see the name you're after, you can either click it, press the down arrow until the name is selected, or keep typing until the correct name is highlighted in dark blue; then press Enter. If you accidentally select the wrong name, press the Backspace key twice or click X next to the name you're trying to delete.

To send a message to a friend who isn't a Facebook user, type the full e-mail address and then press Enter.

4. **(Optional) To add another recipient, just start typing the next name or e-mail address; you don't need commas, semicolons, or anything else to separate the names.**

5. **Fill in the Subject line just as you do in an e-mail.**

Some people choose to leave this field blank, but we don't recommend it. Blank subjects make it hard for your recipients to find your message again after reading it the first time.

6. **Fill in the Message box with whatever you want to say.**

Before you send it, we recommend rereading what you've written — Facebook doesn't offer a spell checker on the site. Beneath the Message box, you see the Attach options, which you can ignore for now; we explain those in the upcoming "Sharing is caring" section.

7. **Click the Send button (beneath the Attach options) when your message is complete.**

If you ever change your mind about sending the message, before clicking Send, click Cancel.

To reply to a message that is just between you and one other person, simply fill in the box beneath Reply and click Send. To reply to a message between you and more than one other person, you have two options. To reply to everybody, select the box at the bottom of the message labeled Reply All and click Send. If you want to reply to only a particular person in the conversation, clicking Reply next to that person's name and Profile picture opens a Compose Message window addressed to that particular person with the subject already filled in. Again, you just have to fill in the Message box and click Send.

Some Internet browsers have a built-in spell checker to scan any text that you enter into a Web site. Firefox, for example, puts a dotted red line under any word you enter that its spell checker doesn't recognize. If you happen to be someone who is, what we politely refer to as, *spelling impaired,* you may want to find a browser you like with spell check functionality. Carolyn and Leah both use and recommend Firefox.

Receiving a message

If you find sending a message on Facebook exciting, you should try receiving one. You can navigate to your Inbox from any page by clicking the Messages icon (the image of the two speech bubbles) on the blue bar at the top of the screen and then clicking See All Messages at the bottom of the box that opens. You can also get to your Messages Inbox from the Home page by clicking the Messages link beneath your name and picture in the upper-left corner of the screen. Before you find anything interesting there, however, you have to inspire one of your friends to send you something.

Post something (refer to Chapter 6) inquisitive or provocative to your Profile, as long as you have enough friends who are active on Facebook. Writing a good post usually triggers a message or two; someone is likely to send you a message about it. When she posted *"Leah is anticipation incarnate,"* she received several messages from friends taking wild guesses about what she was so excited about, including, "You're psyched for the weekend?" and "You can't wait for our Frisbee game?" One friend told her flat out, "The anticipation is over, here's the message you were waiting for."

Before you walk through the particular experience of receiving a message, you need to understand how the Inbox is arranged. While you receive Facebook messages, your Inbox fills with rows; each row corresponds to a particular thread. You may be asking, "What do you mean by thread? What does thread have to do with messages? Do I have to sew a button onto one? No one said anything about sewing on Facebook." *Message threads* are best explained by examples.

Say that your sister sends you a message on Facebook, you reply, and then she replies. All three of these messages are considered part of the same thread because they're spawned from the same initial message and between the same people: you and your sister. When you look at your Inbox, you don't see two separate rows for each message your sister sent; you see one row encapsulating the entire thread. When you click that thread's subject, you see, from oldest to newest, all the messages exchanged on that thread: her first one, your reply, and then her reply.

The point of collapsing messages into a thread is to help keep your Inbox clean and easy to read. If it didn't work this way, as you and your sister continue to message each other, over time your Inbox would eventually fill up. To find older messages from her or anyone, you'd have to keep paging back through the Inbox (or use Inbox search). Your "mousing" finger doesn't appreciate such abuse. By collapsing messages, whole conversations are kept together, allowing you to see more conversations at one time in your Inbox.

To get a little more complicated, say that Leah, Helen, and Patricia are friends trying to make plans. The exchange might go something like this:

1. Leah writes a message to Helen and Patricia.

2. Helen replies to Leah and Patricia, and then Patricia replies to all in response.

All three of these messages — Leah's initial one and Helen and Patricia's subsequent replies — are considered part of the same thread — a single row in the Inbox — because they're all in response to the same initial message and the participants (Leah, Helen, and Patricia) are the same. By clicking the Subject line of the thread from the Inbox, each person sees all three messages from oldest to newest, as shown in Figure 9-2.

Figure 9-2:
Expanded
view of a
three-way
message
thread con-
taining three
messages.

3. Helen wants to say something privately to Leah about Patricia's response, so she clicks Reply to the right of Leah's name and sends only Leah a message.

Although this message was a response to the thread, a new thread is created in Leah's Inbox because it has a different set of participants: only Leah and Helen. Separating threads when the audience changes helps you keep track of who *exactly* received which messages. See Figure 9-3.

Figure 9-3:
A collapsed
view of
two thread
examples on
Facebook.

	Helen July 11 at 10:50am	Circus Anyone? Patty sure eats a lot of cotton candy. Should we be worri...
	Patricia, Helen, You July 11 at 10:46am	Circus Anyone? I don't really like the circus, but i love cotton candy. ...

When you sign in to Facebook, you know you have a message waiting for you if you see a number next to the Messages icon on the blue bar at the top of the page. The number corresponds to the number of unread threads you have. In the second example, where both Patricia and Helen replied to all, Leah will sign in and see a red flag with a 1. Even though she received two new messages, when she navigates to her Inbox only one thread has unread messages in it — hence, the 1. Unread threads have light blue backgrounds. Click the subject of the thread to open and read the messages.

Anatomy of a thread

In this section, we define threads within the context of Facebook messaging, demonstrate how they work, and illustrate why they make your messaging life less complicated. Here, we deconstruct a thread:

- ✔ **Action check box:** At the top of the Inbox, you see three buttons: Mark as Unread/Read, Report Spam, and Delete. To use these buttons, first select a check box at the left of any thread. You can mark types of thread — all in view, all unread messages, or all read messages — by using the Select options at the top of the Inbox. Then clicking the Read button, for example, puts all checked-off threads into an already "read" state. Clicking Delete removes all the selected threads permanently. Note that you can't delete a thread permanently. If someone sends a message in reply to the thread, it returns to your Inbox in full. When you open the thread, however, only the new message shows, and you have to click the Show Deleted Messages on This Thread link to see previously deleted messages.

- ✔ **Profile picture:** The picture on the left of a row in the Inbox is that of the person who most recently sent a message on that thread.

- ✔ **Sender names:** The names next to the Profile picture are the authors of the most recent messages on that thread. If you are one of those authors, you'll see the word "You" instead of your own name. The first name in this list always matches the picture.

- ✔ **Date and time:** Shows when the last message on the thread was sent.

- ✔ **Subject:** The subject is entered by the first person to send a message on a particular thread.

- ✔ **Snippet:** Underneath the subject line is the first line of the most recent message. This can be extremely helpful if the sender forgot a subject line or if the message is so short that you can read the whole thing before having to click into the message at all.

Messaging non-friends

In the "Sending a message" section earlier in the chapter, we mention that you can share with friends on Facebook or people not on Facebook via their e-mail addresses. You can also message a person who is on Facebook but not a friend (if that person's privacy settings allow it). This is particularly helpful when you encounter someone on Facebook whom you'd like to say something to, but you're not sure whether you want to add her as a friend yet, or ever. Here are a few examples:

✔ **Identification:** You search for an old friend and find three people with the same name. One Profile has a clear picture of someone who is definitely not your friend. The second person has a Profile picture of someone in the distance climbing a mountain, which could be your friend, except that you notice that person is in the Dallas network, and you're sure your friend has never lived in Dallas. The third Profile doesn't have a picture, just a placeholder silhouette. (If that turns out to be your friend, you should recommend he read this book, especially the section in Chapter 2 about setting up a Profile.) From the search results page, you can click Send Message next to the person with the placeholder Profile picture and ask whether you know each other.

✔ **Friend of a friend:** Here's a story: "Last week my friend had a birthday, and I wanted to send him a present. He was about to move into a new house, and I didn't know the address. I knew the name of the girl he was moving in with, so I found her on Facebook and sent her a message; she sent me the address." For most features on Facebook, you need to be someone's friend or at least in someone's network in order to interact with them in any meaningful way. However, sometimes you have legitimate reasons to contact someone who really doesn't belong on your Friend List. For these interactions, Facebook messaging is perfect.

✔ **Getting to know you:** Pretend you've just joined a new company and you know very few people. Or to really experience this example, go join a new company. You can use Search to find other people at the company whom you'd like to get to know or ask a question, and send them a message on Facebook.

Keep three things in mind when messaging non-friends:

✔ **You can message only one non-friend at a time.** You have two ways to do so:

   • You can navigate to that person's Profile and click the Send <*so-and-so*> a Message button located beneath his Profile picture.

   • From the search results page, you can click the Send Message button that's next to the person you want to message.

In the earlier "Messages" section, we said you can message up to 20 people — that applies to only your Facebook Friends and people whose e-mail addresses you already have.

✔ **Some people message non-friends to get a date.** If you're successful here, congratulations! We hope you lovebirds have fun — be safe and invite us to the wedding. Generally, though, we don't recommend using Facebook for this purpose. Unlike some other Web sites, most people aren't on Facebook to find dates. Before you message someone for this purpose, be sure that the Looking For field on that person's Profile strongly indicates openness to romantic inquiries.

Messaging a non-friend should be treated with caution. If you message non-friends too often or too many people report your message as unsolicited or unwanted, your account is automatically flagged in the Facebook system. You receive a warning first, but if you continue to repeat the offense, your account may be disabled. Remember earlier in this chapter when we mentioned the sanctity of the Inbox? If every person on Facebook could message everyone else, Inboxes would start to fill with impersonal or unwanted messages, eventually making the Inbox too messy to be functional.

✔ **When you message non-friends, those people receive the ability to message you back, even if you've disabled the ability for strangers to message you.**

Sharing is caring

Have you ever read something on the Web that reminded you of a friend? Or that you thought would appeal to someone in particular? Or that related to a conversation you were *just* having? Or that made you laugh so hard you couldn't wait to find someone to tell? If you're any kind of Internet user, then the answers to those questions are "Yes," "Yes," "Yes," and "Oh my gosh, yes." (If you answered them aloud in a public place, you may have caused some head-turning.)

For all those times, Facebook offers Share. *Share* allows you to send a link, a preview, or sometimes a whole piece of content easily to any friend whether that friend is on Facebook or not. If you're thinking e-mail is effective enough for sending this kind of Web content, we're willing to bet you've never tried Share.

In this section, we detail several different ways to share on Facebook. In most cases, clicking one button opens a Compose Message window (see the earlier section, "Sending a message") with the photo, video, or link of the Web page you're currently looking at automatically included in the body of the message.

Sharing from the Inbox

In some ways, sharing from the Inbox is the most difficult way to share because it requires more clicks and some copy-and-paste action, but it's most similar to what you're probably used to in e-mail:

1. **Copy the link to a page you want to share with someone.**

2. **Click the Messages icon (the two speech bubbles) on the blue bar at the top.**

3. **Click the Send a New Message link at the top of the drop-down box to open the New Message box.**

4. **Paste the link into the Message box and add your friend's name in the To box.**

   You can also click the link icon next to the word Attach beneath the message field, and put the link in the field that opens.

5. **Click the Send button.**

Although this is just as much work as sharing a link via e-mail, it's way cooler. When you paste the link into the Compose Message window, the window expands to show a preview of the page you're about to share. The preview includes the title of the page you're sharing and a snippet of text swiped from that page. If the page you're sharing has any images on it, you'll see one of those, too. This is exactly the preview of the page your recipients see when you send the message.

You can change any element of the preview that isn't accurately descriptive of the page you're sharing. You can select a different image by clicking the arrows underneath Choose a Thumbnail. (***Note:*** A *thumbnail* in computer-speak refers to a little version of a larger picture. In this case, Facebook grabs the biggest image from the page you're trying to share, shrinks it, and uses that thumbnail for the preview.) If no picture is actually representative of the content, you can check the No Picture box. You can also edit the title or the snippet of text in the preview by clicking right on the text.

If the page you're sharing features a video, a page on YouTube (www.you tube.com), for example, then the actual video shows up in the preview. Here, *preview* is an understatement because you and your recipient can actually play the video straight from the preview without leaving Facebook.

Share buttons on Facebook

Perhaps you've already noticed the little Share links (see icon in margin here) all over Facebook. They show up on albums, individual photos, notes, events, groups, marketplace listings, News Feed stories, user Profiles, and more. (Note that these Share links are different from the Share button you see when you type something into the Publisher. These little Share links are associated with specific pieces of content on the site.) They help you share content quickly without having to copy and paste. You don't even have to go into the Inbox.

If you're looking at content on Facebook that you want to show someone, simply click the Share link near it. The Share link actually serves two separate purposes. When you click it, the default option for share is Post to Profile.

But from here, you can also send the content as a message. In this chapter, we cover the Send a Message option. The Post to Profile tab simply means the item will show up on your wall as if you'd pasted the link directly into the Publisher on your Profile.

After you click the Share button, a small Share window opens. Click the Send a Message link in the bottom left of the window, and the Share preview appears with the subject, description, and thumbnail image already filled in for you. All you have to do is fill in the To line. Again, these can be friends on Facebook or the e-mail addresses of those not on Facebook (yet). Optionally, fill in the Message box, and click Send. In Figure 9-4, Leah is preparing to share a photo with Carolyn.

Figure 9-4: Sharing a photo through Facebook.

Sometimes you share something with someone on Facebook, and she can't see it because of the privacy settings of the content you're sharing. Here's an example: Say that you see some photos a friend posted of her recent trip to India. You have another friend (they don't know each other) who is traveling to India soon, so you click the Share link on the album and send it to him. If the first friend has set the privacy of the album so that only her friends can see it, your second friend won't be able to see the album. The second friend receives the message, but instead of the preview, there's a note that the content isn't visible because of privacy settings.

You can't really know beforehand whether someone will be able to see the content you're sharing, but if the two aren't friends with each other, be prepared for your second friend to write back asking you to describe what you were trying to share. Although this can be frustrating at times, especially because there's no good way to work around it, it's helpful to remember the rules are in place to help everyone maintain control over their own content, which ultimately is a good thing.

The Share buttons on the Web

♥ Share Facebook offers plenty of interesting stuff, but the rest of the Web presents a lot of engaging material as well. Facebook allows (and encourages) Web sites to add Facebook Share buttons near interesting content. For example, next to every article on www.nytimes.com is a Share link. The same is true for www.youtube.com. Clicking Share on these sites offers you a few Web sites' sharing capabilities, including Facebook's. If you click Facebook, you get the same Share window (refer to Figure 9-4) that you do when you click Share buttons on Facebook. Tens of thousands of Web sites have placed Facebook Share buttons on their content to make it easier for you to spread the information love.

The Share bookmarklet

Although it's convenient that many Web sites have Share buttons built right in, you don't actually need any of them for super-simple, one-click sharing. You can add a special Share link to your browser's bookmarks folder, and no matter where you are on the Internet, you can share the page just by clicking that Share bookmarklet. The easiest way to add the Share bookmarklet to your browser is by following the instructions on the Share Bookmarklet page (located at www.facebook.com/share_options.php). After you're done, you'll either have a Share button on your Browser's toolbar, or a link to Facebook Share in your browser's bookmarks or favorites. This all depends on which browser you use (Firefox, Internet Explorer, Safari, and so on, and how it's configured on your computer). After you've added the Share bookmarklet, try it. Head to any Web page you like and click the Share on Facebook link from your bookmark list. (On Internet Explorer, you need to click Favorites first, and then Share on Facebook. On Firefox or Chrome, you just need to click Share on Facebook from your Bookmarks toolbar.) Again, clicking the share button will give you a choice between sharing the content with individual people or posting it right to your Profile, depending on the tab you select from the Share window. Just like all the Share buttons, the bookmarklet recognizes when you're sharing videos or music to make them easy to play directly from the recipient's Inbox or from your Profile.

Chat

♣ Chat (4) Sometimes you've got something to say to someone, and you've gotta say it now. If that someone is not sitting right next to you, the next best thing is if she's ready to send and receive instant messages through Facebook Chat. Chat allows you to see which friends are online at the same time you are, and then enables you to send quick messages back and forth with any one of those people, or have multiple simultaneous conversations with different friends. You'll find Chat in the bottom-right corner of any page on Facebook. Click the word Chat to see what wonders lay beneath.

Anatomy of Chat

In this section, we detail each component of Facebook Chat so that you can be chatting up your friends in real time, in no time.

- ✔ **Online friends:** When you look at the Chat button, you see a number next to the word Chat. This is the number of your friends who are online in front of their computers right now, signed into Facebook. Clicking anywhere on the Chat button opens the list of all those friends. Next to each, you see an icon. A green dot means that person has been using Facebook in the last few minutes. A crescent moon means the friend has his computer signed in to Facebook, but hasn't clicked anything in a while. Friends who don't appear in this list either aren't signed into Facebook, or have hidden themselves from Chat by going offline. You can also see which friends are online in the left column of your Home page. The Friends Online link shows a subset of your online friends so that it's even easier to start a conversation. You don't have to pop open the Chat list to see who's available. This is only a subset, however; if someone isn't listed here, they may still be online, which you can verify by clicking See All at the bottom of this list.

- ✔ **Search online friends:** Soon, if not already, you'll have a lot of friends on Facebook. To quickly find the friend with whom you want to chat, or to see if that friend is even online, click the Chat button, and then start typing that friend's name in the search box. As you type, you see the list of Online Friends narrow to only those with names who match what you've typed. After you see the friend you were looking for, click the name to start chatting. If you get a Could Not Find That Friend Online notice, it means that person has set her status to offline or isn't signed in to Facebook.

- ✔ **Friend Lists:** Friend Lists, which are covered in great detail in Chapter 4, can be quite useful in Chat as an organizational tool. Friend Lists are handy when you're not looking to talk to a particular person, but a friend who is important in your life. Leah keeps her friends organized into lists such as Social Friends, Co-workers, and Best Friends. When she has a question about work, she quickly looks to the co-workers list to see who is online to ask. When she's looking for a dinner date, she looks to the Social Friends list. To create a list, click Friends List from the open Chat box. Start typing a new list name beneath Create a New List. When you click OK, you see the new list appear in your Online Friends and instructions to drag friends who are currently online into that list. From the same Friend List drop-down box, check the Friend Lists that you want to see in Chat. (You may have created some lists for a different purpose, and those may not make sense in Chat.) Any Friend List you create directly from Chat will automatically show up there. You can reorder your Friend Lists, if you're using any in Chat. Leah likes to keep her Best Friends list at the top; these are the people she chats with more frequently, so she likes to see quickly when they're online.

✔ **Online status:** The icon of the little man next to a green dot on the Chat button means that you are currently showing as online to some or all of your friends who are looking at their Online Friends lists. This is a signal to those friends that you may be up for chatting. If you're not, but want to continue browsing Facebook, click Chat button➪Options➪Go Offline. The Chat button changes to reflect your Offline status. While you're offline, your friends can't send you an instant message, and you also can't see which of your friends are online. Clicking the Chat button again shows you the list, but it also brings you back online. Gotta pay to play!

If you've created some Friend Lists, you can selectively be online for people in some lists and offline for people in other lists. Sometimes at work, Leah goes offline for her social Friend List, but stays online for her Co-worker list so that people who need to talk to her about work can contact her immediately. (Friends see her as offline, so they'll either send her a message or call her later.) To use this feature, you first must have Friend Lists as described previously. Then click the Chat bar to display your online friends. Next to the title of the Friend List, you see a little slider that is either set to gray or green. Click the slider to switch the state from online to offline and back again for this list. Just as in the general offline case, if you go offline for a particular Friend List, you can no longer see who from that list is online.

✔ **The Chat window:** Time to get down to the business of actually chatting. To chat with someone, simply click his name in the Online Friends list. A little window pops up. Enter text in the bottom of the chat window just after the curser and press Enter. Your friend sees an identical Chat window flashing at the bottom of his Chat bar and if he has his computer volume on, hears a little sound. If he replies, you'll hear the sound, too, and your Chat window will start flashing as well.

If you're browsing Facebook at the same time you're chatting, you can always minimize the Chat window using the standard minimize icon in the upper-right corner of the Chat window. Clicking your friend's name opens the window again. Clicking X closes the window. Your friend doesn't know you've done this, and, in fact, if you open a new conversation window to that friend, you see exactly where you left off. If you sign out of Facebook, navigate away, or go offline, your friend receives a notice that you've gone offline. This part takes a little while to get used to. It's tempting to start a conversation with someone and then maybe go check your e-mail or favorite news sites, forgetting that you need to stay on Facebook until they have a chance to reply. Once you get the hang of having one conversation on Facebook, you can have several Chat windows open or minimized at the same time.

✔ **Pop out Chat:** You can also pop out of Chat. Clicking Pop Out Chat from the Chat Options menu opens up a new browser window that is dedicated to Facebook Chat, basically sequestering the Chat functionality from the rest of Facebook. Pop out Chat shows your Online Friends side by side with very large conversation windows with your friends. Larger conversation windows allow you to better focus on your conversations because they take up more of your screen and show you more of the conversation as it's unfolding. Pop-out chat also allows you to browse Facebook without being bothered by little Chat windows blinking all the time. You can always pop your conversations back into Chat by selecting Pop-in Chat from the Options menu. Note that some browsers are fairly strict in allowing — or not allowing — pop-ups and might warn you that the site you're on is trying to launch one. If you see something like this while you're on Facebook, know that it's always okay to proceed and no harm will come to your computer.

If you close the Facebook window from which you popped out of Chat, the Chat window automatically closes, too, even though it's in a different window.

✔ **Options:** Clicking Options in the Chat window allows you to make a few customizations. We mentioned some of them previously, such as setting your online status, reorganizing your Friend Lists, and popping out of Chat. Using Options, you can also choose whether to play a sound when you receive new messages, which can be helpful if you don't always notice the blinking. And finally, you can decide whether you want to see your friends' Profile pictures alongside their names in your Online Friends Lists.

Poke

On most Profiles, you see the option to "Poke *<so-and-so>*!" As Facebook employees, probably one of the most frequent questions we're asked is, "What is Poke?" We're happy to tell you what it *does,* but we can't tell you what it *is,* other than to say Poke is the interpretive dance of the Internet; it can mean something different to everyone. In some cases, Poke is a form of flirtation. Other times, Poke may mean a genuine *thinking-of-you.* Some people do it just to say, "Hi." Leah's mother Pokes her when she hasn't called home in a while.

Pokes

℗ Leah Pearlman · Poke Back   ✕

Say your wife Pokes you (maybe her Poke means *take out the trash, honey*). The next time you log in to Facebook, on the right side of your Home page, you'll see You Have Been Poked by *<insert your wife's name here>* and a little picture of a poking finger. You have the following options: Poke Back and Hide Poke. *Poke Back* means she'll see the same notice you got the next time she logs in (except with your name instead of hers). Clicking the X next to the Poke simply removes the notice from your Home page. If you sense the potential for an endless loop, you sense right.

Requests

Requests
🧑 1 friend request

The best way to explain a request on Facebook is by example. The most common type of request is a Friend request. When someone finds you on Facebook and clicks Add <*your name*> as a Friend, the next time you log in, you'll see (in the right column of your Home page and on the Friend Requests icon on the blue bar) that you have a request waiting for you. Other types of requests are invitations to attend events and join groups, or to join a game, and plenty more. Whenever you have a request waiting for you, it shows in this same location on your Home page. If you don't see the Requests section on your Home page, you have no pending requests.

Although sending a request is a private affair, often the response to the request is public. For example, if you request that someone add you as a friend, only that person will know about the request until that person accepts your friend request; then others will see in their News Feeds that you two are now friends. Similarly, no one sees your invitations to join a particular group, but if you act on that request by joining, this information generates a News Feed story to your friends.

Unlike a message, you can't explicitly send a request. Requests are only generated in the context of other actions. For example, if you invite someone to an event (see Chapter 11), a request is automatically sent to that person. If you tag people in someone else's photo (see Chapter 8), a request is sent to the photo owner. If you specify that you're in a relationship with someone in particular, a request is sent to that person to confirm your claim. You also receive a request if someone wishes to join a closed group or event you administer. (For more about groups and administrators, see Chapter 10.)

Notifications

Sometimes rather than reach out *to* you on Facebook, your friends reach out *about* you. For example, say that you attend a Michael Franti concert with a friend. The next day, your friend may write a note about how mind-blowing he found the concert, and because you were there next to him having your own mind blown, he tags you in the note. (See Chapter 8 for details on Note tagging.) Your friend wrote the note about you, but he doesn't have to tell you he wrote the note about you because Facebook notifies you when you're tagged in a note or photo. It's a way of letting you know that someone's thinking or talking about you. When you have a tagging notification, you see a little red flag on the little "globe" icon near the upper-left corner of the blue bar on the Home page; the number inside the icon lets you know how many new notifications you have.

Clicking the Notifications globe icon opens a drop-down menu showing the last several notifications you've received; clicking See All Notifications takes you to the Notifications page, where you see all the notifications you've received for the past seven days.

Here are examples of other kinds of useful notifications:

- When someone tags other people in a photo you uploaded, tags you in note, or tags you in a photo
- When someone has written on your Wall or on the Wall of a group or event that you administrate
- When someone leaves a comment right after you've commented on a photo, note, or posted item
- When someone replies to a post that you made on a discussion board
- When someone comments on one of your notes, posted items, or photos that you've taken or that you're tagged in

 You can stop receiving notifications from any application by following these steps:

1. **On the left of the blue bar, click the Notifications globe icon, go to the Notifications page, and select See All Notifications.**

2. **Click X next to the type of notification you no longer want to receive and choose Hide All, or in the column on the right, deselect the check box next to the application you don't want to hear from anymore.**

3. **To receive these notifications again (and see any you've received in the last seven days from that particular application), simply reselect the check box.**

Notifications is kind of an overloaded term on Facebook. The kinds of notifications we describe in this section are those you receive on Facebook when someone talks about you. (They all show on the Notifications tab in your Inbox when you log in.)

Email Notifications, however, refer to the e-mails you receive when anyone is talking about you or to you, as in all the preceding examples, including messages, pokes, and requests. These notifications ensure that you know when something of interest is going down on Facebook — even when you're not logged in. To see the full set of notifications and to select which types of e-mail notifications you want to receive, click Settings on the blue bar and then click the Notifications tab. Select all check boxes you find relevant to you, and click Save Changes when you're done.

Public Displays of Affection: Comments, Publisher, and the Wall

So far, we've been talking about the kind of communication that takes place between specific people, in private. Private conversations are perfect for discussing topics relevant to only a few people, confiding in friends, or getting to know (and spending time with) someone specific. This section talks about a different kind of conversation — the kind you have among friends at a party where anyone may jump in or at a concert or bar where others may overhear. These conversations cover topics of potential general interest, unspecific to a particular group of people within the bounds of one's friends or networks. In the real world, we tend to have more conversations that are private. This is not because we're all gossips and secret-keepers. It's because the existing modes of communication, until now, have only facilitated private conversations. A phone call, e-mail, post card, or instant message, for example, always engages a specific set of participants. Facebook supports the aforementioned private conversations, but also offers new ways to communicate to enable the open conversation.

In this section, you read about how Facebook allows you to have conversations in a public way that encourages any of your friends to jump in if the mood strikes. Facebook encourages openness by the way it allows more information to flow to more people, which deepens and strengthens relationships.

The writing's on the Wall

Have you ever thought someone was so great that you wanted to look at him and say, "You are *so* great," and then turn to the world and say, "World, isn't he *so* great?" That's the spirit of the Wall. Every user, you included, has a Wall on his or her Profile page where friends (or anyone else they've permitted) can write things to or about him or her that the whole world can see. To write on someone else's Wall, simply navigate to that person's Profile. If it's not selected already, click the Wall tab next to the Profile picture, write your message in the box labeled *Write Something,* and then click Post. When you write on someone's Wall, remember that this generates a News Feed story that any one of your friends may see. If you don't see a *Write Something* box, the person has restricted access for those people who can write on the wall.

The spirit of posting on someone's Wall is to say nice things about that person in public. In practice, different people in different situations do Wall-writing for different reasons. Some people use the Wall to have basic back-and-forth conversations similar to how other people use messaging. Others use the Wall as a place to comment on a change to someone's Profile. If you change your status to something intriguing like <*Your Name*> *is keeping a secret,* expect a friend or two to ask about it on your Wall. If you change your relationship status, add new favorite bands, or update your Profile picture, you'll probably get feedback on your Wall as well.

A Wall practice that is nearly universal among Facebook users is the "Happy Birthday!" Wall post. Assuming you leave your privacy set so that your friends can see your birthday on your Profile (you can hide the year), they will also see a reminder on their Home pages as your big day approaches. On the actual day, you can expect to receive Wall posts all day long wishing you a happy birthday. If this doesn't happen, either you need more Facebook friends or you need to buy this book for some of the friends you do have.

When you look at a friend's Wall, you'll notice something *very familiar.* In Chapters 2, 3, and just about every other chapter, we mention the Publisher — the list of actions that lives on the top of your Home page and Profile into which you can publish any piece of content for the world to see. Figure 9-5 shows the different links and buttons that appear here, and the following lists describes how they work:

Figure 9-5:
The
anatomy of
a Wall on a
Profile.

> 🖳 Write on Wall   ○ Ask Question   🖾 Add Photos   ◁┘ Post Link
>
> Write something...
>
>   **Share**

✔ **Write on Wall:** Clicking this link will open the box that prompts you to enter free form text on your friend's wall. Leaving public comments on someone's wall instead of sending a private message is a great way to show that you're proud of your friendship or some activity you did together that you want the world to know about.

✔ **Ask Question:** If you're on someone's profile and you want to know something about them specifically, click this link and then type your Question. "When is Carolyn coming home from India?" for example might illicit answers from her friends like " Not soon enough!" or perhaps give you the actual date. (Chapter 8 has more details about the Questions application.)

✔ **Add Photos:** Lets you upload a photo to your friend's Profile, or else snap a real-time photo from your webcam if you have one. All the steps to uploading a photo to your friend's Wall are revealed when you click this button.

✔ **Post Link:** Works just like the Attach button in the Inbox. (See the earlier "Sharing from the Inbox" section.) Click Post Link and then paste a link into the box. This puts a Share preview directly on your friend's Wall, along with any comments you add.

✔ **Share:** This button will pop up just after you've written something and enables you to submit the text you wrote in the box on the Wall. If you change your mind after you've posted, click Remove (located next to your Wall post).

Care to comment?

Leaving comments is another form of public communication. You can leave a comment on a photo, a video, a note, or various other things just by writing in the Add a Comment box beneath the object (some objects have a Write a Comment link that you have to click first to see the box). Leaving comments has the double-nice property of giving feedback to your friend about their content *and* attracting other's attention to the content when the comment shows in other people's News Feed.

Broader audience

Sometimes you have something to say, but no one in particular to say it to. For those times, use the Publisher — the big empty box at the top of the Home page that asks you, "What's on your mind?" We cover the Publisher in Chapters 2 and 3, but mention again it here in regard to communicating with your friends because sometimes putting a message out there for the world to see can be the best way to get a conversation started. Sometimes people use their status to help connect in person: *Leah is at Starbucks if you want to join.* Sometimes, they use it to keep everyone informed of things they need to know: *Carolyn is off to Spain — don't expect her to reply to anything.* Often, it's a reflection of mood that may strike a chord with someone else, but you can't know who till you post: *Akhil loves having a brother.* And sometimes, people write whatever they want for whatever reason:

> *Dustin is checking off tasks.*

> *Cari can't find the orange.*

> *Justin is downward-facing dog.*

When you post something, it shows on your Profile and in your friends' News Feeds, so remember: If you write something intriguing like *<Your name> is about to pop the question,* you'll probably hear about it from your friends.

Part III
Getting Organized

"Jim and I do a lot of business together on Facebook. By the way, Jim, did you get the sales spreadsheet and little blue pony I sent you?"

In this part . . .

When we talk about organization, we aren't talking about cleaning up your desk so all the piles of paper sit at right angles to each other. No, we mean the idea of getting organized around an idea, a common interest, or even a common time.

In this part, we go in depth into how you can use Pages and Groups to organize people around beliefs, favorites, and even around slogans. We also talk about how to organize your life (and the people in it) into conveniently planned Events. The best part about organizing on Facebook is that it can often lead to organizing off Facebook.

Chapter 10

Creating and Joining Groups on Facebook

In This Chapter

▶ Getting to know Groups

▶ Finding a Group

▶ Creating and administering your Groups

*H*umans are social animals. Although you spend plenty of time tweaking and massaging your Profile, the real value of Facebook lies at the intersections of its massive network: more than 200 million people in every country in the world meeting up with the people they care about for a virtual cup of coffee. Can you foot this bill? We'll get the next one.

The coffeehouses on Facebook are known as *Groups.* Every 30 seconds, a new discussion is started in one of more than 10 million Groups on Facebook, on topics ranging from The Beatles to global warming to Ottawa University's Class of 1958 reunion. If you can't find the Group you're looking for, you can create and host it yourself. Like everything on Facebook, you decide who can participate — from ten of your closest friends to everyone in the world.

Getting Going with Groups

Like Photos, *Groups* is an application built for you by Facebook. You can access this application's Home page (see Figure 10-1) by clicking Applications, located in the far-left column on your Facebook Home page, and then selecting Groups. The page that appears shows you what's new in the Groups scene on Facebook, in terms of which of the Groups that you participate in have been updated. You can also click the Friends' Groups option that appears beneath Groups to see which Groups your friends have joined recently.

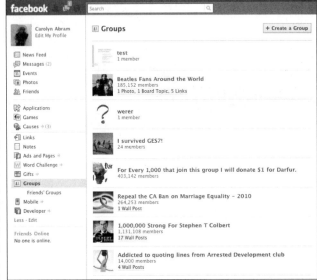

Figure 10-1:
Find out
what hap-
pened
recently in
the Groups
you and
your friends
care about.

Joining a Group

The best way to understand a Facebook Group is to look at one from a member's perspective. We're using the Beatles Fans Around the World Group, where more than 100,000 fans congregate, as an example. To find this Group, just follow these steps:

1. **Type** Beatles Fans Around the World **into the Search box and press Enter.**

   Note that Groups on Facebook may share similar or even identical names. If you're having trouble finding it, the address is `www.face book.com/group.php?gid=2204708817`. The Group is shown in Figure 10-2. (More information about searching for Groups comes later in the chapter in the section, "Searching Groups.")

2. **Click the Join link at the top of the page and become an insider.**

   If you don't want to frolic in strawberry fields forever, don't worry; we show you how to leave the Group when we finish.

Joining a group doesn't grant access to your profile to anyone who couldn't see it before. The only indirect consequence of joining a group is that a story about you joining will appear on your Wall. Additionally, you'll start to see updates from that group in your News Feed on your Home page. Furthermore, a story about your joining the Group may appear in your friends' News Feeds. None of these consequences occurs if the Group you join is secret, which is a concept we discuss in the section, "Creating Your Own Groups," later in this chapter.

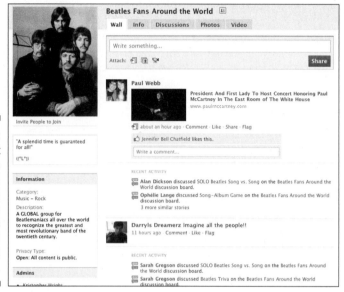

Anatomy of a Group

The first thing you see when you visit a Group is its Home page. Just as your Profile provides a summary of you (not to say that *you* could ever be summarized), this page provides an overview of what's happened in the Group recently, including snapshots of the most recent photos, videos, and member comments.

In bold, at the top of every Group's Home page sits the most important bit of information: the Group name.

Depending on privacy settings (see the later "Creating Your Own Groups" section for more on this), you may be able to see all of a Group's contents before joining it, even though you can't post new content. That's the case with the Beatles Fans Around the World Group because the administrator has chosen the most flexible settings.

In many ways, a Group is similar to a Profile shared among its members. A Group's Home page is divided into a wide right column and a thin left column (plus a column of ads and recommended material on the right side of the page); each column contains a number of different sections. Each section is delineated by a blue title bar and contains the most recent content posted in that section, such as the last few photos or discussion topics. To see everything posted to a section, click See All on its title bar. A group administrator may decide to hide certain sections for his Group, although we purposely chose this Group because it contains all the possible sections.

The right column offers the following tabs across the top:

- ✔ **Wall:** The Wall you see when you click this tab may look a little different than the Wall you are used to encountering on your friends' Profiles, but its purpose is the same. It is the perfect mechanism for casual, free-form commenting. In Beatles Fans Around the World, members often use the Wall to verbalize passionately their gratitude for 50 years of great music. They aren't trying to start discussions.

- ✔ **Info:** This tab may contain one or all of the following sections:

  - *Basic Info:* This section provides the basic details of the Group, such as its name, category, a description that outlines its purpose, and the type of privacy established. The Category includes a type and subtype, which must be standard Facebook categories. For Beatles Fans Around the World, for example, the type is *Music,* and the subtype is *Rock;* you can click either word to see other Groups belonging to the selected type.

  - *Contact Info:* If the Group represents a real-world group (for example, the National Breast Cancer Foundation), the Info tab may also contain the organization's contact information, such as a physical address or an Internet address. Because the administrator of this Group isn't an official representative of the band and has no public presence, he has decided to jokingly specify the address as *151 E. Broad St.* in homage to Paul McCartney's album, *Give My Regards to Broad Street.*

  - *Recent News:* This section discusses recent events, such as a re-release of a classic Beatles album. This section appears only when the Group administrator provides recent news.

- ✔ **Discussions:** Home to lively conversations and debates among members, the Discussions tab is the nexus of a Group. Each topic in a discussion board represents a new area of the broader Group dialogue where particularly insightful or provocative topics can garner hundreds or thousands of responses. For instance, as you can imagine, the "What's your favorite song by The Beatles?" topic has kicked off quite a heated debate. We can't imagine why because everyone knows the answer is "Hey Jude."

- ✔ **Photos:** As you might guess, this tab contains photos that are of relevance to the Group. In this case, fans of The Beatles have posted more than 2,000 of their favorite photos of their beloved band. Only a selection of the most recent photos is shown on the Group's Home page, but you can click See All to view the rest of them.

  In some instances, these photos are of Group members posing with the band long ago. Such photo sharing is a staple of many Facebook Groups. For instance, visit Facebook hiking Groups, and you see members sharing pictures of their most recent conquests. Group members can leave comments on these photos just as your friends can comment on the pictures you post to your Profile.

✔ **Video:** Like photos, videos enrich Groups by moving them beyond mere discussion. On this tab, fans of The Beatles tickle their memories with clips from the band's golden years. Viewing videos is very similar to viewing photos. The most recent videos are shown on the Group's Home page, and you can click See All to view the rest. To watch a video, click it. Group members can also leave comments on videos.

Whew. You'd think that'd be enough, but settle down: We've got another column to go! The left column contains information that may be interesting to members but is probably less important than the things we just discussed. It includes

✔ **A picture:** Group administrators can choose any picture they like to represent the Group on the Home page, but they have to be picky: They get only one.

✔ **Action links:** Just as your Profile contains a set of important actions (such as View Photos) beneath your picture, a series of action links follows the Group picture. These include View Discussion Board (which is a shortcut to the See All link of the Discussion Board section), and either Join This Group or Leave Group, depending on whether you're already a member of the Group. If the Group is *closed*, you may join only with a Group administrator's approval, in which case the link reads, Request to Join Group. If you're the administrator of a Group, you see additional administrative options here.

If the Group administrator chooses to allow it (the administrator of Beatles Fans Around the World has), you also see a link to Invite People to Join.

✔ **Information:** The information box includes a category for the group that the group administrator has determined, as well as a description and a notice about the type of privacy the group uses. As we mentioned, the administrator of Beatles Fans Around the World chose the most flexible settings possible in his effort to attract fans of The Beatles. This means he exposes the existence of the Group to everyone and allows anyone to see the Group, join it, and invite others to join. This set of permissions constitutes an *open* Group. A Group may also be *closed* or *secret,* as we discuss in the section "Step 1: Group Info," later in this chapter.

✔ **Officers (optional):** If a Group has any officers, the Officers section lists its names, primary networks, and titles. Because this concept doesn't really make sense in Beatles Fans Around the World (the administrator has not designated any officers), the section doesn't appear. For Groups that have real-world counterparts, like a school newspaper, the officers section can accurately represent the Editor-in-Chief, Business Manager, and so on. For Groups that are less serious (as many Facebook Groups are), you'll often notice officer designations like "Chief Dummy" and "Dummy-in-residence." See the upcoming "Managing your Group" section for more information about officers.

✔ **Admins:** The Admins section lists the names and primary networks of all the Group's administrators. Whoever creates a Group is automatically the administrator of that Group, meaning he writes the Group's information, controls its privacy settings, moderates its discussions, and generally keeps the Group running smoothly. He can also promote other members to administrators to grant them the same privileges. See the upcoming section, "Managing your Group member list," for help with promoting members to administrators.

✔ **Members:** This section shows you other Facebook members who are part of the Group. If any of your friends are in the Group, they're listed first, followed by other people who belong to your networks (if you have any). This reflects the belief that the people close to you are always more interesting than strangers.

Remember: Groups don't influence the basic Facebook privacy model, so you're not able to see the Profile of a fellow Group member unless she's already your friend, is a friend of your friend, or belongs to one of your networks.

Beatles Fans Around the World has more than 150,000 members, which is impressive, but far from the size of the largest Facebook Groups, which boast more than one million members (such as "When I Was Your Age, Pluto Was a Planet"). Of course, more than 500 distinct Groups about The Beatles exist throughout Facebook, each with its own member base and personality. Because it's so easy to create a Group on Facebook, a prime benefit of Groups is: One size need not fit all.

✔ **Events:** You may not see this box if the Group has no upcoming events. If it does, you see not only the box, but also the name of the upcoming event. Group administrators can invite all members of a group to a particular event, which we talk about in the "Creating a Group event" section at the end of this chapter.

✔ **Photos, Videos, Links:** In addition to the tabs for photos and videos at the top of the page, many groups have small boxes in the left column that feature recent photos, videos, or links that people have posted recently. Beatles fans are always finding new articles, pictures, or compilation videos; by looking at these boxes, you may see something that would otherwise been buried on the Wall.

✔ **Share:** The Share links scattered throughout Facebook allow you to quickly share with your friends interesting content that you find, either by sending it to them in a message or by posting it to your Profile. The Share button allows you to share a link to the Group (along with a preview containing the Group's name, description, and picture).

If the Group is *open,* you may want to use the Invite People to Join link to send an invitation to join rather than a mere link. If the Group is *secret,* you can't share a link to the Group with anyone who isn't already a member because the Group's privacy settings don't permit it. (See the upcoming section, "Step 1: Group Info," for more information about open and secret Groups.)

There's one little link we've skipped over here, and that's the Report Group link. This is what you'll look for whenever you encounter a Group you consider offensive. See the "Finding the Group for You" section, later in this chapter, for more information about reporting Groups.

Adding your two cents (or more)

The best way to get started with a Group is to contribute to the discussions that are already taking place among its members. Click a topic that sounds interesting in the Discussion Board section and dive in. ***Remember:*** You can click See All on the section title bar to see all the ongoing discussions for the Group rather than just the most recent ones displayed on the Group's Home page. If you don't see a topic that strikes your fancy, start your own by clicking Start New Topic.

After you reply to an existing topic or start your own, Facebook helps you keep up with the conversation in a number of ways:

✔ Facebook sends you a notification whenever someone replies to one of your discussion posts. By default, this notification arrives not just on Facebook but also via e-mail. You can turn this off if you don't want it; see Chapter 9 for more information on notifications.

✔ The Groups page (which you get to by choosing Groups in the left column) displays a list of your recently updated Groups in its main column. The yellow-highlighted text indicates the Group's content that changed.

✔ As always, your Home page, especially your News Feed, is a great way to keep up with what's happening in your Facebook universe.

Finding the Group for You

Groucho Marx once said that he wouldn't want to be part of any club that would have him as a member. He probably wouldn't be happy about Facebook, which has millions of public Groups that would readily accept him, you, or anyone else who'd like to join. This section helps you pinpoint the Groups that cover your interests, whether you search for specific Groups, browse Groups, or check out Groups that your friends like.

Searching Groups

If you already have a topic in mind, the following is the fastest way to find Groups that cover it:

1. **Click within the Search box.**

   The Search box sits in the big blue bar at the top of every Facebook page.

2. **Begin typing the name of a Group you want to find, such as** Cat Lovers, **and then either select from the list of choices that pops up or click "See more results for" at the bottom of the menu.**

   The search results contain content from all over Facebook, such as Profiles, Groups, Pages, and Events.

3. **Look for the Groups category on the left side of the Search page and click on any of the Groups in that space to learn more.**

When an administrator creates a Group, she may restrict access to a Group by network (if she has one) or by changing the Group access type to *closed* or *secret,* as we discuss in the upcoming section, "Creating Your Own Groups." Facebook displays only the Groups that you have permission to see in the list of search results.

Narrowing your search

If you're having trouble finding the Group you're looking for, you can try refining your search by Group type.

To filter your Group search results, first make sure you are looking at *only* Group search results, and follow these steps:

1. **After performing a search, click the Group icon in the left column.**

2. **In the right column, above the search results, click the down arrow next to Show.**

   By default, you are shown all group types.

   The menu displays different types of groups, such as Common Interest or Music.

3. **Choose the category type you are looking for.**

   This menu has sub-types for the original category you chose.

4. **Choose any relevant sub-types and click Filter Results again.**

Filtered results can sometimes be a little funky because they rely on people to classify their groups correctly and people don't tend to take this classification seriously. Group search filter options are shown in Figure 10-3.

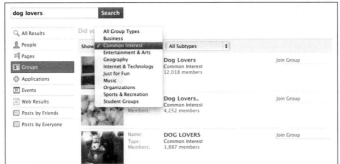

Figure 10-3:
The Filter
Groups by
Type drop-
down list
helps you
filter your
Groups
search.

You can also narrow your search more quickly by adding words to your search phrase to make it more specific. For instance, searching for *Cats the musical* rather than *Cats* returns results that are more relevant to the topic of interest.

Regardless of whether the search filters help, you can clear them and return to the original results list by clicking the original Groups filter on the left side of the Search page. You can also return the Group Type menu to All Group Types, which resets the page to your original results.

Checking out popular Groups

When you go to the bookstore to find an interesting book, you're not at the mercy of the staff. Your friends, co-workers, classmates, and neighbors — who know you better than anyone — can guide your search by telling you which books *they* enjoyed. Groups are no different, so don't worry if you're having trouble finding good ones; your friends and networks are here to help.

When you click the Groups icon in the left column of the Home page, you see an option to view Friends Groups. From there, you can see a running list of Groups recently joined by your friends. Your friends don't manually suggest these Groups to you; Facebook assumes that your friends join Groups that interest them and automatically pushes those Groups to you. To see all Groups recently joined by your friends, click the See All link on the column's title bar or the See All Recent Groups Joined by Friends link at the bottom of the list.

Reporting offensive Groups

If you stumble upon an offensive Group in your travels, you should report it to Facebook so that the company can take appropriate actions. To report a Group, follow these steps:

1. **Click the Report Group link at the bottom-left corner of the Group's Home page (right above the Share button).**

   You see a form like the one shown in Figure 10-4.

2. **Fill out the report by choosing a reason for the report and include a comment that explains why you feel the Group should be removed.**

3. **Click Submit.**

Figure 10-4:
If you find a
Group that
is offensive,
Facebook
is here to
help.

Facebook removes all Groups that

- ✔ Contain pornographic material or inappropriate nudity
- ✔ Attack an individual or Group
- ✔ Advocate the use of illicit drugs
- ✔ Advocate violence
- ✔ Serve as advertisements or are otherwise deemed to be spam by Facebook

Many Groups on Facebook take strong stands on controversial issues, such as abortion or gun control. In an effort to remain neutral and promote debate, Facebook won't remove a Group because you disagree with its statements.

Creating Your Own Groups

If you can't find the Group you're looking for on Facebook, or even if you can but you just want one with a different personality or member list, you're welcome to create your own. As a Group's creator, you're by default the *Group administrator,* which means that you write the Group's information, control its privacy settings, moderate its discussions, and generally keep it running smoothly. You can also promote other members of the Group to administrators to grant them the same privileges, and then they can help you with these responsibilities.

Here are the steps you follow to begin creating a Group:

1. **Choose Groups from the Applications menu on the left-hand navigation bar to navigate to the Groups page.**

2. **Click the Create a New Group button at the top right of the page.**

Creating a Group entails at least one step — specifying the Group's name and other basic information — and you have the option of completing one additional step: customizing how your Group appears to its members. Once you've created a group, Facebook will prompt you to create a member list and invite your friends. It will also make available a number of options for customizing your member list and group, all of which we'll go over in the "Managing your Group" section. Facebook divides the process into two screens, one for each step, and highlights the current step at the top of the page. We discuss each step in depth in the next few sections. You can edit any property of a Group except for its name at any time after its creation, so don't fret too much about getting things just right your first time around.

Although you can't manually delete a Group that you create, Facebook automatically deletes Groups that have no members. If you're the only member, simply leave the Group and poof — the Group is gone. If there are other members, you (as administrator) can remove them from your Group using the Members dashboard. See "Managing your Group" later in this chapter.

Step 1: Group Info

The Group Info step asks you for the following information about the Group. Some information may not be relevant or desirable for the Group you have in mind. You must enter the information designated as *required,* as shown in Figure 10-5.

- ✔ **Group Name (required):** Enter the name of the Group you wish to create, such as Beatles Fans Around the World. If you want people whom you don't know to join your Group, choose specific names. This helps your group be found in related searches. For instance, if you're starting a coffee lovers of California group, calling it just that (Coffee Lovers of California) means that people searching for "Coffee" or "Coffee + California" will find your group and know that it's for them.

- ✔ **Network:** This option is applicable only to people who belong to work or school networks. If you belong to one of these, you have the ability to limit accessibility to only people in that network. For example, you may want to limit people who can join your company's basketball team's Facebook Group to only people from your company. Use the Network drop-down to limit membership to a certain network. If not, your Group is visible to everyone, although you will be able to prevent people from interacting in other ways that we cover later in the chapter.

Figure 10-5:
You need
to enter
only four
basic bits of
information
to get your
Group up
and running.

✔ **Description (required):** A brief overview of the purpose or mission of the Group. This is similar to an organization's charter and is one of the first things a user sees when looking at your Group and determining whether to join.

✔ **Group Type (required):** A broad category that describes the focus of your Group, such as Music. You must also choose a subtype that further narrows the focus, such as Rock.

✔ **Recent News:** Anything that's happened recently that may be of interest to the Group's members. For Groups reflecting real-world organizations, this may be information about recent organizational activities posted for the benefit of members who didn't participate (say, the outcome of a blood drive). For Groups uniting people with a shared hobby or interest, such as hiking, this may be pertinent news about the activity, such as the temporary closure of a popular hiking trail. *Remember:* You can update this information at any time.

✔ **Office:** If your Group represents an organization that operates on a work or school campus, you can enter the colloquial location of the organization's office here, such as Tressider Building, Second Floor. If your Group has a broader audience for whom such an intimate description would not be helpful, you can enter a more precise physical address in the Street and City/Town fields, as described later in this list.

✔ **Email:** The e-mail address of a person or organization that's pertinent to the Group. It isn't necessary (and may be undesirable) to list your own e-mail address here. As the administrator, your name is listed under the Admins section of the Group's Home page, and members always have the option to send you a Facebook message.

✔ **Website:** The address of a Web site that's pertinent to the Group. If the Group represents a real-world organization, such as the National Breast Cancer Foundation, this address is typically the organization's official Web address, such as www.nationalbreastcancer.org. If the Group brings together fans of a particular television show, this address often points to the television show's official home on the Web.

✔ **Street:** If the Group represents a real-world organization that has a physical office, you can enter its street address here.

✔ **City/Town:** If the Group represents a real-world organization that has a physical office, you can enter the city or town of the office here. This field and the Street field in the preceding bullet constitute the most important parts of a physical address.

Step 2: Customize

Figure 10-6 represents the customize page, where you can edit what members will see and be able to do on your Group's Home page.

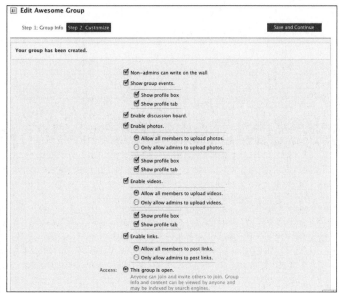

Figure 10-6:
Make your
Group your
own.

Here's what you can do:

✔ **Options:** A mixture of options that control which sections appear on your Group's Home page and, where applicable, who can add content to them. We explain these sections in "Anatomy of a Group" earlier in this chapter.

- *Non-administrators Can Write on the Wall:* As we discuss in the "Anatomy of a Group" section, group Walls are gathering places for recent links, discussions, and posts from group members. If you are running a group that is more about you communicating to a lot of people, as opposed to people all communicating with each other (for example, a charity or non-profit that you organize), you can uncheck this box so that only you and other administrators can post to the Wall.

  If you are running a group for a non-profit or charity, you may also want to consider creating a Facebook Page instead of a Group. We talk more about how Groups and Pages compare in Chapter 12.

- *Show Group Events:* One of the cool integration points of both Groups and Events is that a Group can host an Event, which means you can automatically invite all members of that group to your event (if you're an administrator). If you choose to show Group Events, the events you create will be shown on the Group Home page. You can choose whether you also want to show a profile box and/or a tab about your Group's Events.

- *Enable Discussion Board:* Shows the discussion board. Groups are typically used to host discussions among members, so you probably want to keep this enabled.

- *Enable Photos:* Shows the photos section. If you decide to show this section, you may also decide who may add photos to it. By default, all members of the Group may add photos, but you can restrict this to administrators by selecting Only Allow Admins to Upload Photos. You can also choose whether you want photos to be collected in a profile box, tab, or both.

- *Enable Videos:* Shows the videos section. If you decide to show this section, you may also decide who may add videos to it. By default, all members of the Group may add videos, but you can restrict this to administrators by selecting Only Allow Admins to Upload Videos. You can also choose whether you want videos to be collected in a profile box, tab, or both.

- *Enable Links:* Shows the Links section. If you decide to show this section, you may also decide who may post links to it. By default, all members of the Group may post links, but you can restrict this to administrators by selecting Only Allow Admins to Post Links.

✓ **Access:** When you designate a network for your Group, you indicate the broadest set of people who are allowed to join it. You can further restrict this set via one of the three access settings that Facebook offers:

- *This Group Is Open:* This default setting allows anyone to view the Group's content. Only members in the Group's network (which is everyone if the network is Global) can join the Group. Group members can also invite members of the network to join.

- *This Group Is Closed:* Anyone in the chosen network can see the basic Group information, but only members can see the photos, discussions, and so forth. People who want to join must request membership, and you, or another administrator, have the opportunity to approve or deny these requests.

- *This Group Is Secret:* People can join the Group only if you or another administrator invites them. They cannot request membership; they won't even know of the Group's existence because it won't appear in search results or on the Profiles of its current members. Therefore, only members can see the Group description, discussions, photos, and so forth. The Group's network has little effect here given these additional restrictions on membership.

When you finish customizing your Group, click Save at the bottom of the page. If you have an open or closed Group, you see a prompt asking you if you wish to publish a post to your Wall (and, therefore, to your friends' Home pages), as shown in Figure 10-7. Click Publish if you want your friends to see the Group.

Figure 10-7:
Publish
to your
Wall for
additional
distribution.

Now, pass go, collect $200. Your group has been created. You are taken to the Invite People page, which we describe in the next section. You can also check out what your group looks like by clicking "Back to <Group Name>" in the top-right corner of the page.

Managing your Group

When you finish creating your Group, you may want to do a number of things — invite people to join, add a profile photo to represent your group, take a nice long nap in a hammock. All of these things can be done and re-done at any time, which is why they are not officially part of group creation. At the same time, if you're eager to get people talking and congregating, you might want to at least invite friends to join before succumbing to the sweet siren song of nap time. You can access most of these options at any point in time by clicking Edit Group, located beneath your Group profile picture.

Inviting friends to join

Facebook assumes that the first thing you want to do after creating your group is to invite people to join. Therefore, immediately after completing the Customize step just described, you are presented with a friend selector for sending invitations. You can see this friend selector in Figure 10-8. Notice that the options at the top of the page are no longer numbered steps but Customize, Officers, and Members tabs. You are on the Invite tab.

Remember that if you designated your Group as open or closed, it's not necessary for you to invite people; they may discover the Group on their own via News Feed, the Search feature, the Groups section on their friends' Profiles, or many other sources. However, if you chose to create a secret Group, these invitations are the only means through which someone can discover and join your Group.

Inviting people to your join your Group takes just a few seconds:

1. **Invite your friends who are already on Facebook by selecting them from the Friend Selector, as shown in Figure 10-8.**

   The Invite Members page displays *a Friend Selector,* which is a grid of your friends. To select any friend, you simply have to click her face or name. If you know exactly who you're going for, you can start to type her name into the field labeled Find Friends. The grid filters down as you type. Select your friends whenever you're ready.

   When you invite a Facebook member to join your Group, he receives a Facebook request from you. Depending on his notification settings, he may also receive an e-mail from Facebook regarding your invitation. Note that Facebook doesn't send the invitation to your friend as soon as you select him in the list. Keep reading for instructions on actually sending the invitation.

   You can double-check your member list by clicking the Selected view of the Friend Selector (found in the upper-right corner above your friends' faces). If you accidentally selected the wrong Blake Ross, you can undo the selection by clicking his face again.

2. **Invite friends who aren't yet on Facebook to join the Group by typing their e-mail addresses (separated by commas) into the box labeled Invite People via Email below the Friend Selector.**

   Can't remember their addresses? No problem. Click the Import Email Addresses link to open a window that enables you to select their addresses from your e-mail address book, assuming Facebook supports your e-mail provider (it supports the most popular ones). This process is very similar to the Friend Finder process outlined in Chapter 4. Forgot some folks? Enter more addresses into the box and click Add again.

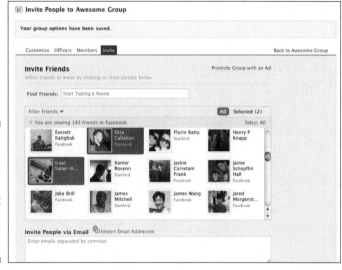

Figure 10-8:
Inviting
Facebook
friends to
your Event
is as simple
as selecting
them.

3. **(Optional) Include a message with your invitation by typing it in the box below the invitee list.**

   Although optional, this adds a personal touch and makes your invitation more persuasive.

4. **Click Send Invitations.**

   The invitations are sent to the people on the list. Forgot some people? You can repeat these steps as people start to join. Many of these steps appear as action links under the picture on your Group's Home page. These actions are visible and available only to you and other administrators; if you recall, you did not see these special links when viewing the Beatles Fans Around the World Group earlier in this chapter.

Designating Group officers

Many Groups reflect real-life groups or clubs that have members serving in various leadership roles. Administrators can mirror these positions in a Facebook Group by designating members as officers and assigning titles, such as Secretary or Treasurer. To promote members to administrators, see the "Managing your Group member list" section later in this chapter.

When your Group has officers, an Officers section appears on its Home page listing their names, primary networks, and titles. Group officers don't have the same privileges as administrators or any more administrative rights than regular members do.

To designate officers of your Group, follow these steps:

1. **Click the Edit Group link under the picture in the left column of your Group's Home page.**

2. **Click the Officers tab at the top of the Edit Group page.**

   You see two lists: a list of the officers (and their positions) followed by a list of non-officers.

3. **Promote a non-officer to an officer by clicking the Make Officer link next to her name.**

4. **When Facebook prompts you, enter a position (such as Secretary) for the officer-to-be.**

   You can enter any position you want, so it can be as silly or serious as your personality (and your Group's personality) dictates.

5. **Click Add to promote the member to officer or Cancel if you changed your mind.**

   A notification is sent to the member letting her know about the change.

6. **To change the position of an existing officer, click Edit next to his name in the Officers list. To demote an existing officer back to a regular member, click Remove Officer.**

Managing your Group member list

After you have members in your Group, you can use the Group member list to remove (and even permanently ban) undesirable members, promote your most trusted members to administrators, or demote your existing administrators (if any) back to regular members:

1. **Click the Edit Members action link under the picture in the left column of your Group's Home page.**

   A list of all Group members appears. Next to each name are two buttons: an X and a button that says either Make Admin or Remove Admin, depending on the administrative status of each person.

2. **Use the link to the right of each member name that corresponds to the action you wish to take.**

   If you want to make someone an administrator, click Make Admin. If you want to remove someone's administrative responsibilities, click Remove Admin. If you want to remove someone, click the X. When you remove someone from a Group, you also have the option to ban her permanently. This is extremely useful in the case of a Group member who is harassing others or being abusive within the Group.

Uploading a picture

The photo you choose to represent your Group will be featured prominently at the top of it, as well as in search results across the site. For that reason, people frequently try to find a photo that best explains what the Group is all about. For members of Facebook Ultimate Frisbee, it's a team photo. For Beatles Fans around the World, it's a picture of The Beatles. To add this image, follow these instructions:

1. **Hold the mouse over the gray question mark currently representing your group.**

   In the top-right corner of the picture, a Change Picture link appears.

2. **Click Change Picture.**

   This opens a menu of options, including the option we care about, Upload a Picture.

3. **Select Upload a Picture.**

   A dialog box appears, as shown in Figure 10-9.

Figure 10-9:
Upload
a Profile
Picture for
your Group.

> **Upload a Profile Picture for Awesome Group**
>
> Select an image file on your computer (4MB max):
>
> (Choose File) no file selected
>
> By uploading a file you certify that you have the right to distribute this picture and that it does not violate the Terms of Service.
>
> Cancel

4. **Click the Browse or Choose File button to open your computer's standard interface for finding a file.**

5. **Navigate to (and select) the picture on your computer that you want to use.**

   The picture you choose must meet the file size and type requirements outlined on the page. If you're not sure whether your desired picture meets the requirements, select the picture and continue with these steps. Facebook notifies you if the picture you choose can't be used.

   Once you've selected your photos, your Group will automatically update to display its new look.

You can also use a webcam to take a photo to use as your Group profile photo. Simply select "Take a photo" from the menu opened in Step 2 and follow the onscreen instructions.

Messaging your Group members

Although you can use your Group's discussion board and its Wall to communicate with your members, there may be times when you want to guarantee that members read your messages. Facebook messages are just the ticket because they appear in your members' Facebook Inbox, and (depending on notification settings) your members may receive an e-mail notification about them. (Because of Facebook restrictions on spam, this option may not be available to you if your Group has a very large number of members.)

To send a message to all members, click the Message All Members action link under the picture in the left column of your Group's Home page. You're taken to the standard Facebook Compose Message window. Complete the rest of the process as if you were sending a message to a single friend of yours (for a refresher on sending messages, check out Chapter 9). To your members, the message appears to originate from the Group rather than from you personally, and they're not able to respond to it.

Creating a Group event

Your Group is open around the clock, but what if you want to gather your members in one place — either online or offline — at one time? For instance, you may wish to convene your Scrabble Lovers Group for a friendly tournament. (Although, have you ever witnessed a Scrabble tournament? They get intense.) In such cases, you may create a Facebook Event to host the details of the gathering and send the invitation to your members.

Although Facebook offers the Events feature to all of its users, it gives special capabilities to Group administrators for scenarios like this. By clicking the Create Related Event action link under your Group's Home page picture, you can create an Event that has the Group — rather than you personally — listed as the host in the Event and its invitation. Furthermore, you can easily add all of your Group members to the Event's invitation list by checking the Invite Members check box just above the Add Personal Message section. See Chapter 11 for more information about Events.

Chapter 11

Scheduling Your Life
with Facebook

· ·

In This Chapter

▶ Getting to know Events

▶ Finding the Event for you

▶ Creating and administering your own Events

· ·

*T*hink about the worst birthday party that you ever had — the big kickball party during the hurricane when the clown was three hours late (and a little drunk) and none of your friends showed up because your mom (hands full with a torrential downpour and drunken clown) forgot to invite them.

Facebook can't do anything about clowns or the weather (as of publication time), but the invites would've happened if your mother used Facebook Events to plan the party. Facebook removes the hassle of hosting an Event — creating and sending the invites, managing the guest list — and allows you to focus on preparing the Event itself.

Not much of a party planner? No worries. Facebook also handles the planning of smaller, more impromptu Events. You can easily collect a crew for dinner or for Frisbee in the park. And if that still isn't enough, hundreds of Events in your area are on Facebook every week. This chapter shows you how to find the best of the best for this weekend.

Getting Going with Events

Like Photos and Groups, Events is an application built by Facebook. To access its dashboard, click Events in the left column. This brings you to the Events page and opens up additional menu options for Events. The Events page (shown in Figure 11-1) that you land on displays all upcoming birthdays and Facebook Events that have you on their guest lists. This includes Events you were invited to and Events you joined.

Just in case you change your mind, even Events you said you aren't attending appear in the list. To change your RSVP, click the link that displays your current response on the right side of the Event listing.

To see more information about an Event, click its title to view the Event's Home page, which contains a detailed overview of the Event. Facebook also embeds a summary of the most important information — the Event's date and time, your RSVP, and which friends (if any) are attending — directly into the Event listing, as shown in Figure 11-2. Wherever you find an Event listing on Facebook — say, in the Events browsing tool or a list of search results — this information is displayed.

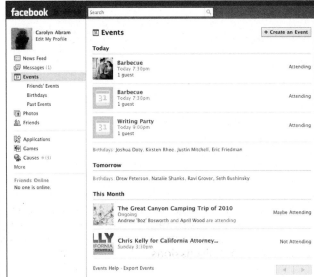

Figure 11-1:
The Events application's dashboard.

Figure 11-2:
An Event's listing displays a preview of the most important info.

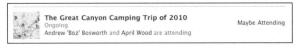

When you are through looking at upcoming events, you can also use the sub-menus on the left side to navigate to more specific kinds of Events, including the following:

- ✔ **Friends' Events:** Lists the Events that your friends are planning to attend. Each listing includes the names of the friends attending the Event. As always, click the Event title to view the Event's Home page.

- ✔ **Birthdays:** Although these aren't Facebook Events in the sense that they have an Event Home page, your friends' birthdays are important real-world events that you don't want to miss. This tab lists all of the birth-days in the current month, as well as what age your friend is turning (if that information is available).

- ✔ **Past Events:** Lists Facebook Events that had you on their guest lists, regardless of whether you attended them. Facebook doesn't delete an Event's Home page after the Event occurs. Instead, the Event's Home page, its photos, videos, and other media remain for posterity as a chronicle of what transpired.

Anatomy of an Event

An Event is represented on Facebook through its Home page, such as the one shown in Figure 11-3. A Home page evolves throughout the life cycle of an Event. Before the Event takes place, its Home page serves as an invita-tion and offers critical information for attendees, such as the Event's date and location. An Event's Home page also tracks who will or might attend the Event so that its host can plan accordingly. After the Event is over, the Home page serves as a water cooler for attendees to share their experiences in the form of photos, videos, and discussions.

An Event's Home page is divided into two columns (in addition to the right column, which houses Facebook Ads and other unrelated content). Each column is further divided into sections or boxes. At the very top of the page, you can see the Event's photo (at the top of the left column) and the Event's name (at the top of the right column).

The right, or main, column of the event shows the following information, starting at the top of the page and working down:

- ✔ **Attendance Status:** If you've already said you'll be going to an event, right below its name you'll see a sentence reading *You are Attending* (or maybe attending, or not attending, depending on your response). If you haven't responded yet, you'll see three buttons: I'm Attending, Maybe, and No. Click whichever is appropriate to RSVP.

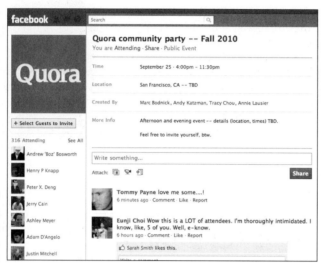

Figure 11-3:
An Event's
Home page.

✔ **Share:** The Share link scattered throughout Facebook allows you to share interesting content quickly with your friends, either by sending it to them in a message or by posting it on your Profile. The Share button allows you to share an Event along with a preview containing the Event's name, description, and picture.

If the Event is public, you may want to use the Invite People to Come action link to send an invitation rather than a link. (See the upcoming "Creating Your Own Events" section for more information on open Events.) If the Event is private, you can't share a link to the Event with anyone who isn't a member because the Event's privacy settings don't permit it.

✔ **Event Type:** Next to your attendance status and Share link, you'll see a notice about whether the event is public or private.

✔ **Event Info:** This area is further divided into convenient sections to show you the when (time), where (location), who (created by), and what (more info) of the event.

✔ **The Wall:** The Event Wall, like the Wall on your Profile, is where event guests can leave messages, photos, videos, and relevant links for all the guests to share. In general, the Wall is where people explain why they can't make an event, or where they express their enthusiasm about coming to an event.

The left column, which is topped by the Event photo, contains information about invitations. If the event is public, you'll see a button just beneath it that you can click to Select Guests To Invite (refer to Figure 11-3). Clicking this will bring up a friend selector that you can use to invite your friends as well.

We go over the friend selector later in this chapter when we go through the event creation process.

REMEMBER

Just because you *can* invite more people to an event, it doesn't necessarily mean you *should*. Make sure your host is okay with you extending the guest list (a good use of the Event Wall) before you blast your whole friend list.

The rest of the left column is dedicated to guests: Who is confirmed as attending, who is maybe attending, who hasn't replied yet, and who has declined to attend. The Confirmed Guests list is on top and shows you names and thumbnails of guests. If you're not sure if you want to go to a party, this section might help you make up your mind. If you're more curious who *isn't* going, you need to click on the Not Attending section to view that list.

Going to the after party

When you get home from that birthday party or book club meeting, return to the Event page to post any photos or videos you shot. Click into the Publisher at the top of the Wall and select options to add photos, videos, or links. Figure 11-4 shows the process of adding a video to an event. This works the exact same way as the Publisher on your Home page does. For more information about adding content via the Publisher, check out Chapter 8.

Note that you can post this sort of content only if the Event administrator allows people to do so. Keep an eye on your own Home page to see when other guests post their photos and videos, which usually happens in one big flurry of activity a day or two after the Event. After all, there's nothing more rousing than a video of your book club in action.

Figure 11-4:
Adding
videos to an
Event.

Finding the Event for You

With more than 200 million people on Facebook, it's no surprise that, at any given time, there are hundreds of Events in your area. Facebook gives you a number of tools to help you find the best ways to spend your weekend.

Searching Events

If you have an Event in mind, the fastest way to find it is to search.

1. **Click within the Search box.**

   The *Search box* is the text box in the top-right corner of every page, on the big blue bar.

2. **Enter the topic of an Event you want to find, such as** Dave Matthews Band, **and press Enter to begin your search.**

   The search results contain content from all over Facebook, such as Profiles, Groups, and Events.

3. **Click the Events tab in the left column to retrieve only Event results.**

To filter your search results by date or type, use the filters that appear at the top of the results once you have selected Events as the search filter (see Figure 11-5).

Figure 11-5:
Browse Events to find one that suits your fancy.

If the search filters don't help, clear them, and return to the original results list by clicking the Hide Filters link, which appears in place of the Show More Filters link on the gray bar at the top.

Checking out popular Events

Face it — nobody wants to go to *That Party.* The one where nobody shows up but you, and you're stuck reassuring the host — "It's probably the weather, because, you know, who wants to go to a party when it's partly cloudy out, anyway?"

Fortunately, Facebook gives you an easy way to see which Events are popular among your friends and networks. The Friends' Events tab on the Events page shows you Events that your friends are attending soon that you can attend. Your friends didn't manually suggest these Events to you; Facebook simply assumes that your friends join Events that interest them and automatically pushes those Events to you.

Just because you found a public event through search, doesn't mean you should definitely show up for the party. People sometimes use public events to get their friends — and not some random person who ran a search for "Barbecue" — to learn about an event. A good general rule is that if you would be considered a "crasher," you probably shouldn't go.

Creating Your Own Events

Tired of being a *guest?* Ready to be in charge? Want to host your own Event, have complete control over the guest list, and almost single-handedly decide who among us is *in* and *out?* Follow this simple step:

> **Take a cold shower.**

Now that that's out of your system, get down to business — the business of organizing and hosting fun Events. If you're planning an Event that's not happening for a few days or so, we recommended starting with the Big Events section. If your Event is more spur of the moment, or perhaps has already started, we recommend skipping ahead to the Quick Events section.

Big Events

Whatever actions have transpired before you log in to Facebook — a conversation about how awesome a surprise party would be, a sudden urge to give all of your friends free food in honor of the season — after you've logged in, creating an Event is easy. To begin, take the following steps:

1. **Click Events in the left column of the Home page.**

   This takes you to the Events dashboard.

2. **Click the Create New Event button at the upper-right side of the page.**

   This takes you to the Create an Event page, as shown in Figure 11-6.

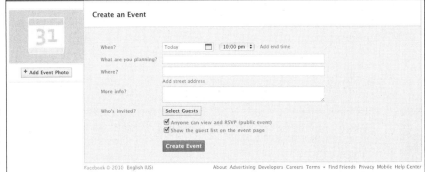

Figure 11-6:
Create your
Event here.

3. **Fill out your event's info:**

   There are a number of fields you can fill out. We note which ones are required below:

   - **When? (required):** By default, Facebook assumes you are an impromptu party planner, so this box will show a party happening later today. Click the calendar to change the date, and use the drop-down menu to select a time.

   - **End-time (click Add End Time):** In case you're worried about your guests overstaying their welcome, you can include an end time in your invitation.

   - **What are you planning? (required):** Enter the name of your event, such as *Jenny's 25th Birthday.*

   - **Where?:** Though not required, professional party planners have noted that telling people where to go is generally necessary if you want people to show up. This isn't always the street address, but the name of the venue, like *Mark's house* or *Olive Garden.*

   - **Street, city/town (click Add Street Address):** The street address of the location where the Event is taking place. Once you expand this section, you will need to enter the address separately from the city or town where the Event is occurring. When you type the city or town, the field tries to autocomplete as you type. If you specify the street address and town, Facebook displays a View Map link that your guests can click to get directions.

• **More Info?** You can include any information you think is relevant in this space — a brief overview of the Event, such as why you're holding it, what the attire is, and why someone should come. This description is one of the first things a guest sees when looking at your Event and determining whether to attend.

4. **Click Select Guests to begin to invite friends.**

   Doing so brings up the Friend Selector (shown in Figure 11-7). Simply click on a friend's name or profile picture to select them. Click again to take them off the list. Use the search box at the top to filter down to a friend by name. When you are done, click Save and Close.

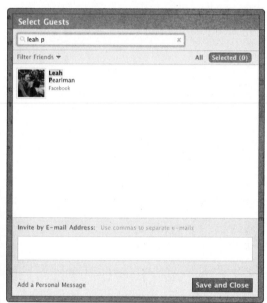

Figure 11-7:
The Friend
Selector
helps
you invite
guests.

You can invite friends who aren't on Facebook by adding their e-mail addresses to the box at the bottom of the Friend Selector.

5. **Choose whether you want a public or private event using the Anyone can View and RSVP check box.**

   Public events are ones that anyone can see and join without invitation. If you aren't holding an exclusive event, this is usually the right choice, since it allows friends you might have forgotten to invite to see the event and add themselves to the guest list. For parties that you don't want everyone to know about, uncheck the Anyone Can View and RSVP box to keep it private. Only people you've invited will be able to see it and RSVP.

6. **Decide if you want to show the guest list using the Show the Guest List on the Event Page check box.**

Keeping your guest list visible is a nice way for friends to know who else is going to an event. This makes it easy for them to coordinate rides or plan presents, or whatever it is people do before your parties. If you don't want people to see this because of your friends' VIP status, uncheck the Show the Guest List on the Event Page box.

7. **Add a photo for your Event.**

Adding a photo to represent your Event makes it look pretty and inviting to your guests when they see the Event — both on the Event Home page and in invitation requests. Big, official Events often have their flier as the picture. To add an image, follow these steps:

a. *Click Add Event Photo, which is under the big calendar icon on the left side of the page.*

b. *Click the Browse or Choose File button to open your computer's standard interface for finding a file.*

c. *Navigate to (and select) the picture on your computer that you want to use.*

The picture you choose must meet the file size and type requirements outlined on the page. If you're not sure whether your desired picture meets the requirements, select the picture and continue with these steps. Facebook notifies you if the picture you choose can't be used.

d. *Click Upload Picture.*

The picture you selected now appears in place of that sad blue calendar icon.

8. **Click Create Event.**

Voilà! Event created. Invitations sent. And you didn't have to lick a stamp. You land on your Event's Home page. Welcome home.

As soon as you click Create Event, all of your guests will receive the information you just filled out. Double-check to make sure the time, date, and spelling are all correct before clicking.

Did you forget someone? People are asking for directions? Don't worry, we'll show you how to add to and edit your event in the "Managing your Event" section.

Quick Events

Although taking the time to find an Event picture and invite your friends and coordinate all sorts of logistics is worthwhile for that extra-special day, what about all of the ordinary, run-of-the-mill Events that transpire every day? All

of the coffee shops or park benches or dinners at your favorite cheap restaurant that would simply be better if you had a few friends along? Facebook
makes these Events easy to plan by letting you create Events directly from
your Home page.

The Events box is located at the upper-right corner of your Home page. It's
where your friends' upcoming birthdays and the upcoming events you are
attending are listed. You can also create an impromptu event from here.

To create an Event from the Events box, follow these steps:

1. **Click the What are you planning? prompt at the top of the Events box.**

   This step expands a few very familiar options, as shown in Figure 11-8.

Figure 11-8:
Quick Event
creation
from the
Publisher.

2. **Fill out your Event's Title (what are you planning?), Time, and
   Location (where?).**

   For example, your Event may read:

   Iron Man 2

   Today, 9:00 p.m.

   Shoreline Multiplex

3. **Invite people from the Who's Invited field.**

   Click in the Who's Invited box and start typing a friend's name. As you
   get to the friend you want, press Enter. Your friend's name will appear
   below this field, as shown in Figure 11-9. You can invite as many or as
   few friends as you want.

4. **Choose Privacy by clicking the lock icon.**

   Like any other event, this one can be either public or private. Making an
   event private means only people you invite will see it.

5. **Click Create Event.**

   The Event immediately appears as an Event in your Events box, with
   links to invite more people or add details. The Event is immediately
   posted to your Wall and to your friends' Live Feeds. To you, it appears
   as shown in Figure 11-9.

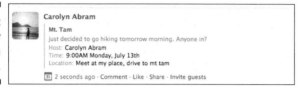

Carolyn Abram

Mt. Tam
just decided to go hiking tomorrow morning. Anyone in?
Host: **Carolyn Abram**
Time: **9:00AM Monday, July 13th**
Location: **Meet at my place, drive to mt tam**

2 seconds ago · Comment · Like · Share · Invite guests

You'll notice that if you click through to the Event, it has the same Event page described earlier in this chapter, just with more empty fields. If you have extra time, you can fill these out in the same way you would edit an Event you created way ahead of time, by clicking Edit Event below the picture.

Additionally, creating this Event generates a post that will go into your friends News Feeds (assuming you kept the Event public). Your friends will see links to RSVP, Like, or Share the Event.

Managing your Event

You can do a number of things when you finish creating your Event and people start to join. Many of these steps appear as action links under the picture on your Event's Home page. These actions are visible and available only to you and other administrators. This section outlines the additional power you wield as an Event administrator.

Editing your Event's Info

Need to update the event time or add info about a dress code? You can do this at any time by clicking Edit Event on the far top right of your event page, above where the ads in the right column are. This will take you back to the Create Event page, which is now called Edit Event, though all the fields are the same. You can edit everything about the event. Just remember to click Save Event when you are done.

Canceling the Event

As they say, the best laid plans . . . go oft awry. If your life has gone a bit awry and ruined your event plans, not to worry, it's easy to cancel your Event and send apologies to your guests. After clicking Edit Event in the upper right of the Event Page, you see the now familiar edit Event page, with one addition: a Cancel This Event link in the lower-right corner (sort of parallel to the Save Event button). Clicking Cancel This Event brings up a pop-up confirmation window, as shown in Figure 11-10.

This confirmation window also provides you with a space where you can let your guests know the reason for the cancellation. Write up a short note and click to confirm that you really want to cancel the Event. This will send an e-mail to all of your guests with the cancellation and your note, so no one accidentally shows up, party hat on, only to be disappointed.

Figure 11-10:
Party's off?
Cancel it on
Facebook.

Cancel Event?

We will email everyone who was invited that this event has been canceled. You may add a note below if you want:

Are you sure you want to cancel this event? This cannot be undone.

Yes, I'm sure   No, Thanks

Messaging your Event's guests

Rain delay? Halloween canceled? Keep your guests up-to-date about the Event by sending them a Facebook message. These messages appear in your guests' Facebook Inbox, and depending on their notification settings, they may also receive an e-mail notification.

To send a message to guests, click the Message Guests link on the far upper right corner of the event page, under the big blue bar, but above the ads column. You're taken to the standard Compose Message form with one addition: an Attendees drop-down list that allows you to indicate which guest list segment you want to message (everyone, those who are attending, may be attending, or haven't responded). Complete the rest of the process as if you were sending a message to a single friend. (If you need help with that process, see Chapter 9.)

Managing your Event's guest list

After guests RSVP to your Event, use the Event guest list to remove (even permanently ban) undesirable guests, promote your most trusted guests to administrators, or demote your existing administrators (if any) to regular guests.

1. **Click the Edit Guest List link under the picture in the right column of your Event's Home page.**

   The Guest List page is shown in Figure 11-11.

Figure 11-11:
The Guest
List page is
your one-
stop shop
for keeping
tabs on
your cur-
rent guests
and inviting
more.

2. **Use the link to the right of each guest name that corresponds to the action you want to take.**

   For instance, to make a member an administrator, click the Make Admin link. As an administrator, the member has the same privileges discussed in this chapter as you do for this particular Event.

   You can also use the X to remove a guest from the Event. If you select this option, you can also choose to ban that person permanently so he may not rejoin the Event in the future. Banning someone is useful if the person is posting offensive content or otherwise stirring up trouble.

You can also invite more people by clicking the Invite People to Come link, which opens a friend selector, just like the one you used when creating the event. If you're running a big party, the Print Guest List option will help your bouncers keep the riffraff out.

Chapter 12

Creating a Page for Your Business

In This Chapter

▶ Understanding Community Fan Pages and Official Fan Pages

▶ Determining whether a Facebook Page is appropriate for your business

▶ Creating and maintaining a Facebook Page

▶ Tracking how your promotional efforts affect your business in real time

*P*icture your town or city. Besides the occasional park or school, it's primarily made of buildings in which people live (like houses) and buildings in which people buy things (like stores). When you drive around town, you see all sorts of activities happening — whether people are throwing a Frisbee around, arguing politics over a cup of coffee, or working out. The world we live in is composed of people, the stuff they do, and the stuff that they need or want. People have real connections to all this stuff: the shops, the brands, the bands, the stars, the activities, the passions, and the restaurants and bars — everything that's important. Facebook is all about people and their real-world connections; the social map wouldn't be complete without these types of relationships.

Facebook offers a way for these non-people entities to be represented as part of your life: *Facebook Pages.* We know, "page" is a pretty common word on the Internet, so we'll always capitalize the P in Pages when we're talking about these official ones. There are two types of Pages, *Community Pages,* which are collectively managed and curated by its fans, and *Official Fan Pages,* which are managed and curated by official representatives of any business entity.

We'll spend this chapter helping you understand the world of Pages. If you just want to know what these things are that you've been liking and that have been showing up in your Profile and News Feed, check out the next section, "Pages and You." If you are looking to represent your small business, brand, band, or anything else on Facebook, start with the "Why Create a Facebook Page?" section and read on from there.

Pages and You

When you're thinking about interacting with Pages of any sort, the most important thing to keep in mind is that they are just like the Profiles of your friends, except when you "friend" a Page, it doesn't get to see your private info. You can do many of the same things with Pages that you can do with friends — write on their Walls, tag them in posts, and so on.

Anatomy of an Official Fan Page

The anatomy of Pages should feel pretty familiar to you, as they are meant to be just like Profiles. So if you read Chapter 6, most of the following will be a good refresher. Figure 12-1 shows a sample Facebook Page from the New York Times.

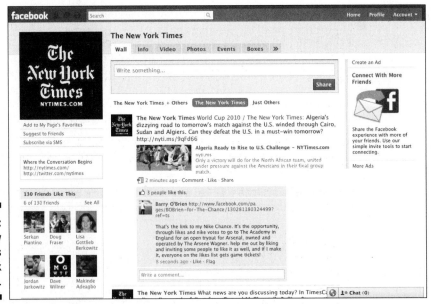

Figure 12-1:
The New York Times's Facebook Fan Page.

Across the top from left to right:

✔ **Profile picture:** Just like you and your friends, Pages choose one photo to represent themselves across the site. Usually, it's a logo or an official press photo.

✔ **Like button** *(not pictured):* Before you become a fan, you will see a "like" button sitting next to the Page's name. Click this to connect with the Page (see the next section for more on this topic).

✔ **Wall (and Publisher):** The Wall is the heart of a Page — it's where the Admins can post updates and where fans can leave Wall posts and comments. Note that there's a publisher here just like on any of your friends' Profiles and that you can see filters for viewing the Wall more prominently. You can choose whether to see just posts from the Page itself, or to view those of its fans.

✔ **Info tab:** The Info tab for Pages tends to be slightly less important, but it is a valuable resource if you ever need basic information such as the hours a business operates or its physical address.

✔ **Application tabs**: Just like your Profile, admins of Pages can add tabs for any applications, including Facebook ones like Events, Photos, and Video. These provide easy routes for fans to view more content or see what's new.

Down the left side, from top to bottom:

✔ **Action links:** Right below the Profile picture is a "Suggest to Friends" link. Additionally, if you've already liked a Page, you'll see a "Subscribe to Updates via SMS" link, which enables you to see status updates from that Page on your phone.

✔ **Bio box:** Just like on a Profile, this bio box provides an overview or context for the rest of the Page, often in the form of a mission statement.

✔ **People who like the Page:** More casually known as *fans*, people who like this Page are broken up into two categories: Friends who like the Page and Everyone who likes the Page.

✔ **Application boxes:** Just like on Profiles, Pages can display their rich content sorted by type, using these boxes located on the left side of the screen.

✔ **More Action links:** At the bottom of the Page are links that you'll need more rarely. They are still important to know about, since they include both Report, which you'll want if you find an offensive Page or one that violates your Intellectual Property, and Unlike, which you'll want if you want to remove your affiliation with a Page. There are also links here to create your own Page and a Share button.

Community Pages

Community Pages, or Pages that don't have one official admin, are fairly new additions to the Facebook universe. These tend to represent a wider range of things, from basic activities to political statements. Often, the object represented by Pages is something that simply can't be owned by a corporation or individual — things like "sleeping" or "Ultimate" or *Pride and Prejudice* (though, interestingly, a new movie version of *Pride and Prejudice* would almost certainly have an Official Page, as opposed to a Community Page).

A sample Community Page is shown in Figure 12-2.

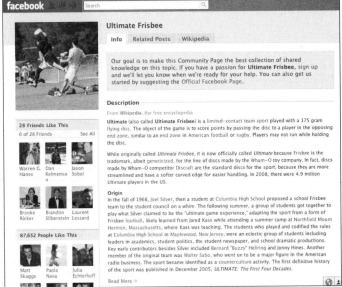

Figure 12-2: The Community Page for Ultimate Frisbee.

Community Pages differ from Official Pages in key ways. First and foremost, they don't have a Wall. Instead, they have a Related Posts tab, which shows posts your friends have made mentioning a particular topic or idea, as well as Global posts (posts set to Everyone) that people across Facebook have made. Additionally, Community Pages often pull basic info from sites like Wikipedia to explain the topic they are representing.

As we mentioned, Community Pages are fairly new to Facebook, so there will probably be additional functionality added over time. In the meantime, they function mostly as badges on your Profile, added to your likes and interests.

Connecting and interacting with Pages

Wherever you go on Facebook, and in many places across the entire Internet, you'll see links and buttons prompting you to "like" something. You can like photos, statuses, comments, articles, Web sites, videos . . . if it's online, you can probably like it.

You can also like Pages. And doing so is the way that you become a *fan*, a person who likes a particular Page. Being a fan accomplishes a few things:

- ✓ **News Feed subscription:** Once you like a Page, you may start seeing its status updates and other posts in your News Feed. If you don't like what you're seeing, you can always hide that Page from your News Feed.

- ✓ **Updates subscription:** Liking a Page subscribes you to receive *Updates*, basically messages from Pages. These Updates go to a special section of your Inbox reserved for them, so they don't interfere with the messages from your friends. If the Updates you get are annoying or too frequent for your taste, you can always unsubscribe.

- ✓ **Access to the Wall:** Just as when you add a friend, liking a Page lets you write on its Wall, usually with the ability to add photos, links, and videos.

- ✓ **Profile display:** It's important to keep in mind that when you like a Page, it appears in the "Likes and Interests" section of your Profile, and by default, this section is visible to Everyone. If you want to keep up with a Page, but don't want your friends to know, you can hide individual Pages from the Edit Profile pages (refer to Chapter 6 for specific steps on how to do this).

So what does this all mean for you? Basically, once you like something, you're starting a relationship with it that can be as interactive as you want, or as hands-off as you want. Frequently, people like a lot of Pages simply as a signifier or badge on their Profiles. Just because you like *30 Rock,* you might not care about articles about it, or interviews with the cast. And that's fine. On the other hand, if you like reading those sorts of things, or interacting with other fans on the Wall, you can do that as well. It's a pretty flexible system.

Why Create a Facebook Page?

Before we can answer why you should create a Facebook Page, first think about other things you can do to achieve success for your business:

- ✓ **Offer a quality product or service.** Differentiated products attract repeat customers and referrals.

- ✓ **Locate your business on a busy street or in a dense shopping area.** Highly trafficked locations translate to attention and accessibility.

- ✓ **Clean and decorate your shop, carefully design your Web site, or dress up for a performance.** Quality presentation gains trust from customers.

In the end, all of these are examples of things businesses do to achieve growth: namely, growth of a loyal fan base. Giving your business a presence on Facebook ultimately has the same purpose: driving growth.

Then again, lots of things *can* drive growth. Handing out flyers on the street, placing coupons in a newspaper, or running a commercial during the Super Bowl may get you customers. The trick is to figure out which, of all possible promotional efforts, has the biggest bang for your buck. We think we know the answer.

Speaking of bucks, it's time to get the uncomfortable money stuff out of the way: Facebook Pages are free. All you need is access to a computer and the Internet, someone who knows how to use Facebook, and a little time. Setting up your business Page can take five minutes or several hours, depending on how advanced you want to get. If that sounds daunting, remember that it would take several hours to make, print, and distribute flyers — and even longer to create a Web site or film a commercial.

Following are several goals you may have for your business. Throughout this chapter, we show how Facebook Pages help you achieve each goal.

- ✔ Engage your customers and fans regularly and in compelling ways. When they think of your industry, they think of you. When they think of you, they feel like they know you. Even if you represent a large corporation, they feel like they understand the human side of the equation.

- ✔ Provide customers and potential customers with an accurate source of information about the business, such as an e-mail address, product details, or hours of operation.

- ✔ Communicate new promotions, products, and updates with as many customers as possible while alienating as few as possible.

- ✔ Encourage customers to provide both positive and negative feedback so you can continually improve.

- ✔ Enable your customers to communicate with one another about your business, product, or band in productive ways.

- ✔ Impress your customers so much that they come back again and again — and tell their friends to do the same.

Facebook Pages offer a suite of features that work together to help you achieve these goals. If you're in a position of promotional authority for a business and have even one of the preceding goals, you can find value in creating a Facebook Page.

Pages versus Profiles versus Groups

In real life, how people interact and communicate with their best friends, favorite bands, or local neighborhood associations is unique. Additionally, the needs of a person, versus a band manager, versus a group organizer in terms of connecting and sharing are also different. This is why people, businesses, and Groups all have unique types of presence on Facebook. The way people interact with these entities on Facebook reflects those real-world differences. Because Pages, Profiles, and Groups offer different features and functionality, we want to make sure that you understand each type of presence. Then, based on your specific business goals, you can pick the presence (or presences) best for your goals. Before we highlight the specific functionality differences on Facebook, first think about the real-world differences between people, businesses, and groups:

- ✔ **Communication:** Communication with a friend is usually a conversation, where you say something, and then she responds, and so on. And frequently, these conversations are very personal, with each member contributing equally. With a business, however, communication is often unidirectional: For example, your favorite band tells you about a new CD, or your favorite store announces a sale. Comparatively, communication within groups tends to flow among all members with equal authority, relevance, and interest to all members.

- ✔ **Access:** You are welcomed and encouraged to walk into a café or bookstore at any time during posted business hours. Quite the opposite is true when entering a friend's home unannounced. Additionally, a group usually meets at formalized meeting times agreed upon by all members (or a governing body) and at a venue accessible to all.

- ✔ **Information:** People are particular about which people know what information about them. Groups have varying degrees of privacy, depending on the group, but they generally fall into two buckets in which information is shared: only among members or with the general public. With the exception of strategic future plans and some financial details, businesses usually want as many people to know as much about them or their products as possible.

These kinds of real-world differences determine the differences in design and functionality of a person, a Group, and a business presence on Facebook.

Table 12-1 details the specific differences among these types of presence on Facebook.

Table 12-1   Comparison of User Profiles, Groups, and Pages

Profiles	Groups	Pages
Have one Administrator: you.	May have many admins, as arbitrarily appointed by the creator or other admins.	May have many admins, which are the appointed authority of the business.
Represent a real person.	With the exception of copyrighted material or hate speech, represent anything. Seriously.	Represent a real business or promotional entity.
Have friends. Friendships need to be confirmed by both parties. Only friends can see private information.	Have members. Member requests may be reviewed or automatic, depending on the Group's setting.	Have fans (a.k.a., people who "like" your Page). Fan requests are automatically approved. The available information is the same for everyone.
Can send messages to other people, and up to 20 friends. If people are friends, they can always message each other.	Permit admins to message up to 500 members. Members can reply to the Group admin. Members must leave the Groups to opt out of messages.	Allow admins to send bulk messages to all fans. People cannot reply to these messages and can opt out of them.
The person behind the Profile may make choices about what — if anything — is globally visible.	Can restrict privacy to members or opt to be globally visible.	Can restrict privacy based on age, but are otherwise always globally visible.
Must approve all friend requests.	May choose to review membership requests, or accept automatically.	Automatically accept all fan requests.
Can block people for inappropriate behavior.	Can block people for inappropriate behavior.	Can block people for inappropriate behavior.
Can publish content, use applications, and customize with additional tabs.	Can publish content, use applications, and customize with boxes.	Can publish content, use applications, and customize with additional tabs and boxes.
Have no access to aggregate information about Profile views and interactions.	Have no aggregate information about the page views and interactions with the Group.	Have detailed insights about how people view and interact with a particular Facebook Page, aggregated and broken down by demographic.

Who should create a Facebook Page?

Simply put, anyone who is in a position of promotional authority can build a Facebook Page. Small-business owners, event promoters, and advertising agencies can create a Page on Facebook to get attention and engagement from people. Facebook Pages are designed and optimized for the legitimate business seeking legitimate attention.

Popular categories for business Profiles include

- ✔ **Local businesses:** Such as restaurants, bars, clubs, shops, and recreational spots.

- ✔ **Big name or national brands:** Such as those that distribute products or provide a service. Starbucks, Verizon, and Coca-Cola are examples.

- ✔ **Nonprofit or government organizations:** Such as schools and religious organizations.

- ✔ **Specific products:** Such as certain car models, business mascots (for example, Ronald McDonald), or high-end designer clothing lines.

- ✔ **News, media, and entertainment companies:** These entities can create Pages for their brands or their various offerings, such as movies, TV shows, and magazines.

The preceding list demonstrates that Pages are equally suited for businesses as well as for their products. The NBA, for example, has an NBA Facebook Page as well as a Facebook Page for each of its teams. CBS has a Facebook Page, as does each of its shows. The reason why many businesses promote themselves in this fractured way is because people may identify with particular parts of their business but not the business in its entirety. Creating different Pages for the different entities with which people may connect is important for maximizing engagement. Conversely, you want to avoid over-fragmenting your audience. For example, Six Flags amusement parks don't have to create a Page for every ride, Radiohead doesn't have to create a Page for each album, and Starbucks doesn't have to create a Page for every beverage.

Who shouldn't build a Facebook Page?

A Page, just like a user's Profile on Facebook, represents a real identity and is managed by the real-life appointed authority of that entity. For example, if you're not Chuck Norris (or his PR person), you can't create a Facebook Page called Chuck Norris. And if you didn't write or publish *Fight Club* (or weren't hired by someone who did), you can't create a Page for it. It doesn't matter how much you love *lite-mocha Frappaccinos, extra whip-cream;* unless you're the marketing rep for Starbucks, you can't create a Facebook Page for them. Well, you can, but your Page — and/or your account — may end up being disabled.

Living In the Gray Netherworld between Pages and Profiles

You may have, by now, noticed a distinction between representing one person and representing a collection of people. So, while it's easy to choose between creating a Profile for the Dave Matthews Band and creating a Page for the Dave Matthews Band, it may be harder to choose what to do if you want to create something for just Dave Matthews.

Celebrities and public figures do have to make a choice about which service best fits their needs. In general, there are two relevant questions to ask if you find yourself in the public figure predicament:

- ✔ **Will I be the only one managing my online self?** In other words, do you have a staff assistant who is charged with keeping your Facebook presence up-to-date? Or will you be doing all of your own Facebooking?

- ✔ **Do I also want to share more privately with my real-life friends?** Some people want to have it all: They want to publish a photo album from the family reunion (even if that family has a last name like Norris) and keep it private, while still publishing interesting articles, thoughts, and less private photos to the world at large (especially the world that is pretty sure Chuck Norris can sneeze with his eyes open).

If the answer to both questions is yes, chances are you should still consider building a Profile. You will be the only one able to access it, and you can use the Publisher privacy controls we describe in Chapter 6 to choose who sees what.

If the answer to both questions is no, you should create a Page. It will give you the most flexibility in terms of who can manage it, and everything will publish to everyone — no special settings necessary.

If you answered no to the first question and yes to the second question, you probably want to create a Facebook Page for your staff to manage and a Facebook Profile just for yourself. The Page represents the public you, and a Profile can become the space where you share just with your friends and family.

If the answer is a combination of yes and no, a Page is again the more flexible, simple way to go, especially if it turns out managing your Page is time-consuming and you change your mind on the answer to question one.

Creating and Managing a Facebook Page

A Facebook Page isn't equivalent to an account. Rather, it's an entity on Facebook that can be managed by many people with their own distinct accounts. This section will take you through all the steps of Page creation, administration, and maintenance.

Before you get started, however, we recommend you read the Terms of Service for Page Owners at www.facebook.com/terms_pages.php. First of all, the TOS clarifies some of the expectations for owning a Page and who can create a Page for their business. There are also a few notes about who can see your content when you create a Page and age restrictions on your Page. We cover all of these topics throughout this chapter, but the TOS provide a nice summary. If you violate these Terms, your Page may be disabled, which will be very bad for your business. On the same note, if you create a Profile to do the work of a Page (as we describe here), that Profile will almost certainly be disabled for violating the user terms of service (which you can read at www.facebook.com/terms.php).

Creating a Page for your business

If you haven't already created an account on Facebook, we highly recommend that you do that first (although you don't have to). If you don't want to, you can start the process at Step 2 in the following steps; before completing Step 6, however, you're asked to create an account. The account you create here is a lesser version of a full Facebook user account, but it's still your account. You're asked to enter your e-mail address and birth date, and you should enter accurate information. That way, if you ever decide that you want a personal Profile, upgrading the account you create here is much easier than starting from scratch.

Pages can have multiple admins. If you plan to have other people managing the Page you're creating, they can do so from their accounts. There's no reason to share the e-mail address or password with anyone. In fact, doing so violates the Terms of Use. We hope we've gained your trust enough at this point of the book that you trust us here: ***Use your real e-mail address and birth date.*** This information won't be revealed to anyone else, and it makes your future interactions on Facebook much easier.

1. **Navigate to www.Facebook.com and log in with your username and password.**

2. **Scroll down until you can't scroll any farther and then click Advertising in the footer menu.**

   The page you land on (www.Facebook.com/advertising) gives you an overview of the Facebook integrated advertising system. Pages are free, but ads are not. That being said, when you are just starting out with your Page, advertising can be worth the investment to help you build a base of connections and subscribers. Find out more about advertising in Chapter 15.

3. **Click the Pages link, located just below the top menu.**

   You're welcome to read the copy on that page or click the Learn More link, but there's nothing there that's not in this book. (After all, we wrote both.)

4. **Click the Create a Page button.**

   It's the green button in the upper-right quadrant of the screen. This starts the Create Page workflow.

5. **In the Official Page section on the left side of the page, specify what kind of business you're trying to promote, as shown in Figure 12-3.**

   The reason for making an accurate selection here is twofold:

   - Depending on the category you choose, your Facebook Page is created with a very specific set of fields and functionality. For example, specifying that your business is a restaurant allows you to specify your hours of operation, and specifying that you're a musician gives you instant access to a discography.

   - You can help users find and identify you.

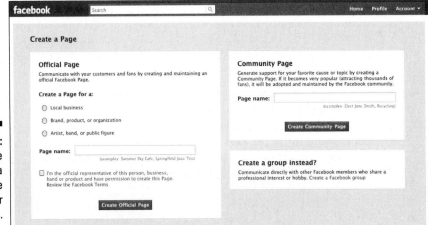

Figure 12-3: Categorize and create a Page for your business.

6. **Enter the name of your business.**

   When you name your Facebook Page, it's important that you sign up with the exact name of your business, just like you need to sign up for Facebook with your real name.

   Good examples of names for hypothetical Facebook Pages are

   - Amazon
   - Anthony's Pizza
   - Stephen Colbert
   - Buffy the Vampire Slayer

   Bad examples of Facebook Page names are

   - **Amazon's Facebook Page:** Like a user's Profile, Facebook Pages are an online representation of your business. When users navigate to your Page and click Become a Fan, they're a fan of your business, not the Page. When you send fans an update, you're sending it on behalf of the business, not the Page. The Page isn't a destination: It's a means. When people interact with your Page, they're actually interacting directly with your business, and it's important that the name reflects this.

   - **Anthony's Pizza at 553 University Ave.:** Just like the thousands of Joe Smiths on Facebook, there may be hundreds of Anthony's Pizzas — but that's okay. People use the content on your Page, such as your photos or local address listed in your information fields, to identify the Anthony's Pizza they're after.

   - **Stephen Colbert, Politician & Comedian Extraordinaire:** Stephen Colbert is welcome to specify his profession in his information fields. Additionally, in the body of his Page, he can declare himself *extraordinaire* over and over. However, his brand is his name, and that should be the name of his Page: *Stephen Colbert.*

   - **Buffy the Vampire Slayer Is Awesome:** Buffy *is* awesome, and this would make a great name for a Facebook Group or a Facebook Community Page. However, there's no real-life entity with this name (that we know of); therefore, there shouldn't be a Facebook Page with this name.

7. **Authorize that you are an official representative of your business and click Create Page.**

   As soon as you click Create Page, you're the proud admin of a Facebook Page. You're not done, though. Now you have to configure and customize. Both of these processes are complicated enough that we're punting those explanations to a separate numbered list.

If all the excitement has gotten the best of you, continue on to customize your Page right away; the next section guides you through that process. If you plan to take a break, you need to know how to get back here.

When you follow the preceding steps to create your first Facebook Page, you automatically have a new application added to your account called Page Manager (if you've ever run an ad, it may also be called Ads and Pages). Whenever you're logged in to Facebook, look for it in the Applications Menu (on the left side of the Home page), and click this link to access, edit, and manage your Page. Page Manager is also where you go to see all the user-engagement statistics, which we talk about in the "Know-It-All" section, at the end of this chapter.

Making your Page yours

Since its beginning, Facebook has operated under a different principle than most of its competitors. Many other sites encourage people to customize their online presence with backgrounds, colors, layouts, and songs to express their individuality. Facebook encourages people to express their individuality through the content they publish on their Profiles rather than through visual (or audio) display. The same is true for Facebook Pages. Most of the customization of your Page comes from what you say, link to, publish, and add as tabs for people to interact with. Businesses that are used to branding and customizing their Web sites may find this limiting, but think of the trade-off. Potential customers who arrive at your Facebook Page know exactly how to get the information they need and how to interact with your Page because they're already familiar with the format. The unified look and feel of Facebook Pages is designed for ease of navigation and to provide a seamless experience for Facebook users. Rather than view these limitations as a disadvantage, try distinguishing your Page by offering rich and engaging content and functionality.

We mention earlier that while creating your Page, you're asked to categorize your business. This category determines which information fields and default applications appear on your Page. Keep reading as we summarize the information fields as well as all the default applications that your Page may start with.

After completing the steps in the preceding section, you see your clean slate of a Facebook Page. An example is shown in Figure 12-4. At the top is your business, brand, or band's name, beneath which are two tabs waiting to be filled in with rich, informative, engaging information.

Figure 12-4:
A newborn
Facebook
Page —
after
creation,
before con-
figuration.

Much of your Page can be edited from the Page itself. Some behind-the-scenes settings, however, need to be edited from what we're calling the *Control Panel.* We call out whenever you need to go to the Control Panel, which you can do by clicking Edit Page right beneath your Profile picture.

People connect to your Page similarly to how they connect to other users, by clicking a big Like button next to your name. By default, when a user clicks that button, she starts receiving your posts on her Home page in News Feeds. We call this *subscribing.* We refer to your fans as connections, customers, and patrons a bit interchangeably, but when we talk about subscribers, we always mean people who see your posts in their News Feeds when they log in.

Getting your bearings

As you look around your newly minted Page, all gangly limbs and blank spaces, you may notice something. It looks . . . just like a user Profile. It has an Info tab and a Wall tab and a Publisher. There's a space for a Profile picture and a bio box running down the left column. Why, it's practically the same as a user Profile. If you don't feel like you're yet comfortable with the user Profile, we recommend skipping back a little bit to Chapter 6, because we're going to breeze through a bunch of the stuff we cover there in this section. But just as we do in that chapter, we're going to first talk about the main tabs, and then the other cool things you can do with your Page.

Information

The very first thing that we recommend doing is to set up a photo for your Page. This brings your Page to life, helping your fans identify you when they find you in Search or read about you in their friend's News Feeds. Set your picture by clicking Edit in the upper-right corner of the Profile Picture box; then follow the instructions to upload a photo. The column in which the Photo is placed is 396 pixels wide and can be up to three times the width of your picture. Keep these dimensions in mind when trying to make or choose a high-quality photo for your Page.

Most Pages have three information sections within the info tab: Basic, Detailed, and Contact.

- **Basic information:** Here, enter information that is core to your business. For Basic information, bands list members, local businesses list their address, and big name brands usually list their Web sites, for example.

- **Detailed information:** This includes information fields unique to your type of business. This is where bands list their influencers, clubs state their dress policies, and movie studios list the awards they've won for certain films.

- **Contact information:** This one is pretty self-explanatory. Depending on the type of business you have, you can enter an e-mail address, phone number, and, in some cases, a mailing address.

Clicking Edit Information in the upper-right of the info tab should expose all of these sections for editing. The more fields you fill out, the more people know about you. Any field that you don't fill out simply won't appear when people visit your Page.

The Wall

Whereas the Information tab lets people know about the basics, the Wall is where people get to know the real you. If you have a personal account with a Profile, the Wall will feel very intuitive. Check out the Wall for the satirical magazine *The Onion* in Figure 12-5 to get a feel for how a Page can use its Wall to showcase what's new and exciting.

The Wall is where people who have connected to you will land when they visit your actual Page. The content you publish on your Wall will also feed into their Home pages, assuming they've subscribed to your posts. In other words, it's a very important place to represent yourself honestly and engagingly through constant updates.

In Chapter 6, we describe in detail all the pieces of the Wall and how they fit together to tell the story of you. That story still needs to be told for you, even when you represent some sort of business. People are going to want to hear from you, they are going to want to learn about you, and the place they will go to do that is your Wall.

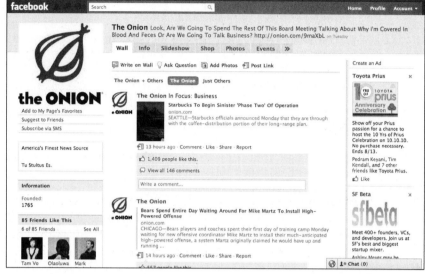

Figure 12-5:
The Onion on
Facebook.

As a Page admin, the most important part of the Wall to understand is the *Publisher.* The Publisher, as shown in detail in Figure 12-6, is where you and fans create the posts that actually appear on the Wall.

Figure 12-6:
Use the
Publisher to
send posts
out to fans.

Facebook for Dummies

Wall   Info   Photos   Discussions   Reviews   Events   **+**

🖼 **Update Status**   💡 **Ask Question**   🖼 **Add Photos**   🔗 **Post Link**

🔒 ▾   Share

The basic steps for using the Publisher are as follows:

1. **Click in the text field.**

   You'll see a few icons extend beneath you.

2. **(Optional) Select the icon that represents the type of media you wish to add.**

   If you want to add a link, click Link. If you want to add a photo, click Photo. You get the idea. If you don't want to add any sort of attachment, that's okay, too. In fact, it's quite common. Text-only posts are referred to as *Status Updates.*

3. **Type your comment, either to explain your attachment or just to say whatever it is you're thinking about.**

4. **(Optional) Target your update by clicking the People icon next to the Share button.**

   You can limit who can see your status by location and language. This is especially useful if you have some sort of local announcement that applies only to people in certain countries or cities.

5. **Click Share.**

Congratulations! Your Page is officially published. Posts you create here are sent as News Feeds for your subscribers to enjoy.

Wall Settings

Unlike user Profiles, Page admins have some control over how their Walls appear by default. From the Control Panel, you can open the Wall Settings section (shown in Figure 12-7) and access the following options:

- ✔ **Default View for Wall:** This setting controls what your subscribers and connections see when they land on your Wall. Some Page admins take great care to post regularly, and having a plethora of Wall posts from eager and enthusiastic fans — though wonderful — can push the newer content from the Page off the Wall very quickly. For this reason, most Pages have a default setting that enables their connections to see only their original posts when they land on the Wall. Page admins who don't have a lot of time to update may consider making both original posts and posts from connections appear together because it keeps the Wall more current, even if they haven't updated themselves in a while.

- ✔ **Default Landing Tab for Everyone Else:** In Chapter 6, we talk about the feeling of landing on the Wall of a new friend and feeling like you just interrupted an incredibly interesting conversation. To prevent your potential fans from feeling that pain, you can opt for them to land on a tab of your choosing.

- ✔ **Auto-Expand Comments:** Comments on posts can be very interesting. If there are a lot of them, however, they can become unwieldy or irrelevant. This option allows you to keep these comments condensed. Users can still click to see them, but they won't show up until they click.

- ✔ **Fans Can Write on the Wall:** We strongly recommend keeping this one checked, but for some industries, it just isn't as possible for users to have the ability to comment at will. If you need to turn this one off, you can do so here.

- ✔ **Posting Ability:** Here is where you can control whether your fans are allowed to add photos, videos, and links as attachments to their posts.

Wall Settings

View Settings

Default View for Wall: [Only Posts by Page ▾]

Default Landing Tab for Everyone Else: [Wall ▾]

Auto-Expand Comments: ☐ Comments on stories will be expanded by default

Fan Permissions

Fans can write on the wall: ☑ Fans can write on the wall

Posting Ability: ☑ Allow fans to post photos
☑ Allow fans to post videos
☑ Allow fans to post links

Figure 12-7:
Wall
Settings.

Applications

We spend a lot of time in this book talking about how applications integrate with your personal Profile. Remember that when you first create your Profile, you have some default applications, as well as more applications that you can use to meet your specific needs. The same is true for your Facebook Page. Most Facebook Pages come prepackaged with a default set of applications, as shown in Figure 12-8. Depending on the category you choose, you may get a few choice extras. You're free to keep any of the preinstalled applications or remove them (with the exception of the Reviews application, which is required for all Pages in certain categories), and you're encouraged to browse and add more applications that you think your customers will find engaging.

Depending on which applications you use, you may want to consider adding a *tab* to feature its content. For example, if you add a lot of photos of your wares, a Photos tab gives people an easy way to see your full history of photo albums, not just the most recent one that may be at the top of your Wall. The same goes for any of the other applications you get by default. Additionally, if you use other relevant applications, you can add those as tabs, too.

To add a tab, click the little + (plus) sign next to the Info tab. This expands a menu and lets you choose which tab you want to add. Remember, this lets you add tabs only for applications you've already added to your Page. (We describe that process in the "More applications" section, a bit later in this chapter.)

Lots of businesses use an application called Static FBML to customize a Welcome or About tab with their own formatting and content. FBML allows you to use rich text markup like HTML to create a custom space. To find this application, search for Static FMBL in the blue bar on top.

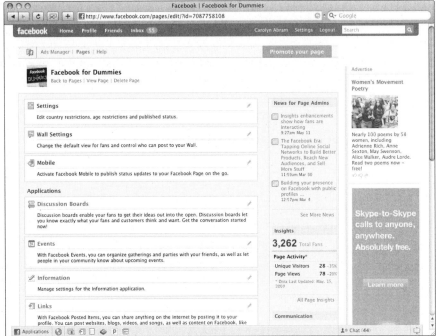

Photos

Use the Photos application to publish albums for your fans to enjoy. If you own a restaurant, you may want to take photos of your most popular dishes, creating one album for breakfast, one for lunch, and one for dinner. Bands may publish albums from their various concerts and events. Brands may use photos to show off people engaging with their products. For example, Nike might show women in Nike shoes, Starbucks might show a kid with whipped cream on his nose, and Blockbuster might show friends watching a movie. Add photos by clicking the Photos link in the Publisher (remember to make sure you're on your Page's Publisher, not on your Profile's).

If you choose, you can set the Photos application to allow people who've connected to you to add photos to your Page. These photos are shown in a separate section from the photos you add, which helps viewers distinguish the content you're adding to your Page from what your fans add. Publishing photos is often a great way to keep your Wall looking really diverse and to generate interesting posts to go into your subscribers' News Feeds.

Events

If you ever host any kind of event for your business, you'll get a ton of value from the Events application. Stores create Events for their big sales, comedians create Events for their shows, and clubs create Events for their special-party nights. To create an Event, click the pencil icon in the upper-right corner of the Events box on the Control Panel. Choose Edit from the menu that appears. This takes you to the Create Event page, where you can fill out the info and upload a photo (see Chapter 11 for more details on Event creation). Finally, send a message to all your subscribers informing them about your event. A bit later, we talk more about what sending messages to your fans entails.

Discussion Board

Every Page comes with a discussion board where your fans congregate and discuss topics relating to your Page. A discussion board takes no setup on your side, which is why there's no box for it in the Control Panel. You can add it as a tab if you want to give people easier access to it. With the Discussion Board on your Page, users can instantly start topics and respond to others.

Video

The Video application for your Page works in a similar way that it does for your Profile (see Chapter 8). Just like with Photos, you can upload videos to your Page. For example, a coffee shop may show a video of a barista making a fancy drink, a singer may show clips from a recent concert, and a movie theater may show clips from an upcoming film. Zappos has added some pretty funny videos that include interviews and short skits done by its employees. It's a great way to put a human face on something very inhuman, like an online shoe store, in the case of Zappos. You can add videos from the Publisher.

Reviews

Besides being a way for you to represent your business or band, Facebook Pages are also a means by which real people get real information about the businesses around them. For this reason, users can count on the Reviews application on each and every Facebook Page in relevant categories. Unlike writing on the Wall (which can only be written on after people connect to you), anyone can write a review on any Facebook Page (although admins can't review their own businesses). Reviews are also different from the Wall in that each user can only ever write one review, although she can update that review if her impression of the business changes.

To do this, you need to first go to the Control Panel (Edit Page) and then click the Edit link (the pencil icon) in the upper-right corner of the Reviews bar. Then select Edit in the drop-down list box.

More applications

At the bottom of the Applications section of your Page's Control Panel is the More Applications box (refer to Figure 12-7). Depending on the category you initially selected for your Page, this box may already be populated with applications that Facebook thinks could be appropriate for your type of business. Restaurants, for example, may be encouraged to add the OpenTable application, which allows your customers to make reservations straight from your Facebook Page.

The Discography application comes recommended for movies and TV shows because many have sound tracks. To discover more about these applications, search for them in the Application Directory (which is covered in detail in Chapter 13), and then click the title to go to the application's About page. From there, if you like what you see, you can choose Add to My Page (you see this link under the Application's logo, with the other action links). To see more apps than those recommended, click the Browse More link at the upper-right to go to the Product Directory. You'll already be in the For Facebook Pages section of the directory, and every application you see listed there can be added to your Facebook Page to increase your fans' engagement with your Page.

Most applications in the Application Directory are built by companies other than Facebook. Although many of them make fantastic applications that can add a ton of value to your Page, some of them may be, um, inadequate. Facebook has rules to protect you from *malicious* applications, but not those that are simply low quality. After adding an application, we recommend that you check how it interacts with your Page and watch how your fans use it. Be sure that an application adds value before you decide to keep it.

Rather than browsing the Application Directory for good applications, some Page administrators check out their competitors' Pages to see what kinds of applications seem to be working well. If you do this and see one you like, look for links to the application's main page in order to add it to your Page.

Settings

The very top of the Control Panel features a box for editing your Page's settings, of which, for now, there are only three, as shown in Figure 12-9:

- **Country Restrictions:** Because Facebook is an international site, it may be helpful to restrict your Page's visibility to only countries that speak the language your Page is in. Additionally, some Page types, like movies, may want to have a different focus or different admin in different countries. For those needs, each Page can be restricted by country.

- **Age Restrictions:** Put an age restriction on your Page in case you're promoting something that's illegal or irrelevant to those under a particular age, such as bars or matchmaking services.

- **Published Status:** This is basically a toggle for turning your Page on and off. You will not want to publish the page to everyone until you feel like it's ready, so after you get your basic information and a few posts up, you can change this to Published (publicly visible).

Some Page types, such as bands, artists, or public figures, may see an additional setting that allows them to change their Page's gender pronoun. If you're a band with more than one member, using *they* makes the most sense. An actress would select *she*. This pronoun is used in sentences, such as those that appear in your Page's Recent Activity. For example, "The Shins added a new album to their Discography," or "Blake Ross edited his Photo Album."

Figure 12-9:
Fine-tuning your settings on a Facebook Page.

Mobile

If you want a little more flexibility in terms of *when* you create posts, you can use your phone as a direct link from the outside world to your Page. For example, you can update your status from your mobile phone, which updates your Facebook Page as well as your subscribers' News Feeds. This type of functionality isn't for everyone, but if you're representing people of any type, these types of quick updates make the Page feel much more authentic. This is the difference between sending a press release detailing a band's most recent concert and sending a short sentence saying, "Minor explosion during sound check. No one was hurt, and the show goes on." Which feels more real to you? Which do you want to pay more attention to?

Mobile for Pages has a few limitations, including the fact that there's only one phone per Page, and only one Page or Profile per phone. In other words, one phone needs to be imbued with the power to update the Page from afar. The phone you select needs to have basic text-messaging capabilities.

Your carrier's normal text messaging fees apply to texts you send or receive as a result of updating your Page via Facebook Mobile. Make sure you're okay with this cost before setting anything up.

After you've selected the phone you're going to use to update your Page, keep it close and follow these steps:

1. **Expand the Mobile section of the Control Panel by clicking Edit Mobile.**

    This is the same pencil icon that always indicates editable content on Facebook. It expands to reveal links.

2. **Click Register for Facebook Mobile Texts.**

    The Activate Facebook Texts dialog box appears, as shown in Figure 12-10.

Figure 12-10:
The first step toward activating mobile for your Page.

Activate Facebook Texts (Step 1 of 3)

Please choose your country and mobile service provider below.*

United States ▾ | Nextel ▾

*If your mobile service provider is not listed, Facebook does not support them at this time.

Next   Cancel

3. **Select your country and your mobile carrier and then click Next.**

    The second screen appears, instructing you on a specific text message you should send to FBOOK (32665).

4. **Send the text message from your phone as instructed.**

    If everything worked, you should receive a text message back from Facebook almost immediately. It contains a confirmation code.

5. **Back on your computer, click Next.**

    The final step for activating mobile appears, as shown in Figure 12-11.

Figure 12-11:
Enter your mobile confirmation code.

Activate Facebook Texts (Step 3 of 3)

In a few seconds, you should receive a text message that contains your mobile activation code. If you haven't received a code after a few minutes, please repeat Step #2.

Enter the code here

Confirm   Cancel

6. **Enter the confirmation code you received on your phone into the designated box within the dialog box. When you're done, click Confirm.**

On your phone, you should get another text telling you that your phone has been confirmed. On your screen, the mobile texts Page appears with some instructions on how to use Facebook mobile as a Page owner.

Now, anytime you want to say something to your fans, you merely need to send a text message from the activated phone to FBOOK (32665) with the text of your post in the message. The post appears on your Wall, the only difference being that it will have a little mobile icon next to it, as shown in Figure 12-12.

Figure 12-12:
Status
updates
from your
phone are
denoted by
a mobile
icon.

Admins

Most businesses have more than one person sharing responsibility for promotion. Perhaps you're the co-owner of your restaurant, or you're part of a marketing team for several companies, or maybe you're the drummer of a band that's sick of the lead singer holding all the cards. Good news: Every Facebook Page can have up to 25 administrators, all of whom can admin the Page through their personal account. This means no password-sharing and no creating fake accounts. Whoever initially creates the Page simply needs to invite all the appropriate people to help administer the Page. Here's how:

1. **Navigate to the Control Panel of your Page.**

2. **In the Admins section in the right column (under which only you are listed), click Edit.**

3. **Invite people to be the administrators of your Page.**

   You can invite any person who already has a Facebook account and with whom you're friends on Facebook to be an admin by entering his name into the Friend Selector at the upper-right of the Invite Admins page. You can enter the e-mail address of any person who isn't on Facebook or with whom you're not friends in the box at the bottom-right. In either case, the person you invite must accept the invitation in order to become an admin.

Promoting your Page

To benefit from the viral nature of Facebook, you must seed your Page with people who want to become your fans.

Tell customers electronically

If you have an existing Web site or a mailing list, you may want to add a link or send a message to alert your existing fans or customers that they can now find you on Facebook. For those in your fan base who already have a Facebook account, they'll probably find that connecting with you there is way more convenient that remembering to go to your site regularly. And having them connect with your Facebook Page doesn't preclude them continuing to visit your Web site; rather, a Facebook Page gives you an extra opportunity to communicate with them about changes and updates on your site.

Tell customers physically

If you have a physical store, try sticking a sign on the window that tells customers to find you on Facebook. As long as they remember your business name and Facebook, they can look you up and connect with your business on an on-going basis.

You can get a vanity URL on Facebook, called a *username,* that will enable your customers to navigate directly to your Official Page. For example, our Page is www.facebook.com/facebookfordummies. If you want a username for your Page, and you have at least 25 fans, navigate to www.facebook.com/username. Remember to think ahead when you claim your username: You want something memorable and also something that will help distinguish you if you are a local business. You can have only one username, so make sure it's one you like.

Tell your friends

If you run a business, you probably already spend a lot of time marketing it to your friends. We'll go out on a limb here and hypothesize that you don't enjoy sending mass e-mails or constantly promoting your business to your friends and family. You never know who really wants to hear about it or who is just being polite by not complaining. Directing your friends to your Facebook Page solves two problems. They can choose to become a fan of your Page, and then they can choose whether to receive updates. This means the following:

- ✔ You update only those people who want to hear about it.

- ✔ You seed your Page with a slew of fans whose actions on your Page serve as passive referrals when their friends read about it in News Feeds or Highlights.

To share your Page with your friends:

1. **Navigate to your Facebook Page.**
2. **Scroll to the bottom and click Share.**
3. **Add up to 20 of your friends in the To line and welcome them to your Page.**

You can also stick the link in an e-mail. We don't recommend messaging your friends more than once in this way, though. If they want to hear from your business, they'll become a fan; if not, they're probably not great customers, anyway.

Advertise

In Chapter 15, we introduce you to the world of advertising on Facebook, with a special emphasis on how to advertise your Facebook Page. The beauty of advertising your Page on Facebook is that you're already targeting the audience most likely to understand what your Facebook Page is all about. Also, from the audience's point of view, it's a smoother experience to click an ad in Facebook, which navigates to another Facebook page. This is very different than how most Web advertising works, where clicking an ad opens a whole new window into a whole different Web site.

Engaging your fans

If you've read this chapter up to this point, you have your customized Facebook Page and are ready to drive traffic to your business. Now may be a good time to get up, take a little walk, a nap, or make a delicious turkey sandwich (extra cranberry, hold the mayo). You're done with the basic work required to allow people to find out about your business and connect with it.

To gain real attention and interaction, though, you can do a lot more. ***Remember:*** The richer your Page and the more you engage your fans, the more actions they take (and the more they have warm fuzzy feelings when they think of you), which generates News Feeds and Highlights stories for all their friends to see, thus giving you more visibility and attention.

Publish rich content

By *rich,* we mean informative and fresh. The more new and useful content you add to your Page, the more reason your fans have to come back and check it out. Here are some ideas to keep fans (that is, customers) lingering on your content:

✔ **Publish authentic status updates:** These short posts go into people's Live Feeds and News Feeds and remind them that you exist. However, if your posts get annoying, others are likely to hide you from their Home page and other lists. Be as real as possible: User posts range from deep and thoughtful to silly to quirky; yours can also run the gamut. If it's raining and that changes something for your business, let your customers know. If you're in a band and you just landed in a new city, let your fans know. If you found an article that's relevant to your fans, let them know. If you're just starting on the second edition of a book on how to use Facebook, let your readers know. Don't end every post with a link to buy your particular good or service. Every once in a while, that's fine, especially if you're offering a discount or sale, but too much and it gets annoying.

If you already use Twitter to publish status updates about your business, you can import those tweets into Facebook automatically. This means that your fans, followers, and subscribers will get your blast, regardless of their preferred medium. You'll see a button to link your Pages to Twitter at www.facebook.com/twitter.

✔ **Publish Photos, Videos, Notes, and Links:** In this way, you give life to your Page, making it grow while your business does. If you sell stuff, you can continually add photos and videos of new products or of people using your existing ones. If you provide a service, you can add videos showing you or your employees at work — say, an expert barista pouring a latte, a sculptor whose fans would love to see him in action, or an auto technician offering tips on good car care. If your fans like what they see, they're very likely to use the Facebook communication tools to show your content to their friends, giving your business more attention.

✔ **Hold Events:** Events will keep your patrons hooked. You use Facebook Events to invite fans to special parties, sales, or promotions. Some businesses hold events *just* for their fans on Facebook. When your fans RSVP your event, their friends may read about it on their Home pages. They can easily invite their friends along as well, or else their friends may just read about it, which is still probably good for your business.

✔ **Talk to your fans on behalf of your business:** Your fans will be writing on your Wall and discussion board, and they'll be writing reviews. Wherever possible, feel free to contribute. If someone writes on your Wall about how they had a bad experience, don't delete it — respond! You can as easily comment on your own posts (or on posts from your fans) as on your Page. In the case of the bad service experience, apologize and tell her you'll give her a free meal or discounted service if she comes back (and shows you her ID, which you'll know because her name is listed next to her Wall post). Other people who see the exchange will be impressed by your level of service.

If you're a shoe salesman and someone asks on your discussion board about finding the perfect shoe, fill him in. This public dialogue has the benefit of informing other customers with the same questions. Any time you write on the Wall or a discussion board of a Page that you administer, your comments are listed on behalf of the business itself, rather than you. This helps viewers trust your voice of authority and doesn't expose your personal account to anyone.

Send Updates

There's a difference between the updates that you publish and the updates that you send. Updates that you publish are usually short, and relevant, and often time-sensitive. They are the types of information that can easily filter down a subscriber's News Feed, and if one gets missed, it's probably okay. Updates that you send are more like newsletters or bulletins. They have some information that you don't want getting lost in the shuffle. Again, it's pretty important to send updates that are relevant; otherwise, your subscribers may opt out.

When looking at your Page, notice the Action links beneath the Profile picture. Only a few may be displayed, but clicking More reveals all the actions you can take, including a link to Send an Update to Fans. Updates on Facebook are different than other types of mailing lists. By clicking this link, you can compose a message that goes out to some or all of your fans. Before writing an update for your fans, however, you should understand how the Updates feature works from the user perspective:

- ✔ **People can opt out of Updates.** When users on Facebook find your Page, they choose to affiliate with it by clicking Like at the top of your Facebook Page. You can comfortably assume that anyone who clicks OK wants to hear what you have to say. If a business ever sends Updates that a particular person doesn't find valuable, he can opt out of Updates by clicking Opt Out directly from the update itself.

- ✔ **Updates are kept separate from Friend-to-Friend messages.** The reason for sorting business updates differently from Friend-to-Friend messages is simple: They're different. We're all familiar with the disappointment that comes from discovering that a new e-mail is promotional. E-mails from our favorite bands or businesses can be very exciting, if not for the fact that we're usually expecting a personal message. Updates are kept in a section of the Inbox called "Updates."

Updates are organized within the Updates tab similar to how messages are arranged in the Inbox (which we describe in Chapter 9):

- ✔ Each line contains an Update from a business, a Profile picture from the business's Page, the name of the Page, the title of the update, and snippet of the message.

✔ A blue dot next to the subject line of an update indicates unread Updates.

✔ The newest Updates are highest in the Updates section of the Inbox.

Okay, so fans experience updates from businesses very differently from how they experience promotional e-mails or paper mailings. What does this mean for you? It means that you should *update your fans.* They said they want to hear from you. The messages you send won't be misconstrued as spam because of the organization in the system, and users have full control to opt out at any time.

In the next section, we show you how to track what effect your updates have on your fans' engagement. Use these metrics to help you monitor what types of updates and what frequency of updates optimize your fans' attention.

Here are a few other things you need to know about updates:

✔ **You can include attachments in an update.** If you add a new photo, album, video, note, event, or other piece of content that you'd like your fans to know about, you can copy the URL for the page where that content lives and paste it into the message. In most cases, the content is automatically transformed into an attachment to your update, just like the Share feature we talk about in Chapter 9. Note that you can attach only one piece of content per update.

✔ **You can target your Updates.** When you're writing your update, you can select the Target Update option beneath Audience. This allows you to target by location, gender, and age. This is especially useful when promoting events, because people in Omaha may think it's a little mean-spirited to post about your 12 concert or performance dates in NYC.

✔ **You can access your sent updates from your Page's Control Panel.** In the right column, just under the Send an Update to Your Fans link, you can click See All Updates.

✔ **Fans who opt to receive your Updates have access to every Update you sent.** The first time someone receives an Update from your business, only that new update is marked as unread. If she clicks through on the row for your business, she sees all the updates that you sent before she became a fan. Cool, huh?

Know-It-All

At the beginning of this chapter, we mention various types of activities that business owners use to try to grow their customer base: running television and radio commercials; putting ads on buses, benches, and billboards; or hiring someone to dress like a chicken and dance outside your door. One of the hardest problems in advertising is figuring out what kind of effect your efforts have on your business. Facebook Insights are dedicated to unveiling this mystery. If you have already set up your Page, follow along with this next section. If you haven't, this section may be the one that convinces you to.

Within 48 hours of publishing your Page, you start to see exactly how people are engaging with it. Click Ads and Pages from the Applications menu to land on the manager application for all of your Ads and Pages. Click on the Pages option at the top of that page, and then select View Insights for whichever Page you want on the subsequent list. This will take you to an *overview page* for that Page, which gives you 24-hour feedback about the current success of your Page. By default, you see two main graphs about your Page's metrics — interaction information and audience information.

The first graphs and stats you see deal with interaction. On Facebook, it's not just about page views or mass reach; the best indicator of your Page's effectiveness is if people are interacting with it. Facebook defines interactions as being a combination of comments, Wall posts, and likes (that is, when someone clicks the little thumbs up that means "I like this" in Facebook-land). In short, these interactions are going to be based on how people respond to the content you post.

The sample graph in Figure 12-13 shows the Interactions Graph drop-down menu and the accompanying demographic break-down for interacting connections.

Figure 12-13: Insights on interactions.

There are two main graphs, The first focuses on Interactions and the second on Fans:

- ✔ **Interactions:** Since Facebook likes to focus on engagement, it believes the most important aspect of your Page's success is how people are interacting with it. By default, this graph shows you the total number of interactions over time. You can also filter it down to more specific stats:

  - **Interactions Per Post:** This graph tracks the average number of comments, likes, and Wall posts generated by each post you publish.

  - **Post Quality:** Post quality is measured by calculating how much engagement results from each post coming from your Page. A high Post Quality score means your posts are engaging and interesting to your connections. That's a good thing.

  - **Posts:** This graph shows how many posts you've created.

  - **Discussion Posts:** This graph shows the number of Discussion topics users have created on your Page.

  - **Reviews:** This graph shows the number of times fans have used the reviews application to rate your Page.

  - **Mentions:** This graph shows the number of times people have tagged your Page in a status update. Tagging your Page creates a link to it from that status, so being tagged is basically a way for users to promote your Page in their status updates.

- ✔ **Fans:** These sets of graphs show you more information about your fan base over time. By default, it shows you your total number of fans compared to the number of fans who have unsubscribed from your Page's updates in News Feed. It also has a few other filters, which you can see expanded in Figure 12-14:

  - **New/Removed Fans:** This graph shows you new fans as compared to fans who have "unliked" your Page.

  - **Top Countries:** This graph shows your growth in the countries where most of your fans are located.

  - **Demographics:** This graph shows your growth along common gender and age demographic groups.

  - **Page Views:** A pretty standard Internet metric, which shows how many times your Page was viewed from day to day.

  - **Unsubscribes/Resubscribes:** This graph shows you people who have unsubscribed from your posts, and people who have changed their minds back and resubscribed. People can be so capricious.

  - **Media Consumption:** This shows the total views for videos, photos, and other content you have added to your Page.

Figure 12-14:
Insights on
fans and
subscribers.

By default, all Insights graphs show you their information since the beginning of time . . . well, since your Page was created, anyway. You can change the time frame to more carefully inspect a particular month, week, or even day. Shrink the time window by dragging either corner of the bar below the graph toward the center. You can then scroll along the timeline.

Part IV
Delving Further into Facebook

The 5th Wave   By Rich Tennant

"Hello—forget the company's financials, look at the CEO's Facebook page under '25 Things the SEC Doesn't Know About Me.'"

In this part . . .

We warn you upfront: By the time you've made it to this part, most people wouldn't refer to you as a "dummy." In fact, your friends are possibly already calling you for help with Facebook. Now that you understand the basics of Facebook, you want to know how to make it even better, even more integrated into your life. And we can show you that.

This part covers taking Facebook everywhere you go using Facebook Mobile, as well as making your experience richer through the use of third-party applications and ads. Hang on to your hats; this is going to be fun.

Chapter 13

Facebook and the Web

. . . .

In This Chapter

▶ Understanding Facebook Platform and the social graph

▶ Seeing how applications can enhance your Internet experience on and off Facebook

▶ Discovering good, trustworthy applications

. . . .

The premise of virtually every *For Dummies* book is more or less the same — break something big into smaller parts, explain those parts, and then show how they fit into the big complicated thing. As each part is understood, the whole is less intimidating, less complex, and more usable. This *For Dummies* book tries to follow that premise, so by now you know a lot about a lot of parts of Facebook. You know about Profiles. You know about friendships. You know about comments. You know about liking things. You know about streams like News Feed. You know about applications like Events or Photos. You know how they fit into using Facebook.

Well, the thing is, they fit into using Facebook, but not only in the way we've described so far. They fit into using Facebook in lots of different ways from lots of different places on the Web. You could, for example, comment on an article on a blog. Or log in to a new site using your Facebook profile. Or find applications that go beyond Events and Groups and on to things like Games or Entertainment. The overarching term we use to describe the system that enables people outside of Facebook's headquarters to mix and match the different parts like a game of pentagram is *Facebook Platform*.

In this chapter, we give you the basic breakdown of what a platform is and how it works for you as a user. We then go into the details of the different types of applications on Facebook and across the Web and talk about how they can benefit you. Finally, we talk about trust and Facebook Platform and how to know if you're dealing with a good application. If you are a developer, check out the sidebar on good traits of applications or look up *Building Facebook Applications For Dummies,* by Richard Wagner, published by Wiley.

Understanding What Facebook Platform Is

The most basic example of a platform is a soapbox. In ye olden times, people would take a crate that soap was shipped in, set it down in the middle of ye olde towne square, step on top of it, and shout out their ideas to ye olde crowde. There are three players here: the soapbox, the person, and the crowde. While you keep reading, here are a couple things to keep in mind:

- ✔ **The soapbox didn't create the ideas.** The ideas belonged to the people shouting, the soapbox literally giving them a platform from which to enumerate their ideas. A person could stand in the middle of a crowd, at the same level, yelling at everyone else, but that person wouldn't be heard as well.

- ✔ **The soapbox means nothing without the crowd.** No matter how high the soapbox boosts you up and allows you to project your voice, if there's no one there to listen, your ideas can't spread.

If you've ever used a PC, you've probably used some version of Microsoft Windows (something like Windows 95, Windows XP, or Windows Vista). Windows is what's known as an *operating system*. It's the graphical interface used to access files and programs on your computer. You don't technically need an operating system. You could manually give your computer text commands to navigate the various files and systems, but that's much harder than using the interface that Microsoft provides. The operating system offers some core functionality that can then be used by various applications.

You've also probably used some version of Microsoft Word. This program was developed by Microsoft. However, you may have other programs on your computer that weren't built by Microsoft — maybe some sort of game, or something like Quicken, which you can use to track your spending. Because both Microsoft and Quicken can build applications, or programs, that work within Microsoft Windows, Windows is a platform for applications — whether built by Microsoft or a third party.

Facebook Platform, like a soapbox or an operating system, also offers core functionality that can be accessed to create applications. Facebook refers to its core functionality as the social graph. The *social graph* is the series of connections — Profiles linked to other Profiles via friendships — that make up Facebook. Information spreads across the social graph in all the ways we've talked about in previous chapters — through messages, posts, and thousands of casual interactions that tell you the most recent information about all your friends based on your closeness and the relevance of the information.

For a long time, Facebook was the only company that could build on its own platform. And it did; it built Photos, Notes, Events, and Groups. All these applications use the connections that exist among individuals on the site to spread more information. These connections are what set Facebook applications apart from other sites, even ones specialized for various applications.

The classic example of this is Photos. Facebook has the number-one photo-sharing application on the Web. Facebook Photos doesn't have all the features of specific photo-sharing sites, like high-resolution storage or anything like that, but it's still more popular than the others. This is because of the connections — your ability to tag your friends in photos. When you do this, your friends are notified, and they look at the pictures. This information is also spread through News Feed, where your friends can see your photos and comment on what they see. This, in turn, makes your friends more likely to use the Photos application the next time they want to share photos.

When Facebook opened up Facebook Platform, it enabled third-party developers anywhere to build applications that fit into Facebook as easily as Facebook Photos fits in. Like the soapbox, Facebook Platform lets application developers get their ideas and creations out to a crowd of people quickly and easily.

The soapbox — the platform — doesn't create the ideas or applications, and the platform means nothing without the crowd. You and your friends are the crowd, which is why Facebook applications can actually be useful to you.

Applications That Live on Facebook

In Chapters 8, 10, and 11 we talk in detail about a few Facebook applications, built by Facebook, that live on Facebook. The biggest difference between these applications and the ones that you'll use and love from outside developers is that you had Photos, Notes, Groups, and Events waiting for you when you first signed up for Facebook. All of the pieces that made these work — tagging, notifications, posts to your Wall, and so on — were already at work behind the scenes.

When you use applications, you need to be a bit of the stage manager for how these applications work. You've been practicing for this moment as you set privacy and other controls on the various applications that Facebook built. Now that the curtain is about to open, you are ready to take command of all these aspects of each application.

Figuring out why to use applications inside Facebook

Well, you certainly don't need to use applications to have a completely wonderful, rich Facebook experience. If you aren't comfortable with applications, or haven't found one that you'd find useful or relevant, they aren't required, and they don't provide you with any Facebook expertise. Plenty of Facebook experts use very few, if any, applications. That being said, there are a few good reasons to use applications:

- ✔ **They offer functionality Facebook doesn't.** Facebook has rules about creating Profiles only for real people, and many a pet-lover over the years has had the misfortune of seeing Fluffy's fake Profile taken down. Dogbook, an application that lets you create a Profile for your dog within your own Profile, means people have the ability to represent this important part of their lives on Facebook, without violating Facebook's terms. Similarly, music-related applications or course-related applications for students have filled the gaps that exist for specific groups of people on Facebook.

- ✔ **They can be really fun.** Do you like word scrambles? Do you like to type? Do you like to pretend you own a restaurant? Do you like Texas Holdem? Really, any game you can imagine is offered as a Facebook application, and it pairs the delight of a game you love with the cutthroat competition that can happen only among friends. For example, a simple typing game like Typing Maniac becomes much more entertaining when you are vying for first place with one of your good friends.

- ✔ **They connect you in new ways to the people you care about.** All of the applications on Facebook help you learn more about people and stay in touch with them in different ways. Whether that's knowing what concerts a friend all the way across the country is going to or finding out that Carolyn is, in fact, Elizabeth Bennet via the "Which literary heroine are you?" quiz application, all of this information enriches your relationships in small, subtle ways.

Getting started: Request for Permission, sir

Before you can start using most applications within Facebook, you need to grant the applications permission to interact with your Profile, account, and information. Most applications achieve this through the Request for Permission page, shown in Figure 13-1.

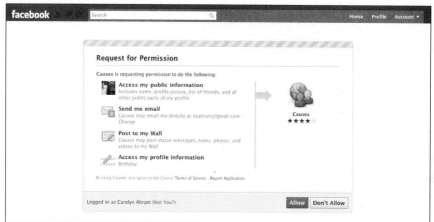

Figure 13-1:
Permission
granted?

The Request for Permission page, shown in this example with the application Causes, has four sections:

- ✔ **Access My Public Information:** Your *public information* is the basic directory information about you that Facebook requires to stay public: your name, Profile picture, gender, and networks, if applicable. Additionally, any information that is visible to Everyone will be counted as public information. If you allow this application permission, it will be able to access all of this information. (You can learn more about controlling this information at the end of this chapter, or in Chapter 5, where we talk about privacy settings.)

- ✔ **Send Me Email:** By default, when you click Allow, Causes will be able to store your e-mail address in their servers, as opposed to accessing it like it does the rest of your information, through Facebook's servers. This allows you to establish a direct relationship with Causes, because they can always get in touch with you, without Facebook acting as an intermediary.

  In general, when you trust an application, this is a good thing. You can get e-mail newsletters and other updates direct from the source without logging in to Facebook. However, if you aren't sure about an application's trustworthiness (though we'll talk about this later), you can click Change, shown in gray beneath the Send Me Email icon. Doing so expands an option to send you e-mails through an anonymous source, as shown in Figure 13-2.

Figure 13-2:
Send
e-mails to
your contact
e-mail or to
a "proxy"
e-mail.

If at any time you don't want to share your e-mail address with a certain
application anymore, you will need to unsubscribe from their e-mail list
through *them* as opposed to through *Facebook.*

✔ **Post to my Wall:** This permission allows an application to post status
updates, photos, and other content to your Wall. An example of a Wall post
might be something like Figure 13-3. Here, FrontierVille is asking if Carolyn
wants to show off an achievement to her Facebook friends. You can remove
this permission later on if an application is taking over your Wall.

✔ **Access My Profile Information:** Here, Facebook defines *Profile
Information* as any part of your Profile or account that is restricted in
any way — in other words, things that are set to any privacy level lower
than Everyone. In the example of Causes, the application needs to know
your Birthday. Pay attention to what fields applications ask for access
to, and make sure the fields they ask for jive with what they purport to
do. Notice how Causes doesn't ask for your photos, your likes and interests, or any other superfluous fields. On the other hand, applications
like Groupcard need access to some of these things in order to build out
personalized greeting cards for your friends.

Figure 13-3:
Wall Posts
gain atten-
tion for you
and for the
application.

If you've reviewed the requested permissions, trust the application, and are excited to get started, click Allow.

Now what? Using applications

Since there are so many different applications, answering so many different needs, it's difficult to tell you what to do next. However, we can tell you some common prompts and on-screen actions you'll be asked to take with applications so that you can decide how you want to proceed when you see them.

Application dashboards

For the most part, once you've allowed an application access to your information, you'll be taken to its dashboard. You can see a sample dashboard, for Causes, in Figure 13-4. The Causes Home page, much like the Facebook Home page or the landing pages for applications for Photos or Groups, is a gateway into the various actions you can take (like creating or joining a cause). When we say that applications "live" inside Facebook, this is what we mean — Causes Home is beneath the main Facebook menu (the blue bar on top), as opposed to taking you to another site entirely.

Dashboards vary widely from application to application, but generally they direct you to take some sort of action. In the case of Causes, it gives you information about popular causes and causes that your friends support and prompts you to choose ones you want to support. You can also start your own causes, donate to other causes, and so on.

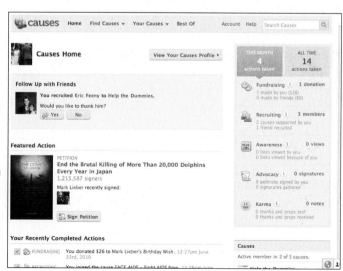

Figure 13-4:
The application dashboard for Causes.

Bookmarks

The left side of your home page displays shortcuts to various parts of Facebook: messages, friends, photos, and so on. Additionally, you can add shortcuts, or bookmarks, to this menu so you can gain quick access to your favorite applications. Applications may prompt you to add bookmarks, and doing so requires a dialog box similar to the one shown in Figure 13-5.

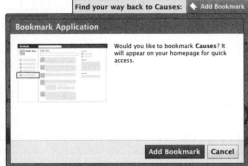

Figure 13-5:
Bookmark
this
application?

Posts to friends' Walls

Just as applications often help you communicate with your friends about specific topics, games, or content, many applications will prompt you to post something on a friend's Wall. The applications can't do this unless you select Post. You can see an example of such a post in Figure 13-6. Here, Carolyn shared something through the application FrontierVille, and it created a Wall post that everyone viewing her friend's Wall can see.

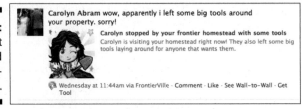

Figure 13-6:
A Wall post
generated
by an appli-
cation.

Profile tabs and boxes

Depending on what's important to you, you can decide which boxes people see in the left column of your Profile and which tabs you add to your Profile.

From your Profile, you can also choose to add a Causes tab. Because tabs are big and very prominent on your Profile, adding them is something you normally do for the applications you care about most and want people to see the most. To add a tab, click the plus sign (+) to the right of your rightmost tab, this expands the Add a Tab menu, as shown in Figure 13-7. You can then select the application you want to add.

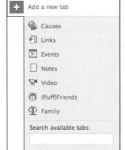

Figure 13-7:
Adding an application tab.

Imagine that the Causes you support and feature on your Profile are a bit controversial. You may not want co-workers, or certain friends, or people who are visiting your Profile for the first time to see your Causes. Facebook allows you to use Privacy to control who sees the Profile boxes and tabs, but keep in mind that these settings don't apply to posts you create. Anyone who can get to your Wall can see posts that you create related to Causes. To set Privacy on this application, follow these steps:

1. **Click Account in the upper-right corner of any Facebook page.**

2. **Select Application Settings from the drop-down menu that appears.**

   This step takes you to the Edit Applications page, which we talk about in the "Managing Your Applications" section later in this chapter.

3. **Find Causes and select Edit Settings.**

   A dialog box similar to the one shown in Figure 13-8 appears.

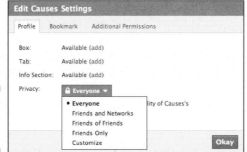

Figure 13-8:
Edit settings here.

4. In the Privacy drop-down menu, choose the visibility level or create a custom setting for the application.

The privacy setting you create here applies only to the boxes and tabs you add to your Profile. It does not apply to posts you create that go to your friends' News Feeds and Live Feeds.

Invitations and Requests

You can invite friends to Events; you can also invite friends to play games or support causes. These are actions you always have to do with some intent, regardless of whether the application was built by Facebook.

The final step of the creation flow for Causes allows you to invite friends to support your cause, and also gains distribution for Causes, because your use of it may imply to your friends that you like the application, making them more likely to check it out as well. Figure 13-9, in a display of both information and meta-ness, shows the confirmation dialog box that you need to approve to send invitations. That dialog box shows what the actual invitation will look like.

Figure 13-9: Sending invites.

Other permissions

There are a number of unique permissions that you can grant to applications that are usually required only by certain types of applications or for certain reasons. For example, a desktop application will usually need a Special Permission to access your info even when you're not browsing the Web.

Keep in mind that although we use only a few applications as examples here, things might be very different for you as you explore applications. Different applications may want to post content more frequently or may strongly encourage you to invite friends. The important thing to keep in mind is that *you* control what applications get to do. You don't have to add boxes or publish posts if you don't want to. Don't be afraid to show your applications who's boss.

Using Facebook outside of Facebook

Imagine all the things you do on the Web. Maybe you buy gifts for friends at Amazon.com. Or perhaps you blog or like to comment on blogs that others write. Maybe you look up movie reviews. Maybe you rent movies through sites like Blockbuster or Netflix. You do any number of things, all of which, we would wager a small sum, would be better if your friends were there.

Wish you had a better sense of whose Yelp reviews you could trust? Looking for a movie recommendation? Don't actually like dealing with strangers on the Web? Welcome to *social plugins*.

A *social plugin* is the blanket term we use to talk about applications that live on other Web sites. These plugins may or may not be similar to the applications you use within Facebook. It may be more accurate to say that these plugins use a Facebook link that you establish to make your experience on their sites more social.

There's no one single application that can explain all of the integration points for social plugins because most applications only need one or two of these points to be called a social plugin. The most important one to understand is what it's like to log in to another site using Facebook, since doing so precedes most of the implementations we discuss (though some implementations use *cookies*, or a way of marking sites you've visited, so you don't need to log in).

Login

The first way Connect can improve your Web experience is to eliminate the need to create a brand new account for every. Single. Web. Site. Ever. The Web forms that ask for your name, your e-mail, and subsequent prompts to upload a Profile picture and find friends — these are things of the past. As an example, we're going to create a new account on Quora, a question-and-answer site.

When you go to the Quora sign-up page at www.quora.com, you'll notice that it allows you to sign up *only* by using an existing Facebook or Twitter account. Clicking the Sign Up with Facebook Account button brings up the Connect with Facebook screen, shown in Figure 13-10.

Figure 13-10: Connect your Facebook account with Quora.

Notice a few important things about this dialog box. First, Carolyn's name is already displaying at the bottom of the screen, because she was already logged in to Facebook when she clicked the Connect prompt. If you aren't logged in to Facebook, you see a Facebook login screen in this space, where you have to enter your Facebook login e-mail and password. Also, if you share a computer with other Facebook users, make sure that the name displaying in the bottom of the dialog box is, in fact, yours.

The second thing to remember is that this dialog box is basically asking you for the same thing that the Request for Permission screen did for Causes — in order to work, this site needs access to your Facebook info. For the most part, sites that use Connect need this info for legitimate purposes, but you should still make sure you trust the site that you're using before you click Connect. WellknownMcgoodreputation.com? Probably okay. SleazyMcSpamerson.com? Maybe do a little more research first.

Figure 13-11 shows the final screen of this sign-up process. Similar to applications on Facebook, Quora builds its own list of users' e-mails, so you can enter any e-mail you want here. Additionally, Quora asks you to create a password so that in the future, you can log in just using your e-mail address and password.

Figure 13-11:
Finish signing up by creating a password.

Now, if you've started using Quora, you probably want to answer a question. Notice how all of your information is prefilled, making it easy to answer a question with your real name and real Profile picture associated with it. In under a minute, you are set up on Quora without e-mail verification, needing to enter your birth date, zip code, or anything beyond your e-mail, new password, and Facebook name.

Plugin Play

There are many social plugins that most Web sites can add very easily. And most Web sites have added some or all of these plugins. In fact, it's hard to visit a site on the Internet without seeing some Facebook presence. The following sections highlight some common plugins you might see as you browse the Web.

Likes

With social plugins, you can like virtually anything, anywhere on the Web. Facebook has made it very easy for companies to add Like buttons to their online content. A great example of this can be seen on the Gawker blog at www.jezebel.com. Alongside every article is the now-familiar thumbs-up (Like) button, as well as statistics about who has liked it. If any of your friends have liked something, you'll see their names. If you like something, it gets shared on Facebook via a recent activity story. You can see a Like button and its Recent Activity counterpart in Figures 13-12 and 13-13.

Figure 13-12:
The Like
button on
a blog.

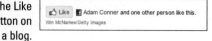

Figure 13-13:
A recent
activity
story about
an article
Carolyn
liked.

Any content you like off of Facebook is shown on your Facebook Profile and may appear in your friends' News Feeds. If liking a controversial article might make waves with some of your friends, you can instead choose to share it as a link and set privacy on that share.

For certain sites, a Like box, such as the example in Figure 13-14 from the Web site www.postsecret.com, shows recent updates from the Web site's Facebook Page as well as a sampling of people who like the Facebook Page.

Comments

Figure 13-15 shows a comment box powered by Facebook. In theory, any blog, whether a big name or just your friend's little hobby, can add a comment box so people can quickly sign in and leave comments. This usually is preceded by a login screen.

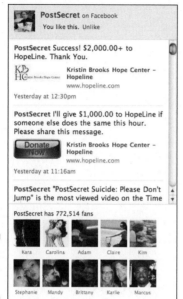

Figure 13-14:
The Like
box.

Figure 13-15:
Comment
on any blog,
anywhere.

Streams

We spent Chapter 7 talking about how important streams — constantly updating lists of activity or content — are to Facebook. Unsurprisingly, streams are very important off Facebook as well. Virtually every news site is a stream of updating posts, so it makes sense that you might want some help from your friends in understanding what to read or pay attention to. There are a few types of stream plugins that help with this:

- ✔ *Recent Activity* **or Activity streams:** Recent Activity boxes on Web sites display recent actions taken by your friends on the Web site in question. In Figure 13-16, you can see an example of Recent Activity — in this case friends liking various articles on a Web site.

- ✔ *Recommendations* **or recommendation streams:** Recommendations shows similar information to recent activity, though instead of what's most recent, it shows what's been liked by the most people in order to show what you might like as well.

- ✔ *Live streams* **or status streams:** Live streams are a very popular integration for various television channels to use during live broadcasts. The first implementation of live streams was actually during the Obama Inauguration, and since then, the live streams of status updates have created an online interactive component to everything from live sports to the Oscars and other award shows. You can see a sample live stream in Figure 13-17.

Figure 13-16: Friends' Recent Activity on another site.

Figure 13-17: Live stream.

Friends

As we say over and over again: Everything is better when your friends are there. That's the philosophy of those Web sites that display a count of friends who have in some way connected their accounts there with their Facebook accounts. You can see a sample of this in Figure 13-18.

Figure 13-18:
Friend box
on an
outside
Web site.

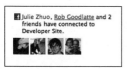

Instant Personalization

With the most recent iterations of Facebook's social plugins, a new category of plugins was announced. It was basically Facebook's way of connecting accounts to trusted partners on behalf of its users. There are only three partner sites at the time of this writing: Yelp, Pandora, and Microsoft Docs.

The idea of Instant Personalization is to make the social aspect of these Web sites completely seamless. As you use Pandora, for example, you see which of your friends like the artists and songs that appear on your screen. You can instantly find all the people on Yelp whose reviews will matter most to you: friends.

Figure 13-19 shows how Instant Personalization might appear to you when using Pandora.

Figure 13-19:
Instant
Personal-
ization on
Pandora.

If you don't use any of the partner sites we mentioned and don't like the idea of your information being shared in this way, you can opt out of Instant Personalization. Go to the Privacy Settings page, click Applications and Websites, and then click Edit Settings next to Instant Personalization. Uncheck the box at the bottom of the page that appears.

Discovering Other Applications

The most common applications you encounter on Facebook are the ones that live inside Facebook and the Connect Web sites that provide functionality elsewhere. However, there are many other categories of applications that you may find use for over time.

Applications for your business

If you are a Page owner, many applications are designed to live on your Page and provide additional functionality for your business. For example, musicians may want to add the Discography application to show off their different albums or the YouTube application so fans can easily share the YouTube videos they've posted from live concerts.

Applications for your desktop

Desktop applications require you to download something to your computer (as opposed to just making information available to the application). These applications often provide functionality like allowing you to read your News Feed and comment on the posts there without having a Web browser open. Or they may take your Facebook events and import them into whatever calendar program you use. In a nutshell, they let you use Facebook outside your browser window.

Applications for your phone

The most basic mobile application is actually just Facebook, itself, which you can learn more about in Chapter 14. However, as social plugins continue to grow, many new mobile applications are being created that allow you to, for example, play mobile games against your Facebook friends on your iPhone. Mobile Platform applications can often feel like a mash-up of Facebook

Mobile and an application that often lives within Facebook. The same features, like posting, commenting, or notifications, make these types of applications effective and relevant as you wander around the world, phone in hand.

Finding Your New Favorite Application

With so many applications, it's hard to predict which ones you'll want to use and which ones will be fun, relevant, and useful to you. We've gone over a few examples here (and for even more of Leah and Carolyn's picks, check out Chapter 16), but the reality is that you have your own tastes, so you may have to do some exploring on your own to find the right applications for you.

You'll probably discover many applications through your friends — posts they create and invitations they send will tip you off on what you may enjoy. And if you want a shortcut to figuring that out, look no further than the Application and Games dashboards.

The Applications dashboard

The Applications dashboard is pretty much just what it sounds like, a dashboard to highlight applications you might want to use. Click the word Applications in the left menu on your home page to get there. You can see Carolyn's in Figure 13-20.

Figure 13-20:
The
Applications
dashboard.

The Applications dashboard has several distinct pieces:

- ✔ **Your Applications:** The Your Applications section is sorted by which applications you used most recently. This is a great place to look if you used an application, didn't bookmark it, and want to get back to it quickly.

- ✔ **Friends' Applications:** This section is really the most important part of the Applications Dashboard, in terms of finding new applications that you might enjoy using. This shows a smattering of friends and applications they've used recently, which means you can see what's popular, interesting, or appealing to you.

- ✔ **Featured Applications:** On the right side of the page are applications that Facebook has chosen to highlight. These applications are often some of the best that the platform has to offer, so this is a good place to start looking for a new application.

The Games dashboard

One of the best aspects of the Facebook Platform is its ability to allow you to play games with your friends no matter where you are in relation to each other. There's a reason "family game night" is such an honored tradition: It's fun, it allows for bonding, friendly competition, and a shared sense of accomplishment. Now, you can bring that to your friends and family on Facebook. Everyone may not be gathered round the table, but the sense of camaraderie is still palpable.

Because of their importance to so many users of Facebook, Facebook has given games its own dashboard. The layout of the games dashboard is very similar to the more general applications dashboard.

- ✔ **Your Games:** This section is sorted by which games you used most recently. This is a great place to look if you were playing a game, didn't bookmark it, and want to get back to it quickly.

- ✔ **Friends' Games:** This section shows a smattering of friends and the games they've been playing recently, which means you can see what's popular, interesting, or appealing to you.

- ✔ **Featured Games:** On the right side of the page are games that Facebook has chosen to highlight. These games are often some of the most popular that the platform has to offer, so this is a good place to start looking for a new game.

We know this sounds silly, but games on Facebook are incredibly addicting. We could tell you how much time was lost writing this chapter due to the discovery of FrontierVille and the relapse into Typing Maniac, but it would be so shameful for us. Suffice it to say, remember to shower and change your clothes every once in a while.

Signs of a trustworthy application

As you explore dashboards and other applications, you will come upon Allow Access and Request for Permission screens frequently. Before you click those buttons, you should make sure you trust the application. To determine that, check out the Application's Fan Page by clicking on its name.

An Application's Fan Page is a rich source of information that helps you know whether the application will behave in a way that is respectful of your information and of your friends. You don't want an application that uses your photos in ways you don't like, nor do you want an application that's going to spam your friends every time you sneeze. Here are some things to look for:

✔ **Your friends are using it:** The first mark of a good application is that your friends are using it. This usually means it's fun, useful, and generally good. One note of clarification: when we say your friends, in this case, we mean *the friends you interact with most on Facebook.* If that guy you met that one time (TGYMTOT) sends you an invitation and you think, "Weird, I haven't spoken to TGYMTOT on Facebook in ages," there's a good chance that this is a bad application using nefarious methods to get invitations sent.

✔ **Its reviews are generally positive:** You can see an overall rating of an application in the Information box on the left column of its Fan Page. Also, click on the Reviews tab. There you can see ratings as well as explanations of those ratings. Lots of comments like "Spammed my friends" or "Too slow" should tip you off that this may not be a good experience.

✔ **It provides some level of support:** Whether through FAQs or responding to Wall posts, good applications respect their users and try to at least help them out a bit if they get stuck. Now, some applications may be developed by one guy in a garage, so their level of support may not be as high as one developed by a big corporation, but the gesture is what signifies a good application.

Managing Your Applications

If you've been trying out every application we've name-dropped so far, you may have found that your application menu has grown faster than a magic beanstalk toward the top of the page. This is fine for now, but depending on how you wind up using applications and how you feel about the ones you've added, there may come a time when you want to change some things.

After you reach that point, there's one place you need to be: the Application Settings page.

The Application Settings page

The Application Settings page lets you control many of the aspects of your applications that we've already discussed in this chapter. You can see what the Application Settings page looks like in Figure 13-21.

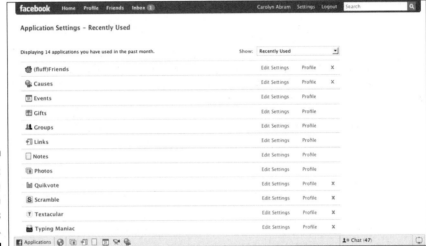

You can get to this page by selecting the Account menu in the upper-right corner of the blue bar and then clicking Application Settings.

By default, when you arrive, you see the applications that you've used most recently. Next to each application's name are three links: Edit Settings, Profile, and a little "x". The "x" can be used to remove an application entirely. Clicking it not only removes any boxes or tabs you have on your Profile, but also removes your authorization of it, meaning that application won't have any access to your info. If you want to use it again, you need to go through the authorization screen again.

The Profile link takes you to that application's Profile (we also call it an Application Fan Page in this book), so if you want to quickly leave a review or check out any information about that application, you can do so from here pretty easily.

The whole purpose of this page, however, is the little Edit Settings link, which accesses the Edit Settings dialog box, as shown in Figure 13-22.

Figure 13-22:
The Edit
Causes
Settings
dialog box.

Most of these settings are aspects of applications we've already talked about, so here's a quick run-down of all of the options and exactly how they change your relationship with that application:

- ✔ **Profile>Box:** If you've previously added a Profile box for this application, this space reflects that. You can remove that box from here or add one if you haven't already done so.

- ✔ **Profile>Tab:** If you've previously added a Profile tab for this application, this space reflects that. You can remove that tab from here or add one if you haven't already done so.

- ✔ **Profile>Info Section:** This setting theoretically controls whether or not you get an additional section on your Info tab related to this application. We say theoretically because it appears to do nothing of the sort. Leave this set to Available.

- ✔ **Profile>Privacy:** This control lets you set privacy on who can see any Profile boxes, tabs, or sections you've added. This doesn't control who can see content that you post to your Wall and friends' News Feeds.

- ✔ **Bookmark:** The bookmark tab has only one setting — if you want to add or remove a bookmark for that application to your Applications menu.

- ✔ **Additional Permissions:** As we mentioned earlier, Additional Permissions cover a broad range of things. The thing to keep in mind here is that any permission you've granted in the past can be revoked from here. Additional Permissions are at the discretion of the developers, if they are needed at all, so you usually won't see options here that you haven't been prompted for before.

When you add a Profile box or tab, that setting controls only the existence of it. To edit the content (or what people are seeing there), you need to go to your Profile or to the application.

You'll notice at the top of the Application Settings page that you can choose different ways to display your applications. You can see, for example, all the applications you've bookmarked, or all the ones you've added to your Profile in one way or another. Most of these categories are covered in the preceding list. If you want to see all applications you've ever used, select the Authorized item in the drop-down menu. Any applications for which you want to revoke *all* permissions simply need to be deselected from any of these views.

The Application Privacy page

The Application Privacy page is where you go to control how your *information* is shared with applications, as opposed to how the application *behaves* on Facebook. You can get to the privacy page by clicking Privacy Settings in the Account menu, and then selecting Edit Your Settings, shown under Applications and Websites.

Five main settings are connected to Applications and Websites:

✔ **What You're Using:** This section may be empty if you're fairly new to Facebook. This section lists all the Web sites and application with which you've linked your Facebook profile. If at any time you don't like how an application is working or you start to feel uncomfortable, you can delete it from here.

✔ **Game and Application Activity:** This controls who will see your name and associated applications on their Application and Game dashboards.

✔ **Info Accessible Through Your Friends:** When your friends use other Web sites and applications in conjunction with Facebook, they may find it useful to see their friend's (that is, your) information. An example of this is a birthday calendar application, which may alert them when a friend's birthday is on the horizon. In this section, you can determine the information about you that your friends can allow sites to access. If you want your friends to be able to use a birthday reminder Web site to remember your birthday, you may want to allow them to give your birthday to the sites they trust. If you never want any application having access to some of your information, the notes you write, for example, then uncheck that box and your friends will not be able to import that information into their applications.

✔ **Instant Personalization:** As previously discussed, Instant Personalization is a way of instantly linking your Facebook account to partner sites. If you don't want Facebook doing this on your behalf, opt-out here.

✔ **Public Search:** This listing refers to a limited view of your Profile that anyone can see if he searches for your name in an external search engine such as Google. Your Public Search Listing shows a portion of the content you've made available to everyone.

Controlling what you see from friends

You know that aunt you have who shows up for family events wearing crazy hats and talking a little too loudly about her opinion of everyone? More than one family member may have listened to her lecture on the virtues of macro-tastic vitamin supplements and responded simply with, "To each, her own." Similarly, you may have some friends on Facebook who just don't have the same taste as you when it comes to applications. Maybe they take a ton of quizzes, which flood your Home page with information you don't find particularly enlightening. Or maybe they are always challenging you to games of Scrabble, and you've been boycotting that game since that one time you got two triples in one word and knew you would never top yourself. Here are a few pro tips that will keep your Facebook just the way you like it.

✔ **Block an application:** If you find an application offensive or it keeps sending you some sort of invites, you can block it from its Page. Simply look below its logo for a link to Block Application. This prevents the application from being able to contact you at all, even if your friends are using it.

✔ **Ignore a Friend's Invites:** Remember that crazy aunt? She may be sending you invites or requests from multiple hat-related applications. Look beneath that request to find a link that lets you ignore all invites from that friend. You can still be friends, but you won't receive all the annoying invites anymore.

✔ **Hide from News Feed:** If you're looking at your Home page and it's inundated with one type of post that you just don't like to look at, use the Hide links (which you can find in the upper-right corner of that post when you mouse over it) to hide all posts for that application. Alternatively, if all the annoying posts are coming from one person using many different applications, you can hide that person.

Best practices for developers

If you are a developer thinking about creating any sort of Facebook application, the best advice we can give you is this: Be excellent to your users. If you need something more specific than that, here are some tips:

✔ **Don't spam.** Users hate spam. If they associate spam with your application, they will probably hate your application.

✔ **Be useful.** People use Facebook as a way to keep in touch with friends and get the information they need about people. If your application is useful, it's more likely to spread virally.

✔ **Be social.** Folks use Facebook to keep in touch and interact with friends and family in a new way. Your application spreads quickly if it has an inherently social aspect to it. People want to connect with their friends. Give them new ways to do so.

✔ **Be clear about what you do.** It's very important that people understand what they're

doing when they add your application or interact with it. No one likes deception.

✔ **Be competitive.** Numerous people are developing on Platform, so distinguish your application from others that may be similar. Make sure it has the absolute best feature set you can build.

✔ **Listen to your users.** Facebook users are passionate and vocal. Use that to your advantage. Read the reviews and discussions on your application's page, take suggestions seriously, and respond to negative posts when you can.

✔ **Be reliable. Be fast.** No matter how good your application is, if a user is always hit with a Down for Maintenance message or has to wait 30 seconds per page load, she stops using your application. Spend time and resources planning on how to scale quickly for a large user base.

Chapter 14

Facebook on the Go

In This Chapter

▶ Capturing and sharing the moment with Facebook Mobile Uploads

▶ Keeping yourself connected with Facebook Mobile notifications and texts

▶ Staying up-to-date with Facebook Mobile Web

▶ Discovering special versions of Facebook designed to work on your phone

*T*hroughout this book, we show you how Facebook enriches relationships and facilitates human interaction. Nevertheless, what can Facebook do to enrich your relationships while you're *not* sitting in front of a computer? Life is full of beach weekends, road trips, city evenings, movie nights, dinner parties, and so on. During these times, as long as you have a mobile phone, Facebook still provides you a ton of value.

We don't propose that you ignore a group of people you're actively spending time with to play with Facebook on the phone (unless of course you *want* to ignore them). Moreover, we don't think you should tune out in class or in a meeting to Poke your friends. We do suggest that knowing the ins and outs of Facebook Mobile actually enriches each particular experience you have — while you're having it. With Facebook Mobile, you can show off your kids' new photos to your friends, or broadcast where you're having drinks, in case any of your friends are in the neighborhood and want to drop by.

Facebook Mobile serves another function — making your life easier. Sometimes you need *something,* say, a phone number, an address, or the start time of an Event. Maybe you're heading out to have dinner with your friend and her boyfriend whose name you can't, for the life of you, remember. Perhaps you hit it off with someone new and would like to find out whether she's romantically available before committing yourself to an awkward conversation about exchanging phone numbers. (Just a heads-up: This conversation can be awkward even *if* you find that person is single. Facebook can do a lot for you, but not everything.)

In this chapter, we assume that you have a mobile phone and know how to use its features. If you don't have a phone, you may consider buying one after reading this chapter; this stuff is way cool. Mobile texts simply require that you own a phone and an accompanying plan that enables you to send text messages. Facebook Mobile Web requires a mobile data plan (that is, access to the Internet on your phone). Facebook Applications require that you own any one of the several types of phones that Facebook can currently support.

Is That Facebook Mobile Web in Your Pocket . . . ?

In many ways, using a mobile phone can augment your experience of using Facebook on the computer. In this first section, we talk about how you can easily add information to and get information from Facebook when you're not physically in front of the computer. These features are primarily for people who do most of their Facebooking on the computer, but sometimes interact through their phone. In later sections, we talk about how you can experience most of Facebook without ever logging on to a desktop or laptop computer.

Getting started

This chapter teaches you almost everything you need to know about using Facebook with a mobile device. However, if you ever find yourself asking questions about it while near a computer but NOT near this book, you can go to www.facebook.com/mobile for much of the same information. To get started with Facebook Mobile, you first need to enter and confirm your phone number into the settings page:

1. **Go to the Account Settings page from the Account menu in the upper-right corner of the big blue bar on top.**

2. **Click on the Mobile tab.**

3. **Beneath Activate a Phone, click Register for Facebook Texts and follow the instructions to activate your phone.**

If your carrier isn't listed in the drop-down list, some features of Facebook Mobile aren't available to you.

After you've activated your phone, and put your phone in your hand, much of the Facebook Mobile experience is at your fingertips.

Mobile uploads

In this section, we show you how to spend only one magical moment to capture, save, and publish the real magical moments in life.

Three types of people can be found at social events. You find the scrapbookers who always remember to bring their fancy-schmancy camera to every gathering. (You know who they are because they tell you to "Smile!" a lot or sometimes say "Act natural.") There's the person who never intends to take photos but who, when the birthday girl blows out her candles, the host spills wine on himself, or someone arrives wearing a hilarious, slogan tee shirt, is ready with the low-quality mobile phone camera. (Hey, it captures the moment, right?) And you have the person who doesn't take photos even though his phone has a camera because "What good is a picture on a phone?" (Where do you go from there?)

For the scrapbookers of the world, we recommend Facebook Photos. After the social gathering, plug your camera into a regular computer, weed out the embarrassing photos, and upload the rest to a photo album. However, if you're the second or third type of person, we recommend you check out Facebook Mobile Photos. With mobile photos, you have no time for weeding, editing, or second thoughts. Mobile photos pave the way to instantaneous documentation.

Here's how to upload a mobile photo:

1. **Make sure you have a phone with a camera and you know how to use it to take a picture and/or take a video.**

   If you're unsure, check your phone's instruction manual, or ask just about any teenager. Leah has a few nephews you can borrow.

2. **Go to `www.facebook.com/mobile` and look beneath Upload Photos via Email for a personalized e-mail address.**

   This e-mail address, of the form `aaa111parsec@m.facebook.com`, makes it possible for you to upload photos to your Profile from your phone. Optionally, you can click Send My Upload Email to Me Now. From there, you can ask Facebook to either e-mail you the address or text it to your phone. Either way, you want to add that personal e-mail address to your phone's contacts so you can easily message it in the future.

3. **Wait for something hilarious to happen and then take a picture or video of it.**

4. **Send an e-mail to the address you just found with the picture or video attached.**

The subject line will be the caption, so choose wisely. ***Note:*** If your phone doesn't support e-mail, but does support MMS (multimedia messaging service, which enables the sending of audio, video, photos, and rich text), you can send your mobile photos or videos to `mobile@facebook.com`.

5. **(Optional) To make any edits or changes to your mobile photos, go to your photo albums and click the Mobile Uploads album. To make changes to your video, go to the Video application and edit there.**

   Note that the default visibility of your mobile uploads is Everyone. You can change this by going to the mobile album from the Photos tab of your Profile, or the Video application from the application bar on the bottom, and adjusting the privacy level.

Mobile texts

You're out and about and realize you need the phone number of someone who isn't stored in your phone. What do you do? Call a mutual friend? What if she doesn't answer? 1-411? What if 15 Robert Johnsons live in your city? For this scenario and several others, you send an *SMS,* or text message, to 32665 (FBOOK) containing a code word that tells Facebook what kind of information you're trying to access. For example, the word *cell* informs Facebook that you're trying to access a cellphone number. The results of your inquiry are sent to your phone via SMS.

To follow along with this section, head to the Mobile Tester:

1. **Navigate to `www.facebook.com/mobile`.**

2. **From the Mobile page, located beneath Facebook Mobile Texts, click Learn More about Mobile Texts.**

3. **On the bottom right of the Mobile Texts page, you can enter text into the field just below the image of a mobile phone to simulate mobile texting.**

The texter tester (say that three times fast), shown in Figure 14-1, is a nice way to learn about how Mobile Texts work without having to pay texting fees, and without using your friends as test subjects.

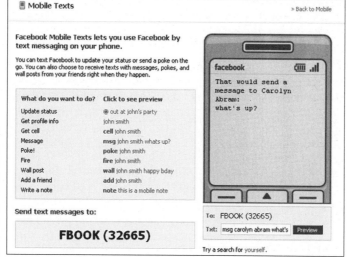

Figure 14-1:
The
Facebook
Mobile tes-
ter lets you
try the Texts
service.

The tester allows you to try various commands and see the result as though it were from a real phone. Typing **Poke Carolyn Abram** into the tester tells you that doing so from a mobile phone would actually Poke Carolyn, but doing so from the tester won't actually do this. The Mobile Text tester is free — Facebook Mobile never charges you for using any feature, although your mobile plan may charge you per text message. Here's the lowdown on what you see in Figure 14-1:

- **Update your status** by typing @ in the body of the SMS followed by what- ever you want your status to be. For example, **@ on a ski lift** changes your status to *<Your Name> on a ski lift.* You receive a text message from Facebook stating that your status has been updated.

- **Get Profile information** for a particular friend by sending the name of the person you're looking for. If Facebook finds an exact first and last name match, you receive the Profile information that person has given you permission to see. For example, if Leah sends an SMS to 32665 containing **Carolyn Abram**, within seconds she receives a text from Facebook containing Carolyn's mobile phone number, e-mail address, status (she's at a party right now), relationship status, and networks.

- **Get someone's cellphone number** by sending a text containing **Cell** fol- lowed by the name of the person whose number you're after. For exam- ple, **Cell Carolyn Abram** returns Carolyn's cellphone number (as long as you have access to it via her Profile). This time, though, if multiple matches appear for the name you entered, Facebook sends you the first four matches and their numbers (if they're listed and visible to you). Again, if the name you're looking for isn't in the list, simply reply with *n* for more results.

✔ **Message someone's Facebook Inbox** by typing **Msg** followed by the first and last name of the person you'd like to message and the body of the message. For example, Carolyn could send a text to 32665 that reads, **Msg Leah Pearlman Stop writing and come to this party.** Leah immediately receives the message in her Inbox.

If you enter a name for which Facebook finds more than one match, such as **Carolyn**, you receive a text message asking, *Which Carolyn?* with a list of the four most-likely matches among your Friends and then your networks. Each result is accompanied by a number. (For Leah, Carolyn Abram is first.) When you see the result you're looking for in the list, reply to that text message with the number associated with the matching result. Facebook then sends you the Profile information. If you don't see a match, reply with *n* to see the next set of results.

✔ **Poke someone** by texting **Poke** followed by the person you'd like to Poke. If Carolyn sends a text message containing **Poke Leah Pearlman**, Leah is immediately poked. Just as with Profile information, if Facebook finds multiple matches for people you might be trying to Poke, you receive a text message containing a list and a request that you clarify whom you're trying to Poke. Reply with the number associated with the right name.

✔ **Post on a friend's Wall** by writing **Wall** followed by your friend's first and last name and the contents of the post. Leah could text **Wall Carolyn Abram I'll come to the party after writing about Facebook Mobile** to let Carolyn and everyone who looks at Carolyn's Wall know why she is late to the party.

✔ **Add a new Facebook friend** by sending **Add** and the person's name. While Carolyn waits for Leah to come to the party, she might make a new friend, named Blake Ross, say. Carolyn can text **Add Blake Ross**. She might have to choose from multiple Blake Ross's, but then the request is automatically sent. Blake can confirm when he's back at his computer. Using your phone to immediately *friend* a person you meet is less formal than exchanging business cards, less awkward (and more reliable) than exchanging phone numbers, and gives you more flexibility later for how you want to get in touch. However, remember that by *friending* someone, you give away access to your Profile, so think twice before you Add.

✔ **Write a note** by texting **Note** followed by the contents of a note to 32665. The best Mobile Notes are often written when someone finds himself trapped in some interesting situation with nothing but a mobile phone. We've seen several Mobile Notes written when someone is locked out of her house, for example. Another popular Mobile Note comes from someone in a long line, such as one for a new Harry Potter book, the latest Xbox release, or the next hot iToy from Apple. Mobile Notes also come from airports, runways, and sporting events — even dentists', doctors', and hospital waiting rooms.

Mobile Texts is currently available only in the United States and Canada. Mobile Texts works on any mobile device as long as it can send and receive text messages and is one of Facebook's supported carriers. You'll know whether the last part is true if you start to sign up and don't see your carrier listed in the drop-down list. Facebook never charges you for any text messages you send, but your carrier might — check your plan to know what to expect on your bill.

What's all the buzz about?

An old wives' tale claims that when you feel your ears burn, someone is thinking about you. (Maybe it just means to back away from the campfire.) Here's a slight modification: Someone, somewhere, is thinking about you when your phone starts vibrating. Turning on Facebook Mobile Texts means that you'll be notified via SMS when someone Pokes you, sends you a Facebook message, comments on your photos and notes, writes on your Wall, or requests to be your friend.

To activate Facebook Mobile Texts, go to the Mobile tab of the Account page; from the bottom of the page, click Edit Mobile account settings and then select the Texts Are On radio button.

The Mobile Texts page (shown in Figure 14-2) offers a number of granular settings:

✔ **Which Text Notifications Should Go to My Phone?**

You actually control the notifications you receive (you can opt in and out of Messages, Wall Posts, Comments, Friend Requests, Photo Tags, and Pokes) from the Notifications tab of the Account page, not from the mobile tab. (a little "click here" takes you straight there). Here, you can also specify whether you want to receive texts only from friends. In other words, you only find out about friends' messages, not strangers' messages, on your mobile phone.

✔ **What Times Should Texts Be Sent to My Phone?**

You can specify what time you prefer to receive text notifications, so for example, if someone Pokes you at 2 a.m., you don't have to wake up for it. (Maybe you *only* want to know who's trying to Poke you at 2 a.m. No judgment here.)

Additionally, you can opt to not receive notifications while you're actively using Facebook, since that can get a bit redundant.

Facebook Text Messages

Texts are:
○ On ◉ Off

Which text notifications should go to my phone?
Click here to manage your mobile notifications.
☐ Send text notifications only from friends

What times should texts be sent to my phone?
○ Anytime ◉ Only from [8:00AM ⬍] to [11:00PM ⬍]
☐ Do not send me SMS notifications while I am using Facebook

How many texts should be sent?
Limit my daily texts to [Unlimited ⬍]

Should a confirmation text be sent when I message, wall post, comment, poke, upload photos, or set my status from my phone?
○ Yes ◉ No

Whose status updates should go to my phone?
Click here to manage your mobile subscriptions.

Figure 14-2: Set up your preferences for receiving notifications on your mobile phone.

✔ **How Many Texts Should Be Sent?**

If you have a mobile plan for which you're charged per text message (and you're exceedingly popular), use the settings that limit the number of messages Facebook sends you per day.

✔ **Should a Confirmation Text Be Sent . . . ?**

You can select whether to receive confirmations about the success of the Pokes, messages, or Wall posts that you send from your mobile phone.

✔ **Whose Status Updates Should Go to My Phone?**

Finally, as covered in Chapter 9, this is another entry point for specifying which of your friends' statuses you want sent right to your phone.

If you subscribe to the status of someone who doesn't spell very well but is conscientious about it, you may receive several texts as he tries to get his status just right.

From this page, you can also jump into your Account settings, change your mobile phone number, or add another number to your account.

Using Facebook Mobile Web

Have you ever noticed how some things are smaller than other things? Bunnies are smaller than elephants; toy cars are smaller than real cars. How about the fact that your mobile phone is much smaller than your computer?

If you haven't noticed *that,* you clearly haven't tried to access the Web on your phone.

Viewing a Web page from your phone can be extremely difficult because the information that is normally spread across the width of a monitor must be packed into one tiny column on your phone. Facebook is no exception to this, which is why the very first tip in this section is this: Never go to www. facebook.com on your mobile phone. You'll regret it.

But fear not, you still have a way to carry almost all the joys of Facebook right in your purse or pocket. On your mobile phone, open your browser application and navigate to m.facebook.com — a completely new window in Facebook designed specifically to work on a teeny-tiny screen.

If you use an iPhone, or a few select phone types, entering www.facebook.com redirects you to iphone.facebook.com, which we talk about in more detail a little later on.

The first time you arrive at m.facebook.com, you're asked to log in. After that, you never (or rarely) have to reenter your login information unless you explicitly select Logout from your session, so be sure you trust anyone to whom you lend your phone.

If you plan to use the Facebook Mobile Web site frequently, we recommend that you have an unlimited data plan that allows you to spend as much time on the mobile Web as you like for a fixed rate. The Facebook Mobile Web site is nearly as comprehensive and rich as the computer version. You can spend hours there and, if you're paying per minute, spend your life savings, too. Currently, Facebook Mobile Web is supported in the United States for people using Boost, Nextel, Sprint, and Virgin USA. Bell Mobility, Aliant, Fido, Solo, Rodgers, TELUS, SaskTel, and MTS support Facebook Mobile Web in Canada. Facebook Mobile Web works with many other carriers besides these, but Facebook makes no guarantee about the quality of your experience if you use a different carrier.

Mobile Home

After you log in, you see the mobile version of the Facebook Home page. Although the design of the mobile site is somewhat based on the design of the regular Web site, it has some significant differences. Some of the differences exist simply because of less space; the mobile site must cut to the chase while allowing you to get more information on a particular topic. For example, the mobile Home page shows only five News Feed stories rather than 25. You can get more stories if you want them, but you'll damage your thumb if you have to scroll through 25 News Feed stories to get to any of the links at the bottom.

The other differences arise because people using Facebook on a mobile phone often have different needs than those at a computer. For example, one of the first pieces of information you find on a friend's Profile is her phone number (if she has it listed), because if you're looking up someone on a mobile phone, you may be trying to contact her by phone.

To follow along with this section, you can navigate to m.facebook.com on your Web browser. Just imagine what you see on about one-tenth of the screen.

The Mobile Web page is shown in Figure 14-3. In this section, we detail what you see on the mobile Home page; we cover the other pages in the following sections.

> **facebook**   Search
> Home Profile Friends Inbox (7)
> You have 4 friend requests
> You were poked by Lyn Lewis. (poke back - remove)
> **What's on your mind?**
>
> Share
> **Events**
> Housewarming Pool Party and BBQ
> Tomorrow 4:00pm
> See All · Create an Event
> **Birthdays**
> Nick Schrock, Kyna Fong
> **News Feed**
> Top News · **Most Recent**
> Nick Schrock › Eric Zamore
> http://www.facebook.com/epriestley?
> v=wall&story_fbid=104702352915845

Figure 14-3: Facebook Mobile Home, also known as m.facebook.com.

From m.facebook.com, you'll see these items in your mobile Home page:

✔ **Home, Profile, Friends, Inbox:** These are the main navigational links you'll see at the top of any Page on the mobile Web. Home brings you back to the page you see when you sign in, Profile takes you to your own Profile, Friends takes you to a list of your friends, and Inbox takes you to your written messages.

✔ **New Messages or Notifications:** When you reach the mobile site, you find whether you have any unread messages, Events, or notifications right at the top of the page. These links only appear if you have something waiting for you. If you have a new message, remember that the name of the sender always links to the sender's Profile, so be careful to select the word *Read* if you want to jump straight to the message.

✔ **What's on Your Mind?:** When you use Facebook from your mobile phone, you're probably not sitting at your home office, workplace, or school. You may be trapped in jury duty, a bachelorette party, or waiting in line for a roller coaster (wheee!). Facebook makes it super easy to spread the news the moment you're doing something that you want people to know or when you want people to meet you:

✔ **Upcoming Events:** If you've received (and have not declined) invitations to Events that are in the next three days, you see the primary information here. If you have no Events in the next three days, this section won't appear on the mobile site. To see your Events, you have to get to them in another way, which we talk about later.

   • *Name of the Event:* Takes you to more information about the Event.

   • *Location:* An extremely handy feature when you can't remember the address of where you're going.

   • *Time:* The start time helps you avoid arriving too early or too late, which is good, because that's embarrassing. The end time helps you plan your after-party activity or arrange for a ride home.

   • *See All:* Shows your upcoming and past Events.

   • *Create Event:* In case you realize at the Party store that you forgot to send invites, you can create your event straight from your phone.

✔ **Birthdays:** If you have any friends with birthdays in the next three days (who have those birthdays listed on their Profiles), the big days show up below statuses on the mobile Home page. If you see none listed, you can probably put away the wrapping paper . . . for now.

✔ **Mobile News Feed:** Shows you the most recent stories that you would see on your computer. To save space, the stories have a little less information than the stories you're used to. Click through to a story to get more information about it. Select See All at the bottom of the Mobile News Feed section to see all the stories your heart desires.

✔ **Bookmarks:** More navigation links to pages you're likely to want to get to: Notifications, Photos, Links, Notes, Groups and Events.

✔ **Search:** The search box on the mobile site is designed to help you find people. When you enter text, the search results show your friends, the people in your network, and everyone else — in that order. There's no full-blown search or browse functionality from your mobile phone, just the search box, which is usually good enough.

✔ **Bottom Links:** Much like the bottom links on the regular site; a catchall of other stuff.

- *Find Friends:* In case your mobile experience is feeling kind of lonely, you can always go find more friends.

- *Settings:* Allows you to opt-in to applications that you'd like to use on your mobile phone. This list contains every application you've added to your Profile. Not all of these applications have a mobile component, but if you check the box next to an application, you get access to that application on your phone if that application adds mobile support.

- *Help:* A misnomer on the mobile site — it's actually more like an About page that explains the value of the Facebook Mobile Web. We recommend that Facebook update this page to make it actually *help*ful.

- *Logout:* The only way to end your mobile session. We recommend that you log out regularly if anyone else has access to your phone.

Mobile Profile preview

Profiles on the Facebook Mobile Web are designed differently than Profiles on the regular site. As we mention in the previous section, a lot of information from specific applications may be absent from your Profile. Moreover, the structure is ordered such that the information you're after is closest to the top. When you arrive at any mobile Profile, you see the most usable and actionable subset of the available information. A See Full Profile link at the bottom gives you access to the rest.

Access to information on mobile Profiles is the same as on the regular site — when you look at your Profile on the mobile site, you see your information, but that doesn't mean everyone has access to it. They have access only to what you specify via the privacy settings on the regular site:

- **Message, Poke, and Call:** These options are at the top of the Profile for quick *thinking of you* (or whatever your Poke means) communications. Your friend is guaranteed to get your message if he has Facebook Mobile Notifications set up, which we talk about earlier in this chapter. A call only appears if he's listed a phone number for himself, and a message and Poke depend on his privacy settings.

- **Status:** At the top of a person's Profile after her name, you see her status and the last time it was updated. When you see that your friend is *at Starbucks, come join,* the time stamp is helpful for knowing whether she updated it one minute ago or four days ago. You can also see how many people Liked or Commented on their status, and you can add to those counts yourself by doing the same.

- **Profile picture:** Next, you see the current Profile picture. Selecting it shows you other photos used as Profile pictures in the past.

✔ **Wall tab:** This is the same as the Wall tab of your Profile on the regular Facebook site. If you're looking at your own or your friend's Profile, it's selected by default. If you're looking at a non-friend's Profile, you have to click the Wall tab link beneath the Profile picture to see the Wall. The Wall tab shows you the last several stories that person (or you, if you're looking at your own Profile) added to her Profile.

✔ **Info tab:** To see the Info tab, you likely have to click the link to it located beneath the Profile picture. This shows the same information you can see on that person's Info tab on the normal site, but reordered to be mobile-friendly. Contact info is right at the top of the Info tab, because when you look someone up on a mobile phone, you're often after a number or address. If the person has his phone number listed here, you can select it to start the call. After that you see all the other information he may have added to his Profile, including his networks and basic info, his favorites, and where he went to school or worked.

✔ **Friends list and Other tabs:** Beneath the main contents of the Profile, you can see that person's friends, as well as jump into any other tab that user may have on her Profile, including her photos.

Mobile Friends List

The Friends link takes you to a list of your friends with the most recently updated statuses. The reason for this default is that when you're out (and on your mobile phone), it's nice to see where everyone else is out and about. At the top and bottom of the page, you have access to a few more filters for viewing your friends:

✔ **Updated:** By default, your phone shows your friends in order of who has updated their profile most recently. In yellow, you'll see what exactly has changed for each friend.

✔ **Phonebook:** Filters your Friends List down to only those friends who have a phone number listed on their Profiles.

✔ **Pages:** This tab shows you Pages you have liked in alphabetical order.

✔ **Everyone:** Shows you an alphabetical list of your friends' names, which you can use to navigate to their Profiles. Just like in normal Facebook search, you can message your friends without having to go to their Profiles.

✔ **Recently Added** *(at bottom of page):* Friends are all your friends in the order in which you became Facebook friends, starting with the most recent one. This is handy when you've recently friended someone, at a dinner party, say, and want to sneak off while she's not looking to learn more about her.

✔ **People You May Know** *(at bottom of page):* These people aren't your Facebook friends, but they can be! This is the same set of people who are featured on the right side of your Home page on the computer.

These are people with whom you have mutual friends or other things in common and whom you're quite likely to know and may want to become friends with. It's not really the kind of thing you'll probably spend much time on while using your phone, but who knows how boring your family reunion might be? You might welcome any distraction.

Mobile Inbox

The Mobile Inbox functions the same as the Inbox on the regular site, but you access it in a compacted view. In the Mobile Inbox, your messages are sorted by the time the last message on a thread was sent. Each thread includes the subject, the sender's name, the time the last message was sent, a snippet of the message, and quick links to Reply, Mark as Read/Unread, or Delete. The Mark as Unread link is particularly handy because often you read a message on your mobile phone, but don't have time or energy to type a response right then. Marking it as Unread reminds you to respond when you return to your computer.

Here's one major design difference between the Inbox on your phone and the Inbox on your computer: When you enter into the mobile thread, the newest message is at the top with the Reply box beneath it. You can scroll down to read the previous messages in the thread. In the regular Inbox, the order is flipped because it generally makes sense to read a conversation from the top of the page to the bottom. When you open a thread on the regular Inbox, the oldest message is at the top of the page, but the page automatically scrolls down to the newest message. This scrolling behavior isn't possible on a mobile phone, so the order of the messages is reversed.

Your Sent messages appear as a separate tab in the regular Inbox. In the mobile Inbox, you access your Sent messages by scrolling to the bottom of the Inbox and selecting the Sent link.

Facebook Mobile for the touch screen

As we mention earlier, if you navigate to Facebook on your iPhone, you actually end up at a completely different version of the site designed specifically for touch screen phones. Because only a fraction of people who use Facebook use it in conjunction with a mobile phone, and only a fraction of those people use it with a touch screen, we're only going to touch on the topic. (Get it? Touch on it? Ha!) If you have an iPhone or similar device, you are (a) cooler than Leah, who had to borrow her 16-year-old nephew's phone to research this section, and (b) you can follow along on your phone. If not, you can skip past this section entirely or go to `touch.facebook.com` on your computer to see what you're missing.

Even if you don't have an iPhone, you can still use the Facebook Mobile App on your iPod touch, and on a variety of other touch devices.

The lowdown on mobile downloads

Facebook Mobile Web sites can be highly useful when you have Facebook needs and are far from your computer. However, they can also be highly . . . slow. The speed of Facebook Mobile depends on the speed of your phone, and when it comes to speed, phones aren't exactly Superman just yet. If you have an iPhone, or a Blackberry, Nokia, Android, Palm, or a phone that uses Windows Mobile, Motorola, or Sony Ericsson, you can probably improve your Facebook Mobile experience by downloading a special Facebook application built specifically for your phone. More details about each are listed beneath the Facebook for Your Phone heading at `www.facebook.com/mobile`.

Touch screen layout

The touch screen site is organized really similarly to the computer version of the Web site except you get about a tenth the functionality. The beauty is that it's the tenth that most people use, most of the time, so you'll rarely miss the rest.

✔ **Home:** The Home page is broken into three sections, News Feed, Events, and Requests. The reason News Feed is the primary view is because it's often nice to know what your friends are up to right now so you have the possibility of meeting up or having a real-time exchange. The reason Events are also front and center is that often when people are out and about using Facebook on their phones, it's because they're at or on their way to an Event. Having the time, address, and attendee list of an Event right in your pocket can be key to making sure you show up at the right place and time.

✔ **Publisher:** At the very top of News Feed, just like on your computer, is a publisher where you can update your status. As mentioned before, this is because when people are out doing crazy things, they often have crazy things to say. In your authors' experiences, mobile status updates are among the most amusing and useful. Right now in Leah's News Feed, a mobile status is letting her know that a couple of friends are having an impromptu picnic near her house. If she wasn't writing a book right now, she'd join them.

✔ **Search:** In the upper-right corner, you have a magnifying glass icon, which is actually a link to search for people on the site. As you type, your phone will start digging up matches for you.

✔ **Profile:** Profiles are organized into the same Wall, Info, and Photo tabs as Profiles on the site; however, each is abbreviated, and any additional tabs that might exist on the real Profile aren't on this version of the Web site. The Info tab has only basic and contact information. To add something to your Wall, you can touch the Publisher at the top of the wall and start typing. The Photos tab features the photos of and by the Profile owner. Again, the brevity here is for readability on a small device.

✔ **Friends:** The touch screen Friends page is organized into three views. The default lists all your friends who've recently updated their statuses. You can switch that to view all friends who are currently online and available to chat. Or you can see all the most recent photos uploaded by your friends.

✔ **Inbox:** This is where you access all your messages. From here, you can compose a new message, delete a message, or reply to one.

Oh the Places you'll go

If you're using an iPhone, your built in GPS enables a nifty extra feature: Places which enables you to let people know where you are -- whether you're at an airport, a restaurant, or home -- by checking in. Your GPS supplies the location, and you can add a status or photo. Simply tap Check In to add your location. After you do so, your friends will see something like "First day of school - CCA Writing Studio." This might seem a bit superfluous because if your friends are across the country (or even the world), it might not matter whether you're at an ice cream shop or the gym. But for your local friends, Places enables all sorts of serendipitous connections to be made. If you arrive at the airport and go to check in, you might notice a section of friends who are already at your location. You can ping them and wait together, or grab a drink before going your separate ways. Same goes for concerts, coffee shops, or anyplace.

Like most other Facebook features, you can also tag your friends in your check-ins. Going to the movies with a few people? Check them in with you and then their friends might be able to save you seats. Remember: Location information is very powerful. Be respectful of people's preferences. If you're checking in to a backyard barbecue, ask your hosts before you tag your coordinates as their home. Places you enter are public; someone checking in down the road will see a place called "Chateau de Smith." Make sure your friends are comfortable with this information being out there. If your friends don't like you to tag them in check-ins, respect their wishes. Additionally, if you are uncomfortable with certain aspects of your location information being shared, use the settings on the privacy page to make the places you go less visible.

Chapter 15

A Different Kind of Advertising

In This Chapter

▶ Understanding the key difference between good and bad advertising

▶ Touring Facebook's advertising solution

▶ Improving your return on advertising investment by managing your ads

There are two kinds of people in America: those who watch the Super Bowl and those who watch the Super Bowl commercials. It's odd that, for a few hours every year, most of us actually seek out advertising, while the rest of the year we resent it. We fast-forward commercials, we change radio stations, we chuckle at the occasional billboard (but mostly we complain about how they ruin the skyline). What's the cause for prejudice? Is advertising inherently evil?

If you're someone who runs a business or is responsible for driving customers to a business, you know the answer is *No*. Advertisers have no malicious intent (usually), and they're not out to annoy, distract, or interrupt us. They simply have a product or service that they believe could improve our lives, if we only knew about it. So they tell us. They tell us three minutes before the end of our favorite TV shows; they tell us with their tee-shirt logos, hood ornaments, and catchy jingles; they stand on the corner with signs that read *Lemonade 5 cents*. And if one person among us responds well to an advertiser's particular message, that advertiser has no problem yelling across an entire crowded room to make sure that person hears it.

Realizing How Advertising Has Improved

Yelling across a crowded room has been the model of advertising for years. Advertisers operate under the somewhat accurate principle that the wider the distribution, the better the chances of reaching someone who cares — that's why Super Bowl slots are the most expensive of the year. It's not because football fans are more likely to buy stuff; it's because more people simultaneously watch the Super Bowl than anything else on TV. More people equals more customers.

However, there is a cost. People have only so much attention to lend to advertising. Therefore, if 2, 3, 4, or 5 million advertisers start yelling across the room, people hear none of it. When too many messages fly, people tune out, leaving advertisers with no recourse other than being the *loudest, brightest,* or *catchiest.* Anyone who has stood in the middle of Times Square in New York City understands exactly what we're talking about. And that has certainly been the model of advertising on the Internet. The flashier an ad, the more in your face, the more distracting — the more likely you are to click it.

Advertising has a bad rap because of this. Every now and then, you see an ad for something you were craving, something that intrigues you, or features something that just entertains you. In those times, you probably don't mind the advertising at all; in fact, you might appreciate it. Nevertheless, 99 times out of 100, an ad is a nuisance, which is how *ad* has practically become a dirty word. Understanding these flaws with the modern advertising landscape led to the formulation of principles for the Facebook Ad system:

✔ Consumers are happiest if they see fewer total advertisements and the ones they do see are most relevant to them.

✔ Advertisers are happiest if they *don't* throw away cash and *don't* dilute consumer attention. In other words, advertisers want to deliver their messages primarily to those people who actually care about them.

✔ When consumers are exposed to relevant, high-quality advertisements, they're more likely to pay attention to advertising on the whole, making each ad that much more valuable.

✔ To get people's attention, advertising is usually weaved into some product or service that already has consumer attention, such as TV shows or Web sites. People enjoy a TV show or Web site more if its ads are relevant, high-quality, and not harmful to the user experience. As a result, they spend more time watching that channel or using that Web site, thereby seeing more total ads. Therefore, responsible TV stations or Web sites are rewarded for good advertising behavior. Customers are happier, advertisers are happier, and the product or service provider is happier.

Advertisers have to yell across the room because they don't know who, in a crowd, may be listening. Now, because each Facebook user enters so much personal information, Facebook can enable its advertisers to deliver their messages only to the people most interested (while completely protecting its users' privacy).

No more yelling.

Imagine Times Square in this model. Rather than everyone looking at thousands of flashy signs, each person would see five or six messages about things that actually interest them, making more room for flowers, and sky, and, we'll go ahead and say it, *no commercialism.*

Defining Social Ads

On Facebook, users see two types of advertising. The first type of advertising is fancy, expensive *engagement units* such as videos and sponsored event invites, which appear on the right side of the Home page. Although these are super-cool and high-performing, they require a direct, personal relationship with the Facebook Sales team and cost a pretty penny. This chapter focuses on the second type of ads on Facebook — self-service social advertising. These are the ads from which anyone who has something to sell can benefit. A *social ad* is an ad that businesses create and upload to Facebook directly to circulate on Facebook. No middleman. Social ads have a number of interesting characteristics:

✔ Social ads appear in the right column on most Facebook pages, under the Sponsored heading.

✔ Social ads are composed of the same set of optional components: a title, a photo, an ad body, and the option for inclusion of social actions (which we explain in the next section). Therefore, social ads are uniform in their appearance, so advertisers must get your attention with content, not form.

✔ Social ads are demographically targeted to users based on information they list in their Profiles, including geography, age, sex, interests, school, workplace or profession, political views, or relationship status.

✔ Using social actions, social ads are targeted to people whose friends have shown an interest in the product or service.

Social actions

Previously in this chapter, we refer to *social actions.* If you haven't heard this term in advertising before, don't be surprised. It's currently exclusive to Facebook. Social actions are best described via examples:

✔ Wiley Publishing makes a Facebook Page (described in Chapter 12) to advertise *Facebook For Dummies.*

✔ At some point, Carolyn publicly liked the *Facebook For Dummies* Page.

✔ Wiley Publishing creates an ad on Facebook. Characteristics of the ad include the following:

- A subject that reads something like, "*Facebook For Dummies*. Do you know someone who needs help understanding Facebook? More help than you can give?"

- A picture of the book's cover.

- A targeted audience of 30–40-year-olds.

In addition, Wiley Publishing *opts-in* to appending social actions to the ad.

✔ Because Carolyn has already pledged allegiance to Dummies, the social ad system tries to show the *Facebook For Dummies* ad to Carolyn's friends who fit the 30–40-year-old demographic.

The system automatically appends to the ad the social action, "Carolyn Abram likes this."

Social ads plus social actions rules

Carolyn's friends are way more likely to be interested in *Facebook For Dummies* if they already know that Carolyn liked it. At the very least, if they're intrigued, they might ask her for more information. When authorized by an advertiser, the Facebook system looks at all the people within the targeted demographic for an ad and then tries to show the ad to people whose friends have already had a positive interaction with that company. Here are a few important points about social advertising:

✔ **No one's actions are ever shown to people who couldn't also have seen that action as a story in their streams.** In other words, the only people who can see the ad with the social action are those to whom Carolyn has made her action visible. By default, liking a Page is a publically visible action, so, most likely, anyone connected to Carolyn will be able to see her story appended to the ad.

✔ **You cannot append a social action to your ad unless you also have a Facebook Page or Application.** Users must have a place to interact to generate the social actions in the ad.

✔ **Even if you opt-in to social actions, this doesn't guarantee that a social action is always appended to your ad.** If there's not enough engagement with your Page, there may not be enough social actions to append to your ad. To increase the likelihood that this happens, you must ensure that your Facebook Page or Application is seeing a lot of activity.

Who uses social ads?

Anyone who has access to a computer, a credit card, and something to promote is a great candidate for using Facebook social ads. People use social ads for all kinds of different things:

- ✔ Drawing attention to your Web site or business
- ✔ Telling people about a new deal or offering
- ✔ Campaigning for an election
- ✔ Promoting a college event
- ✔ Driving traffic to a Facebook Event, Group, Page, or application
- ✔ Raising awareness of a cause
- ✔ Promoting a concert or a new CD
- ✔ Directing traffic to a listing on Marketplace
- ✔ Recruiting for a job opening

Social ads target your ad to an audience as small as a single school or as wide as a whole country, and they're applicable to just about every promotional effort. The only audience Facebook can't currently target is people who don't use Facebook. But you can spread your message to them some other way — dress up like a chicken and hand out flyers in front of your store, perhaps.

Creating a Social Ad

Creating an ad on Facebook is extremely easy; creating a good ad may require some extra effort. In this section, we walk you through the basic how-to of creating an ad on Facebook, while providing lots of tips and tricks to ensure your ad is as effective as possible. We call out what steps are required and what steps are recommended.

Getting started

Log in to Facebook and navigate to `www.Facebook.com/adversting`. You can access this Page at any time by scrolling to the bottom of any Facebook Page and clicking Advertising. You can also click Create an Ad on the right side of any page above the ads that are displayed in the right column. Click Create an Ad to get started.

If you don't have a Facebook account, you can skip the log in part, but you are asked to create a personal account (use your e-mail address, password, and birthday) before completing your ad purchase.

Designing your ad

Figure 15-1 shows where you add some basic information about your ad, as described here:

- ✔ **Destination URL or Facebook Content:** The destination is the landing page for people who click on your ad. If you already have a Web site for your business, enter your business's URL (or the URL of the page you want people to land on when they click your ad). If you're trying to advertise something you have on Facebook, such as a Facebook Page or an Application, select the link below the URL box that says I Want to Advertise Something I Have on Facebook and choose the relevant Page, Application, Group, or Event from the drop-down list. If you want to link your ad to a Facebook page you haven't yet created, hop back to Chapter 12 to set up your page first.

- ✔ **Title/Body Text:** When you enter the ad title in the Title field and body in the Body field, use the preview on the right to see what your ad will look like. You have 25 characters for the title and 135 for the body, so remember to invite your inner editor to the ad creation process. By default, if you are advertising Facebook content, the name of your Page or Event (and so on) will be the title of your ad — a bit limiting to the creative genius in you, but that makes it easier for your customers to know what they are looking at.

- ✔ **Image (Optional):** You can upload a photo — the way your photo shows up in the Preview is how people see it in your ad.

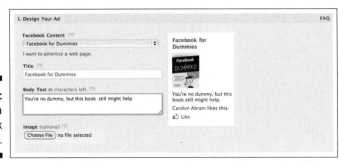

Figure 15-1: Creating a Facebook ad.

After you make your choice, continue on to the next section.

As you're creating your ad, notice the little question mark in brackets ([?]) next to almost every field. If at any point you are unsure about what a field refers to, clicking on the little question mark will bring up an explanation and relevant tips.

Targeting your ad

On Facebook, an engaged man or woman is likely to see ads for wedding photographers, whereas sports lovers may see an ad for coverage of the big game. An older married man may see an ad about anniversary presents, and if you're a 23-year-old female who likes poetry and traveling, don't be surprised if you see an ad for a women's writing workshop in Europe. (Recently, this happened to Carolyn, who was so thrilled by the ad that she went on to get more info about the workshop.)

As we mention at the beginning of this chapter, targeting your ad may be the key to good advertising. If you narrow your message to the people most likely to respond, you pay much less for the same amount of attention.

The goal of targeted advertising is to try to be as specific as possible, without alienating anyone who may be interested. To that end, Figure 15-2 shows the options for the Facebook targeting system, and this list helps demystify them:

Figure 15-2:
Your ad's
targeting
options.

> **2. Targeting** FAQ
>
> **Location**
>
> Country: [?]   United States ×
>   ○ Everywhere
>   ◉ By State/Province [?]
>   ○ By City [?]
>   Enter a state/province
>
> **Demographics**
>
> Age: [?]   18 ⬍ – Any ⬍
> Sex: [?]   ◉ All   ○ Men   ○ Women
>
> **Likes & Interests**
>
> Reading × Reading Books ×   Journaling ×   [?]
> Writing ×
>
> **Suggested Likes & Interests**
> ☑ Writing   ☐ Cross-Stitching
> ☑ Journaling   ☐ Outlander Series
> ☐ Crocheting   ☐ Cross Stitching
> [Refresh Suggested Interests]
>
> Show Advanced Targeting Options
>
> Estimated Reach
> **4,640,420** people
> • who live in the **United States**
> • age **18** and older
> • who like **reading, reading books, journaling** or **writing**

✔ **Location:** If your product or service is relevant to consumers only in a particular location, be sure your ad is shown only to those people. A traveling circus, for example, might make a whole series of ads targeted at different locations to let people know when to break out their clown noses and floppy shoes. If you've entered the United States, or certain other countries, you'll be able to target to state-level or city-level locations as well.

✔ **Demographics:** You can target ads to people of certain ages and genders.

  • **Age:** Specify the minimum and maximum age for your ad. The default is 18 years old because any ads targeted at people under the age of 18 are reviewed before being shown.

  • **Sex:** Selecting either male or female ensures your ad goes to only men or only women. If you check both of these boxes, or if you leave them both unchecked, your ad is delivered to both males and females.

✔ **Likes and Interests:** When Facebook users create their personal Profiles, they enter various terms that describe their likes, activities, and interests. When enough people like the same term, that term is used for keyword targeting. You know a term is valid for targeting if you start to enter it and a drop-down list appears to automatically complete the word. If the word you're thinking of doesn't appear, come up with a synonym. If the word you're looking for *does* appear, you probably still want to come up with a few synonyms and target those as well. For example, if you sell books, you may want to target to *Reading, Read, Books, Reading Books,* and *Literature.*

Play around with this step and see how the audience size estimator fluctuates with various combinations, as well as the "suggested interests" that appear beneath the text field that might help you round out your targeting. The audience size estimator takes the criteria you've entered, and quickly figures out approximately how many people on Facebook match that criteria so you have a rough idea of the audience you're targeting. It's not exactly accurate because calculating the audience fast is quite difficult technically. Also, more than a million people sign up on Facebook daily, so your audience size is shifting constantly.

✔ **Advanced Targeting Options:** Rather than inundate you with a million fields by which you can target your ads, Facebook hides a few of the more specific ones behind the Advanced Targeting Options link right beneath Likes and Interests. Advanced Options include:

  • **Interested In** *(under Demographics)*: You can target people of specific sexual orientations using this field. So, for example, if you're a magazine for gay women, you can make sure that only gay women (or women on Facebook who have self-identified as gay) see your ad.

- **Relationship *(under Demographics)*:** Photographer? Florist? Caterer? Invitation specialist? Yes, you are trying to reach people planning their weddings. You can use this field to make sure only people who are listed as engaged see your ad.

- **Languages *(under Demographics)*:** Maybe you want to reach people who live in the U.S. but speak Spanish for your political cause. Use the Languages field to get to the right people.

- **Education and Work:** These fields allow you to reach the people in a particular life stage, such as high school, college, or college graduate. You can also target people at (or from) a particular school or company. If you're targeting kids in college, you can reach out to a particular graduation year if that's relevant. You can target particular majors. For example, a computer company could create an ad and target it to all the computer scientists and engineering seniors from the top schools, or even target it to people who work at competing companies. If you're planning an alumni event for Amherst College, you can target everyone who is listed as an alumnus of Amherst.

  To specify a specific school, workplace, or major, select the education level and then start typing the name of the school in the field. The name of the school most likely autocompletes for you; if not, it's not in the system and can't be targeted.

- **Connections on Facebook:** This section is definitely advanced in that it probably won't apply to you unless you've already created a few ads in the past. It basically allows you to advertise just to people who have already liked your content (for example, offering a new promotion or coupon to your fans), or the reverse (excluding people who are already your fans). It also allows you to target just the friends of your fans. Notice that you'll need to reenter the name of your Page, Event, Group, or Application in each of these fields. If you manage multiple pages, this is a way to feed off of earlier success. If someone attended your band's event in San Francisco, they might want to see you again the next time you're in town.

✔ **Estimated Reach *(on the right side of the page)*:** As you adjust the parameters of your audience, the Estimate section automatically updates to tell you the number of people you're targeting. As you add more specifications, the number drops. This is good because it means you're focusing your message to a specific audience. If you're too specific with your parameters, however, you may lose your audience entirely. There just may not be many 64-year-old Spanish-speaking South Korean women who like to surf, no matter how much you'd like to advertise to them. If the number dips too low, you should consider relaxing your requirements. In this example, you could expand the age and language requirements or add other hobbies such as swimming or boating. In the Estimate section, you'll see your target audience reflected back to you in plain English. After checking a bunch of boxes and choosing from drop-down lists, it may be tricky to be sure you've targeted correctly. Checking the Estimate section can help reassure you that you've chosen your settings correctly.

We spend a lot of time emphasizing how valuable targeting can be if you have a message that's relevant to only certain kinds of people. However, what if you have a product everyone can enjoy? You still target your ad — with tailored messaging for different people. Say, for example, that you are the promotions manager for a jewelry store. You can create one ad targeted at women with a message about treating one's self, and another ad targeted at men that emphasizes gift-giving. You can be more specific by targeting married men with an ad about buying gifts for their wives or by targeting young men with an ad about gifts for their mothers, for example.

Figuring out campaigns and pricing

Figuring out the price of an ad isn't quite as straightforward as listening to a vendor yell, "Hot dogs, 99 cents, get your hot dogs!" The amount you pay for your ad depends on all kinds of factors, including how you target it, whether you care that people click your ad or just see it, and how you've set your campaign and your budget (see Figure 15-3).

Figure 15-3:
Pricing
your ad.

> 3. Campaigns and Pricing   FAQ
>
> ⦿ Create a new campaign [?]
> ◯ Choose an existing campaign [?]
>
> Campaign Name
> New Ad
>
> Daily Budget What is the most you want to spend per day? (min 1.00 USD)
> 10.00
>
> Schedule. When do you want to start running your ad?
> ⦿ Run my ad continuously starting today
> ◯ Run my ad only during specified dates
>
> Based on your targeting options, Facebook suggests a bid of $1.32 per click. You may pay
> up to this much per click, but you will likely pay less.
> Set a Different Bid (Advanced Mode)

✔ **Account Currency (not shown):** In order for Facebook to bill you correctly, you need to specify your preferred currency. You'll only need to fill this out once. After that, Facebook will remember your preference.

✔ **Account Time Zone (not shown):** Because Facebook's ads charge according to a bid plus a daily budget (more on that in a minute),

Facebook wants to make sure it's on the same page as you about when a "day" technically begins and ends. Thus, you should enter where you are and your time zone in this field. You only need to fill this out once. After that, Facebook will remember your preference.

✔ **Campaign Name:** A campaign refers to one or more ads that you want to run and pay for as a group. You may have created several ads that are targeted differently in order to bring a more diverse audience to your band's concert ten days from now. Grouping all these ads into the same campaign allows you to set a single budget and schedule for the entire group of ads so you don't have to spend time and effort optimizing for the ads that are performing better or worse. The first ad you create on Facebook is automatically put in a campaign. When you create more ads, you're able to add them to various campaigns or create new campaigns.

✔ **Daily Budget:** You're charged based on how many people click or view your ad (up to your maximum daily budget, which you set by entering it into the Budget field). If you set a maximum daily budget of $10 and offer to pay up to 10 cents per click, you hope that approximately 100 people click on your ad. The Facebook Ad system does some fancy behind-the-scenes math to figure out how many people must see your ad to get you your 100 clicks. If the system shows your ad to too few people, you won't end up paying the full $10, Facebook makes less money, and you may not get the response you were hoping for. If the system shows your ad to too many people, you may end up getting some free attention you don't have to pay for. Good for you; not so good for Facebook. The system is constantly being improved to deliver your ad to exactly as many people as it takes to get the response you're willing to pay for.

✔ **Schedule:** You can choose to either start running your ad right away or specify the start and end dates for your ad. When you select Run My Ad Continuously Starting Today, you stop your ad when your goals are met; otherwise, you're charged per day continuously.

Once you have specified your campaign and pricing, Facebook will automatically suggest a bid per click. If you're unhappy with this bid, you can monkey with your targeting options or go to Advanced Mode.

Advanced Mode

The preceding fields are part of what Facebook calls *simple mode*. This mode is the faster and easier one to understand in terms of pricing and starting an ad. If you're a more advanced advertiser, you may want to consider further customization through Advanced Mode, which you can get to by clicking on the Set a Different Bid (Advanced Mode) link, located at the bottom of the Campaign and Pricing section.

✔ **Pay for Impressions/Pay for Clicks:** Advanced Mode lets you opt to pay for views (CPM) instead of clicks (CPC), which will drastically change your bid price. Amazon (www.amazon.com) is an example of a company that would likely choose Pay for Clicks because customers buy products on its Web site.

Other examples of Pay for Clicks advertisers might be application developers who want people to use their applications, bands who want people to try their music, or non-profits who want people to contribute to their causes. Coca-Cola may be the kind of company that would use Pay for Views to simply get its brand and slogan in front of people. Someone selling his car might use Pay for Views after putting a photo and all his contact info in the ad.

✔ **Max Bid:** This field allows you to specify how much you want to bid for a click or a set of 1,000 views. Say that five advertisers want to target men who have the text *tattoos* in their Profiles. All five advertisers bid differently for clicks. Each time men with *tattoos* in their Profiles log in, the ad system shows them the ad from the highest bidder, until that advertiser's budget is exhausted. Then the system shows the ad of the next highest bidder. For each click or view, advertisers are charged the price of the next highest bid beneath their own (except that the second-to-lowest bidder pays 1 cent higher than the lowest bid). If an advertiser bids 10 cents per click and another bids 5 cents and all the others bid 3 cents, the first advertiser ends up paying 5 cents, the second advertiser 4 cents, and all the others 3 cents as well.

Facebook has a lot of users, but it doesn't show each user very many ads. The value in bidding high is that it's the safest way to get the response you're after. The value in bidding conservatively is that you may pay less for the same number of clicks or views. The bid system helps advertisers pay exactly what a click or impression is worth to them. Moreover, the companies that take the time to make highly targeted and quality ads often end up bidding higher than those companies that produce low-quality ads; therefore, users are more likely to see high-quality and relevant ads. Facebook will show you suggested bids so you can understand where you are in the range, and therefore how likely your ads are to be seen.

Reviewing your ad

After you create your ad, target your audience, and set your own budget, it's time to admire all your handiwork on the Review Ad page. Rather than just applauding yourself for a job well done, review all the information carefully to make sure you're getting exactly what you're about to pay for. Speaking of paying for things, when you're done reviewing all the information, fill out the standard credit card information on the bottom half of the page and place your order. But first, we highly recommend you read the advertising guidelines and advertising policy linked on the right side of this page before you begin your Facebook advertising adventures. When you're confident all the information is accurate, click Finish.

After you created a few ads, you may want to create similar ones to those you've already created. Say you're the manager of a small chain of restaurants in California. You may want to run two nearly identical ads: one targeted toward Los Angeles residents, pointing them to your L.A. location, and the other targeted at San Francisco residents, directing them to your S.F. location. Besides these slight differences in targeting, the body, copy, image, social actions, and everything else about the ads are identical. Rather than duplicate your effort, you can make one of the ads first, and then when you come back to create an ad again, click the drop-down menu at the very top of the page that says Copy an Existing Ad. From there, select the first ad you created and watch how every form is automatically prefilled with the information from the previous ad. Then you can simply make the necessary edits and quickly proceed.

Managing Your Social Ads

After you start running an ad on Facebook, you're more than welcome to just cross your fingers and hope for the response you're after. However, with the Ads Manager, if you want to know exactly what kind of responses your ads are getting and if you want to improve the performance of your ads, you can always temporarily stop running ads while you make changes to optimize your efforts. Then when you're ready, you can start running the ads again.

To manage your ads, go back to www.Facebook.com/ads and click the link that says Manage Your Existing Ads beneath the Create an Ad button. You can also sign in to Facebook and click Ad Manager (also called Ads and Pages if you're the admin of a Page, in addition to running ads) in the Applications menu in the bottom-left corner of any Facebook page. You'll land on the Campaigns tab of the Ads Manager. Going down the left-hand menu, you can always easily navigate to the following pages:

- **Pages:** This takes you the Pages Manager. To learn more about Pages and what they might mean for you, refer to Chapter 12.

- **Reports:** Once you've had several ads running over a certain amount of time, you might want to generate reports that you can show to your boss, or yourself, that let you know how effective your advertising has been. You can compare various campaigns over time or see what types of people tend to respond to your ads. You can generate ads in html or as Excel spreadsheets.

✓ **Billing:** This section helps you keep track of how much money you've spent on Facebook ads.

✓ **Settings:** You can change your e-mail notification settings, as well as your basic Account Info from the Settings page. You can also choose to close your ad account from here.

✓ **Learn More:** Once you've gotten up and running on ads, you may have questions or need advice beyond what we've given you here. That's a good thing, young grasshopper. The Guide to Facebook ads will have a bunch of good tips and tricks to take your ads to the next level.

From the Campaigns page, which you land on whenever you click Ads Manager or Manage My Ads, you'll see a list of your campaigns and some basic info about them, as shown in Figure 15-4.

Figure 15-4:
The Campaigns page shows a summary of your ads' performances.

The elements to notice here are

✓ The status of the ad (scheduled, running, or completed).

✓ Budget/Day (which you can change inline at any time; just click on the number).

✓ Clicks and Impressions: As your ad starts to run, you'll see Clicks and Impressions tracked here.

✔ The click-through rate (CTR), which is the average number of times your ad is clicked on each time it is viewed.

✔ The average cost you're paying per click (if your ad is a Cost per Click or CPC ad).

✔ The average cost per million (CPM) to you each time 1 million people view your ads.

✔ Your total spent so far.

In addition, you can specify whether you want to see all these metrics for the last 24 hours, 7 days, or to date, using the drop-down menu above the ad summary tables.

On the front page of the Ad Manager, you see a graph of the performance of your most active ad campaigns. The overview graph shows clicks, impressions, and the click-through rate over time. You can use the Choose a Graph drop-down menu at the top of the graph to isolate any one of these pieces of information. If you're interested in how many people saw your ad, for example, you can select impressions. If you only care about who clicked on it, select Clicks. CTR, or Click-Through Rate, tells you how many people clicked it divided by how many people saw it. A CTR of 0.5 means that one out of every two people who saw the ad clicked it. The bottom of the Overview page shows the performance of your ad today compared to yesterday.

Clicking the name of an individual ad shows you all the detailed information at the campaign level, but this time about the performance of that particular ad in a campaign. This page also shows the preview of the ad and reminds you of your targeting information. From this detailed view of an ad's performance, you can choose to pause or stop your ad at any time.

Between graphs and detailed statistics, the ad management interface gives you all the information you need to help customize your ads to get the absolute best return on your investment. This isn't as selfless as it sounds. If you're having the most success possible, it's likely you're making extremely high-quality ads with accurate targeting; therefore, it's a better experience for Facebook users and a better experience for Facebook. To this end, Facebook plans to continue building these tools to create one of the most robust, valuable advertising networks on the Web.

Spam Is Not Delicious

Good user experience is key to the success of Facebook and, therefore, key to the advertisers who advertise on Facebook. In order to preserve good user experience, Facebook puts most ads through a review process before they're allowed on the site. Your ad must be generally relevant to the people you target. The text and image of your ad must not be misleading in any way. The content of your ad and the site that it links to must be appropriate for any audience. Ads may be rejected for other quality metrics, such as misspellings, too much capitalization or punctuation, and so on. Generally, if your ad is clear and tasteful, you won't have any problems.

Part V
The Part of Tens

"Mr. President, North Korean President Kim Jong-il just sent you a SuperPoke."

In this part . . .

In the earlier parts of this book, we focus heavily on options and hypothetical situations. So, to ensure that you have some concrete examples of what's really happening on Facebook, we present to you the "Part of Tens."

In this part, we don't make claims about what's the *best* of anything on Facebook because every experience is unique. However, you can see how much your taste matches ours by checking out our favorite applications. Additionally, you can see how Facebook has made an impact on people's lives — and how it might just have an impact on yours. In case you forgot some of what you read earlier (we know, it's a lot of info), we include some of the most common questions we get from our family and friends. And finally, we recount some of our favorite anecdotes about people reconnecting via Facebook.

Chapter 16

Ten Great Third-Party Applications

In This Chapter

▶ Typing Maniac

▶ Music by iLike

▶ Digg

▶ Carpool by Zimride

*T*raditionally, Facebook has focused on offering the most general types of functionality that just about anyone would find useful. But, in life, different people have different needs and desires. Students like to know what courses their friends are taking. Athletes sometimes trade exercise tips; some record their workouts. Foodies often swap recipes. Music lovers share new music discoveries; movie buffs rate and review films. In an attempt to be all things to all people, Facebook has empowered the masses to add all the specialized functionality that can transform Facebook from a general social network into a specific, tailored tool for managing one's lifestyle — no matter what that lifestyle consists of. This specialized functionality includes all of the previous examples, tools for students, business people, hobbyists, families, and more. Here's a variety of applications that we think are good examples of what Facebook has to offer.

Typing Maniac

On the surface, measuring the speed of one's typing sounds like something only professional stenographers would want to know. However, Typing Maniac, a game played on Facebook, tests that theory. As words float down the screen, you must type them before they hit the bottom. As you move up the levels, the words get longer and move down the screen faster.

Of course, the part of the game that is most entertaining is that you can track your progress among your friends. As Typing Maniac posts to your Profile about your progress from caveman to alien, your friends are alerted and can start to compete against you. We strongly suggest that you not use this game as a "break" from work, as you will never want to stop playing.

Marketplace

Marketplace is an application that helps you buy and sell used goods. At first, you might think, "Why would I need this when I have Craigslist?" The answer lies in the difference between buying a used car from a friend, or a friend's friend, as opposed to buying a used car from a total stranger. If you've ever brought home a lemon, you understand the difference.

By showing you how you know people who are selling items, Marketplace helps you make choices about whom to trust, and who will give you good quality merchandise. It also helps you, as a seller, get the word out about your merchandise, sublet, or whatever it is you are looking to sell. Your listings can get published to friends, who in turn can pass them on to their friends.

Music, by iLike

Music listening and discovery are two of the most common activities people do online. Functionality related to music (with the exception of Pages for musicians) is notably absent from Facebook, and is certainly a hole for most people, who feel that their music is a big part of their identity.

The Music application, then, allows people to feature their musical tastes front and center through the addition of a music tab. Additionally, through browsing on the Music application, you can find out what your friends are listening to, as well as create Internet radio stations based on the songs and artists your friends listen to. Music also features a dashboard of content from your favorite artists — everything from their tweets to new music videos.

Groupcard

Groupcard is an application that lives on Facebook that replicates the real-world experience of passing a card around to be signed at a party. Groupcard allows you to choose a card type and the basic look and feel of the card and then invite others to sign it. Each person who signs it can select a variety of fonts, as well as pull from his photos to find an appropriate one to send with the card. After everyone has signed, the card then gets "sent" to its intended recipient.

We like Groupcard because, although it's not required for wishing someone a happy birthday or congratulations, it makes the experience of doing so a little more personal and special.

Digg

Self-described geeks out there are probably avid users of Digg (www.digg.com), a news site that allows its users to *Digg* or promote certain news stories that they think are the most interesting or relevant. By connecting Digg with your Facebook account, you can publish your Diggs back to Facebook. This ability means that you can tell your friends, as well as the larger Digg community, what you think is interesting or newsworthy.

Also, if you're not finding anything interesting on the Digg home page, you can see what your friends (who have also connected their Facebook accounts with Digg) have Dugg in the last few days. Another example of how social plugins work to make Facebook, as well as its companion site, more interesting and social.

Graffiti

Graffiti is a simple and beautiful application that allows users to add the ability for their friends to draw pictures for them on their Walls. A friend can leave a little visual gift for another friend, and mutual friends can discover the art in their Home pages.

We like Graffiti because it's a mix of the *thinking-of-you* Poke and the more labor- and time-intensive task of writing a card and mailing it. Receiving a Graffiti drawing is rewarding because someone devotes time to you in a public way, which shows the world that person cares about you and that you are worth their time. Goosebumps.

Carpool by Zimride

The Carpool application allows people to offer and request rides to wherever they need to go. It can be used to organize regular carpools to and from work (especially useful when people at your company have actually joined your workplace network), or to find company for longer, one-time road trips.

There are plenty of other services online that people use to find rides, but what's great about the Zimride Carpool application is that it adds the layer of identity that is easy to find on Facebook, and difficult to find elsewhere. Carpooling with a stranger can be worrisome, but carpooling with someone who has friends in common with you might be more comfortable. Even if that's not the case, the mere ability to check out potential carpoolers and see if they seem like someone you could tolerate being in a car with for a few hours can make a world of difference.

Visual Bookshelf

Visual Bookshelf, an application by Living Social that lives on Facebook, pretty much proves the assertion that a recommendation from a friend is worth more than a recommendation from a stranger. You and your friends can leave reviews and share favorites with each other straight from Facebook. You can feature Visual Bookshelf on your Profile as a box that allows your friends to see what you're reading now. (For example, *Facebook For Dummies*, and it is *amazing*!)

Visual Bookshelf actually has a pretty smart connection with Amazon (www.amazon.com) so that as you see books you want to read, you can easily go buy them and get down to reading and reviewing them.

Lady Gaga

Lady Gaga kind of took the world by storm starting in 2009. She's been a cultural force since then, bringing her special brand of art, music, and "fame" to the top of everyone's playlists. Her Web site, www.ladygaga.com allows her fans to sign in using Facebook and participate in commenting, forums, and connecting with other fans through their shared love of all things Gaga. Fans can also share her content back into Facebook and keep track of her musings on her Facebook fan page. Although the implementation is simple, her use of social plugins keeps her fans connected and engaged with her music and persona.

Restaurant City

If you like games that you play over time and that allow you to make lots of decisions — Monopoly players, we're talking about you — you will most likely love Restaurant City. This game allows you to start a restaurant and hire your friends to work there. As your restaurant makes money, you can hire more of your friends, redecorate, and start to compete with your friends' restaurants. Simple fun, right on Facebook.

Chapter 17

Ten Ways Facebook Uniquely Impacts Lives

In This Chapter

▶ Getting ready to go to school

▶ Meeting people in your new city

▶ Keeping up with the kids

Sometimes people are dismissive of Facebook, saying, "I keep up with my friends by calling them and visiting them. I don't need a Web site to do that for me." This is true. However, we try to make the point throughout this book that Facebook doesn't replace real friendships — it supplements them. You can still communicate and share information with your friends without Facebook; however, it's easier and faster to do with Facebook. Some things are always a part of life; Facebook just makes them better, faster, and stronger.

Keeping in Touch with Summer Friends

Carolyn once spent a summer leading a troop of seventh graders into the wild. After two weeks of backpacking, kayaking, climbing, and bonding, the kids were given a big list of e-mail addresses and phone numbers, said their good-byes, and were packed off to their respective homes. Carolyn (about to return to Facebook headquarters) lamented the fact that the kids were too young to be on Facebook because they almost assuredly would lose that sheet of paper. Carolyn quickly "friended" her co-counselors (who were all old enough to be on Facebook) and keeps up with them through photo albums, notes, and the occasional Poke war. As an added bonus, years later, when her co-counselor needed a reference, he knew exactly where to find her.

Not just for Carolyn, but for thousands of high school students, the best-friends-for-the-summer — who had a tendency to fade away as school and life took over — are now a thing of the past. Camp friends immediately become Facebook friends, and on Facebook, no one gets lost. Plus, it's easy to share the memories of a fun summer via Facebook Photos. If you're interested in finding out what's new with your camp friends, they're only a click away. Additionally, it's easy to plan camp reunions without needing to find everyone's new info.

Preparing to Head Off to School

Everyone has a story about leaving for college. Whether they're dropping off a child or an older sister or heading off themselves, people remember some form of anxiety, nervousness, or blinding fear of the unknown. Who were these people in the hallway or sharing the bathroom? Who was this so-called roommate?

Now, college students go off to school having been introduced to their future dorm mates, roommates, and residence assistants via Facebook. Students can list their residences and easily pick out the people they'll most likely meet on the first day, thus dulling the fear that they won't know anyone.

In the time between acceptance letters and orientation, college freshmen spend their time Wall posting, friending, and getting to know their future classmates. Therefore, they join groups and support one another through a big transition. Suddenly, school is less scary.

Going on Not-So-Blind Dates

Ever been a matchmaker? Ever had a particularly difficult "client" — a friend who has a million requirements for "the one"? Ever been embarrassed because you didn't realize just how picky your friend was until after the date? Enter Facebook. Now, "He's smart, funny, has a great job, lots of cool hobbies, a nice family, and nice friends" can be condensed into a Facebook message with a shared Profile. From there, both parties can decide based on the Profiles — looks, interests, or the combination of all the information — whether they want to go on a date.

Some of our friends have gone so far as to say, "No Profile, no date." Given the circumstances, this is reasonable. Not only do you get a little window into a person's world, but you also prepare for talking about the various interests and activities that you see there. This way, "So I saw you like snorkeling. Where does one do that when you live in Idaho?" can be a much better conversation starter than, "So, what do you do?"

Think of it as *far-sighted* dating rather than blind dating.

Meeting People in Your New City or Town

When Leah moved to California from Seattle, the first thing she did was look up all the people she knew who were in the Brown University network and who also listed their current city as San Francisco. She figured it was as good a place as any to get a handle on what her new social life was going to be.

Many people are making themselves comfortable this way in new cities around the world. Carolyn got the following message from her friend, Shelby, who was living in Abuja, Nigeria, at the time.

> So I was friends with this Marine in Liberia. We lost touch when I left Liberia. He joined Facebook two weeks ago, and requested me as a friend. We started talking again. He put me in touch with a friend who works for the U.S. Consulate in Lagos, Nigeria. I Facebooked her. She found my blog address on my Facebook Profile, and forwarded it to her friend who works for the U.S. Embassy in Abuja.

> Tonight, I went out with this girl from the Embassy and a bunch of other Embassy people. And I have plans (finally!!) for a couple of days next week with these people.

> And all of this is because of Facebook.

Shelby's story is just one example of how Facebook makes moving less of an ordeal — a neighborhood is waiting for you when you arrive.

Reconnecting with Old Friends

Long-lost friends. The one who got away. I wonder whatever happened to her. Have you heard about him? These are just some of the ways people talk about the people they somehow lost track of along the way. Whatever the reason for the loss, this sort of regret can be undone on Facebook. Finding people is easy, and getting in touch is, too.

Many recent graduates exclaim that going to a reunion is unnecessary — you already know what everyone is doing five years later; you found out from Facebook. But even for the not-so-young alums, the Find Classmates and Find Coworkers features provide a direct line to search anyone who's on Facebook that you remember from way back (or not so way back) when.

Facebook gets e-mails every so often about people who find birth parents or biological siblings on Facebook. However, the majority of the time, people are looking for and finding their old classmates and reminiscing about the good old days. Better yet, they are reigniting a spark in a friendship that can last far into the future.

Keeping Up with the 'rents

Face it: Keeping your parents in touch with everything that's going on is difficult. However often you speak, it sometimes feels as though you're forgetting something. And visits often feel rushed, as though you don't have enough time to truly catch up.

Facebook Photos and Video applications are two of the best ways to easily and quickly share your life with your parents. Because you can upload photos so quickly, they can feel as though they were present at the *<insert activity here>*. Whether a dance, party, or concert, it's as though you came home and immediately called to tell them about it.

Additionally, Facebook creates the casual interactions that are so often missing from a long-distance parentship. The *How was your day?* is reinstated by daily status updates. *Good morning* replaced with Poke. If you still don't feel as though you're actually home for a visit, you could add a game like Lexulous, an application that lets you play Scrabble with anyone (at any time) from anywhere in the world. It's perhaps the best way to keep in touch with your parents.

Your parents might want to keep their family separate from their Facebook friends, especially if they use it for networking or professional reasons. Respect your parents' boundaries (as we advise them to respect yours in the next section), and all will be well.

Keeping Up with the Kids

If you've read much of this book, you know (from your authors' gentle reassurances) that everyone is welcome on Facebook and that Facebook is for everyone. If you happen to be the parent of a teenager, you may hear a distinctly different story, something more along the lines of, "Stay out of my life!" followed by the sound of a slamming door.

Well, Facebook *is* for everyone, and it can be a great way to keep up with your children when they go away to college and beyond. Our parents love the ability to look at our photos, Poke us when we haven't called, and say things like, "Your status said that you're stressed. Is everything okay?" If you're looking to be friends with your child on Facebook, here are some tips:

- ✔ **Respect their boundaries.** At some ages, kids just don't want their parents to have access to their social life. Don't be hurt if your child doesn't accept your friend request or doesn't let you see all of her info. Like all relationships on Facebook, share what you're comfortable with, and your kids can share what they're comfortable with.

- ✔ **Don't friend all of their friends unless given permission.** As funny as it can be to say, "See? Johnny thinks it's cool that I'm on Facebook," this can also be really irritating and breaks Rule 1: Respect boundaries.

- ✔ **Have your own social life.** Yes, Facebook can be a great way to feel connected with your child at any distance, but use Facebook to connect with your own friends and share content with everyone — friend and family alike.

- ✔ **Don't worry too much.** Yes, you might see some parts of your child that you didn't know about. Just as you're a wonderful, multifaceted human (as represented by your Profile), so too is your child. Get excited that you're getting to know the person you helped shape.

Assuming that your child accepts your friend request, start keeping up. It's easy to check her Wall if you haven't heard from her in a few days, weeks, or months. A simple status like *Carolyn is writing Facebook For Dummies all the time* can explain a lot of lost phone time. (Sorry, mom and dad!)

Facebooking for Food (or Jobs)

If you've ever found yourself job hunting, you probably are acquainted with the real-world version of *networking.* You ask friends for their friends' numbers and job titles; you take people out to coffee; you go on interviews; you decide whether the company is right for you; you repeat the whole process.

Although finding the right job hasn't gotten any easier with Facebook, a lot of the intermediate steps have. Asking your friends for their friends' info is as easy as writing a note. Better yet, scan through your friends' networks to see whether any of them are working at companies that interest you. After you receive some names, send them a Facebook message (or e-mail, whichever is most appropriate) to set up the requisite "informational coffee date."

After interviewing, a great way to get information about a company is to talk to people who work there. Use Find Coworkers to search people who've listed that company in their Profiles.

The only caveat to this approach is that you're now using Facebook to represent a professional portion of your life. If you contact people via Facebook and they feel a little uncomfortable with the content in your Profile, whether that's your Profile picture, a recent status that can be easily misinterpreted, or a Wall post from a friend that reveals just a little too much information, it could make a bad first impression — just as if you'd shown up to the interview in torn jeans and the shirt you slept in. As a well-educated user of Facebook (because you *have* read all previous 16 chapters without just skipping directly to this one, right?), you're well aware of the myriad privacy settings that enable you to tailor what different parties see and don't see. However, if anything on your Profile might be particularly misunderstood, simply hide it until you sign your offer letter.

Goin' to the Chapel

A small bit of Facebook trivia: There has, in many circles, arisen the idea of *Facebook Official (FBO)* — the act of moving from *single* to *in a relationship* and listing the person that you're in a relationship with on your Profile. For any fledgling couple, this is a big deal for their personal lives; however, becoming Facebook Official also serves notice to friends and anyone who happens upon one's Profile: I'm taken.

Because of this relationship function, Facebook has become the fastest way to spread a wedding announcement to extended friend groups. Of course, people still call their parents and their closest friends, but *everyone* can find out and share in the happiness via News Feed. Congratulatory Wall posts ensue, as do copious numbers of photos with *the ring* tagged front and center.

Once the wedding has taken place, Facebook becomes a wonderland of virtual congratulations as well as photos of the big day (see Figure 17-1). And in case anyone missed it, they can share in the after-party online.

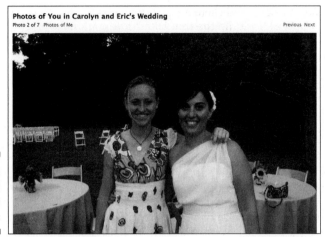

Photos of You in Carolyn and Eric's Wedding
Photo 2 of 7 Photos of Me   Previous Next

Figure 17-1:
Leah and
Carolyn at a
wedding.

Hey, Facebook Me!

Before Facebook, in both romantic and platonic contexts, it was hard to get from "Nice to meet you" to "Will you be my friend?" Now, the simple phrase, "Facebook Me!" expresses this sentiment and so much more. "Facebook Me!" can mean, *get in touch, look me up,* or *I want you to know more about me* but in a pressure-free way. It doesn't mean *take me to dinner,* or *let's be best friends forever and ever.* It's simply a way to acknowledge a budding friendship.

"Facebook Me!" can also be how good friends say, "Keep up with my life; I want you to know about it," which acknowledges that people are busy and that it's difficult to find time to see each other or talk on the phone. However, even when people are incredibly busy, a quick check on Facebook can make you feel connected again and secure that your friend is doing well.

Chapter 18

Ten Questions That Leah and Carolyn Get a Lot

In This Chapter

▶ Is my computer infected with a virus?

▶ How do I convince my friends to join Facebook?

▶ What if I don't want everyone knowing my business?

*H*aving worked for Facebook, Leah and Carolyn often get an insider's look at the specific complications, confusions, and pain points people come across while using Facebook. At dinner parties, group functions, family events, or even walking across the street wearing a Facebook hoodie, someone always has a suggestion or a question about how to use the site. It's understandable. Facebook is a complex and powerful tool with a ton of social nuances, much of which has yet to be standardized. Questions like "When should I send a Facebook message instead of an e-mail?" "When is it OK to request someone be my friend?" and "How do I turn down requests?" are popular questions for which there are no concrete answers because the social norms are still being formed. However, because your authors have heard a lot from friends, our families, and strangers about the experiences they've had on the site, we have been able to form some opinions about and recommendations for some of the fuzzier Facebook questions.

What follows are the questions Leah and Carolyn hear most often from friends and family, often with strain in their voices or pain in their eyes. The goal of highlighting the more complicated questions is to save you the stress of encountering these issues yourself and wondering if you're the only one who just doesn't get it.

Is My Computer Infected with a Virus?

A virus is such a total bummer, and if your computer is infected with one, you have our deepest, most sincere sympathies. But first, make sure you really have one. One of the main ways that people discover they've picked up a virus through Facebook is when a friend receives a message from them that looks like spam. If this situation happens to you, your first step should be to change your password by clicking the Forgot Your Password link from the log-in page, or going to Account settings. Often, viruses hack an account and change the associated e-mail address or password to take control. If you can't change your password, that's probably what happened. If that's the case, contact Facebook customer support immediately by clicking the Help link and searching for "hacked" for related questions and answers. Finally, you should run a virus scan of your computer to help remove any malware that might have ended up on your computer as a result.

Much more information about Facebook-related viruses can be found at www.facebook.com/security. You'll find recommended virus scanners, steps for fixing problems, and information about any new viruses as they crop up. By liking the Facebook security page, you can get information in your News Feed from the Facebook security team, which can help keep you on the lookout for any suspicious-looking links. That, in turn, brings us to the most important reminder about viruses.

The best way to deal with a virus is not to get it in the first place. The best way to *not* get a virus on Facebook is this: Don't click on any links you don't trust. When a friend sends you a link through a message or a Wall post, make sure that the friend's message is significantly personal to your relationship, such as "Hey, Mom, remember how we were talking about the singularity the other day? Check out this video." If it's impersonal, such as, "Hi! Check out this link, you'll like it." That's a vague message that could easily be a virus in disguise. Second, check whether you recognize the domain name of the link. URLs for well-known sites such as www.youtube.com, www.facebook.com, www.flikr.com, and so on are likely legitimate. If you don't recognize the URL, don't click. Instead, write back to your friend and ask him if he meant to send you the message. If he did, no harm, no foul. If he didn't, you've just alerted him that he has a virus, and you should tell him about the Facebook security page and recommend a good virus scanner.

Do People Know When I Look at Their Profiles?

No. No. And oh, yeah, no. When people see stories about their friends pop up on their home page, they sometimes get a little anxious that this means Facebook is tracking everything everyone does and publishing it to everyone else. That's not true. Consider two types of actions on Facebook: creating content and viewing it. Creating content means you've intentionally added something to Facebook for others to look at or read, such as uploading a photo or a video, writing a note, or posting a status. These types of actions are all publishable posts — that is, stories about them may end up on your

Profile or in your friends' News Feeds — although you have direct control over who exactly gets to see these posts. The other type of action on Facebook is viewing content such as flipping through photos, watching a video, following a link, or viewing someone's Profile. Unless someone is looking over your shoulder as you browse, these types of actions are strictly private. No one is ever directly notified about them, and no trace of the fact that you took that action is left on your Profile or in your friends' News Feeds. So now you can check people out to your heart's content.

I Have a Problem with My Account — Can You Help Me?

Carolyn and Leah frequently are asked to help fix the accounts of friends and friends of friends and friends of friends of friends of . . . well, you get the idea. Sometimes the problems are Facebook's fault, and sometimes they are user error, but either way, you'll be surprised to learn that, quite often, we *can't* help fix most account problems. The main reason for this is that many account problems can be resolved only by employees with special access to the specific tool required to fix an account. Here are a few of the account questions we've received recently, and the answers given:

- ✔ **I can't remember my password. Can you reset it for me?** Answer: No can do. Resetting a password requires a special tool — it also requires that an employee verifies you are who you say you are by verifying your answer to your security question. This prevents someone from pretending an account is hers and duping an employee into handing over access.

- ✔ **My account got deactivated because it said I was sending too many messages. Why? Can you fix it?** Answer: Leah recently had this happen to two friends, one who was using his account to promote his music career, and one who was distributing his poetry to many, many friends through messages. This is Facebook spam detection at work. When an account starts sending a lot of messages in quick succession, especially when those messages contain links, this looks a lot like spam to the system. In most cases, the person is warned first, but if the behavior continues, his account is disabled. The only way to have this action reversed is to write in through the Help pages and request reactivation. To write in, click on Help Center at the lower-left of any Facebook Page. Look for a FAQ titled My Account Is Disabled from the Site, and follow the instructions for requesting reactivation. This can sometimes take several days.

- ✔ **I changed my name to a fake one as a joke, and now I can't change it back, can you do it for me?** Again, a special tool is required. Click the Help Center link at the bottom of any Facebook Page, and search for Name Change. The first FAQ gives you directions and a link to write in and request a name change. These requests may take up to a week to fulfill. This example also serves as a heads-up to everyone else. Facebook allows only one name change before requiring people to write in and get permission for a change. This requirement preserves the authenticity of the accounts. During the 2008 U.S. presidential election, many Facebook users added the middle name "Hussein" to show their support of Barack Hussein Obama. The fact that you still see so many at the site with this name reflects the fact that people used up their name changes and can't change them back without writing in.

What Do I Do with Friend Requests I Don't Want to Accept?

This is a tough question. As far as we know, there isn't exactly a social convention for this yet, so the answer to this question is pretty personal. Just know that there are a number of actions you can take:

- ✔ **Many people just leave the request sitting there forever.** Carolyn and Leah don't recommend this action because it just clutters up your account — it's better to make a decision.

- ✔ **Click Ignore.** This is Leah's favorite option. Although people are never directly notified that you've rejected their request, they may notice later that you're not friends and make the correct inference you did not accept. If you do ignore a request, you also need to prepare your follow-up if she asks you about why you ignored her request. Because there is no social convention for this situation just yet, most responses work well here, such as "I'm sorry, I like to keep my friend list down to only my closest friends," or "It's OK. I don't use Facebook often anyway." You can try "Weird, Facebook must have messed up, I don't think I got it," but then you'll have to accept her request when she likely tries again.

- ✔ **If you don't want to accept because you don't want that person having access to your Profile, we recommend adding him to a special restricted Friend List (see Chapter 5).** You can go into your Privacy settings and exclude that friend list from seeing any parts of your profile. Then anyone you add to that list will be restricted. In this way, you can accept the friend request without giving up access to your Profile.

- ✔ **If you don't want to accept because you don't want to read about that person in your News Feed, no problem!** Simply hit Accept. The first time she shows up in News Feed, hit the Hide button at the upper-right of the story. This action removes her from your News Feed for good until you choose to add her back.

What's the Difference between Facebook, MySpace, Twitter, and LinkedIn?

It's likely there are graduate students across the globe writing theses on this particular topic. Needless to say, it's a tough question to answer in a paragraph or casual conversation, so anything you read here is a gross generalization and subject to opinion:

✔ **MySpace has its origins as a tool for local bands to promote their music.** Because many people love music, many people flocked to MySpace (www.myspace.com) in order to connect with their favorite musical artists. A key rule of advertising is to go where the people are, and because so many people were going to MySpace, other businesses and celebrities got involved to garner public attention as well. To this day, MySpace is still oriented toward the relationships between people and media and people and celebrities. The site is designed in a way to make it maximally easy for popular figures to achieve wide distribution and large audiences, or even for everyday Janes and Joes to become popular figures.

✔ **LinkedIn is a tool geared to help people connect primarily for business purposes.** LinkedIn (www.linkedin.com) users try to connect with as many people as they can so that if and when they need a new job or they're looking for someone to hire, they can flip through a vast network of friends and friends of friends to find a reliable lead. People can write and request letters of recommendation for one another, and often recruiters reach out to LinkedIn users whether they're actively looking for a job or not.

✔ **Twitter allows people to engage in real-time sharing.** Whenever a Twitter member has something interesting to share, he blasts out some text, 140 characters or less, that everyone who is "following" him has the option to see. What differentiates Twitter (www.twitter.com) from Facebook is its extreme simplicity and single focus on real-time exchange of ideas. Facebook is a place where you build longstanding relationships with people; you have access to their static content like their phone numbers and photos; you can message them privately or interact with them through groups and events. Twitter is a place where your friends (and anyone else) find out the information you're sharing at any given time, and vice versa. Popular uses of Twitter are link sharing for interesting Web sites and news, short opinions about current events, and enabling people to meet up when two people are out and about at the same time.

I Keep Getting Invites for Those App Thingies — Should I Accept Them?

Here's how your authors would handle this situation: Accept the invitation if the app invite is from a company or Web site you already use and like *or* if you've heard personal accounts from friends that a particular application is worth trying out. Ignore the rest. Your friends won't be offended, or if they are and ask you about it later, you can just tell them you weren't sure what it was. (It's easy to play dumb when you have a copy of *Facebook For Dummies* sitting on your shelf.) Leah personally uses only two or three applications and has probably ignored 30 or 40 requests. The whole notion of applications on Facebook is still a bit of a work in progress — one day, we expect that we'll find more worthwhile applications we can accept, but for now, feel free not to accept anything that confuses you.

How Do I Convince My Friends to Join Facebook?

One sneak attack we don't recommend is creating a fake account for your friend and interacting with his friends on his behalf. This is against the Terms of Use, but we've seen it be highly effective in convincing a hapless victim to come take the reins on an account that's out there acting on his behalf. Careful with that strategy if you want to retain your friendship.

Other methods involve showing (rather than telling) your friend the value by sending him links to the photos you post on Facebook, putting his e-mail address on the invite of event and group invitations, or even sending him links and messages (again, by putting his e-mail address on the To line) from the Facebook Inbox.

You can tell her anecdotally the ways in which Facebook has enriched your life. Maybe you're interacting with your kids more, you're keeping in touch with friends you thought were lost, or you have a place to put your thoughts and photos where your friends might actually see them. You can let her look over your shoulder as you use the site so that she can see the experience herself — ask her questions about whether there's anyone in particular she'd like to look up. The more information she sees about the people she cares about, the more likely she is to take the next step.

One common complaint from people who haven't joined the site is that they "don't have time for yet another computer thing." To this concern, one common response is that Facebook is an efficiency tool that often saves a person time compared to using old-school methods. Messaging can often replace e-mail, and events are easier to coordinate over Facebook. Sharing phone numbers is easier. Sending and receiving links is easier. Finding rides to the airport, restaurant recommendations, and who is heading to the park on Saturday are all faster and easier than trying to use e-mail, phone, or other methods of communication.

Finally, for some people, it's just not their time. No matter what you say, they'll stick their fingers in their ears and sing la-la-la until you start talking about sports or the weather or the circus coming to town next week. You can't force them to Facebook; you have to let Facebook come to them. Over the years, Carolyn and Leah have watched many a nonbeliever eventually cross over and discover the value. Patience may be your only weapon for these diehards.

What if I Don't Want Everyone Knowing My Business?

To those who ask that question and don't have time to read Chapter 5 of this book, which goes into great detail about how to be a private person on Facebook, we simply try to impart the following message: You can be an extremely private person and still derive nearly all the same value out of Facebook as anyone else. All you have to do is learn how to use the Privacy control and lock down all your information and access to your Profile, ensuring that only those you trust can see your info. From there, you can interact in all the same ways as anyone else without feeling like your privacy is being compromised.

Note: Besides learning the Privacy settings and taking the initial time to adjust yours until they feel just right, you will have to do a little extra work to be private on Facebook and still derive comparable value. You'll likely have to put in extra effort connecting with friends, because the more locked-down your information is, the harder you make it for not-yet-Facebook-friends to find your Profile, and the harder it is for your friends to find you, identify you, and connect with you. As long as you're willing to do the work of seeking out your friends and connecting with them, however, your experience should be nearly identical with everyone else's.

I Heard Facebook Owns Everything I Put on its Site — True?

In a legal sense, yes. You also own everything you put on Facebook, and whenever you delete any of your content, it will be deleted by Facebook. What Facebook doesn't own (but you do) is the right to transfer ownership of any of your content to anyone else. So it's completely illegal for anyone else to take your content from Facebook and use it for their own or any commercial use. In early 2009, many Facebook users banded together to express concern about this legal stipulation (which exists for any site you upload content to, by the way). In response, Facebook published a statement of rights and responsibilities that makes a commitment about what Facebook will and won't do with your information. These commitments were voted on by every Facebook user who chose to participate, and the commitments govern the company's use of any material you add to the site. Read about these rights and responsibilities in greater detail at `www.facebook.com/terms`.

Does Facebook Have a Feature That Lets Me Lock Myself Out for a Few Hours?

Short answer: not really.

Long answer: Many people do deactivate their accounts, their reason being "I spend too much time using Facebook." The benefit of such an action is that you're guaranteed not to get notifications about messages, picture tags, Wall posts, or anything else. The downside is that it will cause a lot of confusion among your friends who suddenly can't message you, tag you, or write on your Wall. If they have your e-mail address, they're likely to bug you anyway to ask why you disappeared from Facebook.

The reason it's not a real solution is because all you have to do to reactivate at any time is to enter your password (just like signing in), and you're completely back to normal. So if you're remotely curious how your social group has evolved without you, you might have trouble truly staying away. Which brings us to our next suggestion: Have some self-control. Just like many good things in life, the key to keeping them good is moderation. French fries are delicious, but too many give you a tummy ache. Dancing is a blast 'til your feet are full of blisters. Television is educational and entertaining until it's 3 a.m., you're watching your fifth infomercial, you forgot to feed the cat and put out the trash, and you find yourself wondering what life is all about. Facebook is no different. It's a brilliant utility when used to make your life easier and your social interactions richer. When you find yourself flipping through two-year-old vacation photos of a friend of a friend of a friend of a friend, it's time to blink a few times, step away from the mouse, and go out for ice cream, or dancing, or whatever else it is that gives you joy.

Chapter 19
Ten True Facebook Tales

In This Chapter

▶ Finding true love, a baby, a parent
▶ Facing down terrorists
▶ Electing a president

*W*e hope we've impressed upon you all of the awesome ways Facebook can impact your life and how you communicate and share with your friends, but you may still think we're pretty far from the truth. However, truth is indeed stranger than fiction, and trust us, there are endless possibilities for what Facebook might wind up meaning to you. If you're still skeptical, take the following true tales as our proof, although by all means, imagine us with flashlights below our chins as we tell them.

If you're looking for more stories like these, pay attention to your local news or even national news. More and more, Facebook gets referenced as a source, a cause, or the news itself. Also, poll your friends. Chances are many of them have their own true tales about finding a long-lost friend, reconnecting with an estranged family member, or improving a strained relationship through Facebook.

I'm Kelly — I'm Kelly, Too

According to ABC News (www.abcnews.com), Florida resident Kelly Hilderbrandt (woman) was curious who else in the world shared her exact same name. She went on to Facebook and searched for it. She found exactly one match: Kelly Hilderbrandt (man), living in Texas at the time.

According to she-Kelly, he-Kelly's Profile picture was rather attractive, so she sent him a message, and they began a long-distance friendship. Eventually, they decided to meet in person, and their long-distance friendship blossomed into a romance, and eventually, an accepted marriage proposal.

If you're single, running out of options, and have a first name that could be shared by someone of the gender you prefer to date . . . just know, it might work for you, too.

One Million Voices

If you ever doubted the ability of one person to make a difference, we encourage you to read more about Oscar Morales, the creator of a Facebook group called *"Un Millon de voces contra las FARC."* FARC is a terrorist organization in Colombia that is said to have taken more than 700 hostages. Oscar Morales at first intended just to start a Facebook group, but as it quickly grew (according to the BBC, 250,000 users quickly signed up), it soon became a full-fledged, worldwide demonstration.

As reported in the BBC, in more than 100 cities worldwide, between 500,000 and 2 million people showed up to march in a demonstration. They wore the group's slogan, which roughly translates to: "No more kidnapping, no more lies, no more deaths, no more FARC."

Although it's unclear what the lasting effect of such a demonstration will have on its targets, what is clear is that one person can reach thousands upon thousands of other people. The little diagrams of a completely interconnected world aren't just the stuff of airline magazines; it can happen.

Facing Autism

Barbara Fischkin wrote her story for Facebook as part of Autism Awareness Month. The story was published on the Facebook blog in April 2009. Her son, Dan Fischkin, 21, suffers from a severe form of adult autism. Due to his condition, he had formed very few social connections throughout his life.

His mother once blogged about her son's condition, and a woman with a high-functioning form of the same type of autism reached out to Ms. Fischkin and asked to connect with Dan on Facebook. Due to the specific nature of Dan's autism, Facebook turned out to be a much more comfortable way for him to interact with people. It offers lots of pictures, brief text exchanges, and most importantly, the ability to meet people from all over who understand, from personal experience, what Dan is going through. Through this first friendship, and a group of Facebook members with a similar form of autism, Dan's social group grew.

After a number of months on the site, Dan developed a rich social life, consisting of more than 150 online friends. His mother expresses how watching him interact with friends has taught her much about his social interactions.

Bringing Home Baby

John and Molly Connelly had been looking to adopt a baby for a long time, and they had been through the wringer already. Birth mothers had backed out on them, they'd had trouble with an agency they were using, but they pressed on, deciding to start marketing themselves as parents. They created a Web site and a Facebook group in 2009 called "John and Molly looking to adopt." When Valerie, a woman looking for a good home for her soon-to-be-born child ran a search online for adoptions, John and Molly's group came up.

Valerie was able to get to know John and Molly through their group, their Profiles, and their friends. She agreed to have them adopt her child, and sure enough, in January 2010, John and Molly were able to update their Facebook supporters with good news: They had a son.

Twenty-Year Reunion

As reported on Canada.com, a mother who had given her son up for adoption when she was only 17 later found him through Facebook. She described how she'd wanted to find him her whole adult life, but the nature of the adoption records left her clueless because all she had was a name.

Eventually, a friend recommended that she try to find him on Facebook, where she could look him up by name, and also see a picture that might give her some clue. According to mom, a number of results matched her son's name, but one picture gave him away. She sent him a message tentatively asking about his identity. He, knowing right away that this was the birth mother he'd also been wanting to meet, wrote right back. His adoptive family was supportive of their reunion, and the two have grown very close since their first meeting.

Activism Like an Egyptian

As Facebook spreads across the world, people within every country can be more connected and more organized. This was the case in Egypt, where

Facebook was widely used to coordinate political dissent and activism like marches, protests, and boycotts. In particular, a group of Facebook activists called for one nationwide strike in May 2008 to protest the rising prices of food and other basic commodities. As reported by *The Wall Street Journal*, Facebook activists were detained by the government. Their imprisonment, including that of Esraa Abdel Fattah, was protested on Facebook as well.

The story of activists being arrested by their own government is never a happy one to tell. But the fact is that in this case, such an act was not quietly hushed up; her arrest was not a secret act. Rather, it drew more notice to the cause, and *they could not be silenced.* The fact that so many young people (indeed, people of all ages) had a forum with which to connect — that they could do more than pass out fliers or mark money to let people know about protests and events — speaks volumes about the future of all nations.

Kids with Compassion

As a freshman in high school, Brett Bassock wanted to do something for his grandmother, Elaine Fox, who suffered from Parkinson's. He started a group on Facebook, pledging to donate 17 cents to Parkinson's research for each member who joined. Elsewhere in the world, Michael J. Fox, the actor who has been living with Parkinson's for much of his adult life and has a Parkinson's Research foundation named after him, caught wind of the group. Actor Fox offered to sponsor the 17 cents himself in Grandma Fox's name.

At the time of reporting, the group had more than 6,000 members. At that time, Brett brainstormed other ways he could raise funds in honor of his grandmother. He started a Web site to organize walks for Parkinson's as well as brainstorming how to organize other events. Today, nearly 900 groups on Facebook organize people interested in Parkinson's Research. The Michael J. Fox Foundation has nearly 15,000 members.

Robyn Doolittle of the *Toronto Star* interviewed 13-year-old David Robertson about his use of Facebook for fundraising. At his fifth-grade birthday party, he asked his friends to donate money to the Santa Claus Fund, a drive put on by the *Toronto Star* that collects money to buy needy children gifts at Christmas. David raised $500 from people he knew, so he decided to expand his efforts to include people he didn't know. He started a group, pledging to give $1 to the fund for every person who joined his group. In a short time, his group had 120 members. It's a modest number, but probably a manageable amount when the chief donor makes his money through household chores.

Tons of causes on Facebook raise money and attention this way. It's an important way that charities can be brought to people's attention.

Virtual Support Network

In 2007, monk-led protests in Myanmar led to a massive crackdown on such demonstrations by the ruling junta. The junta tried to restrict images of their actions from leaking to the outside world, but with the Internet and Facebook chugging along, that effort proved to be impossible.

As reported by the Associated Press, the Facebook group, "Support the Monks' Protest in Burma," grew to more than 100,000 members in about ten days. Although it was started by someone in Britain, the group became a storage area for reports of what was happening from within Myanmar. Citizens posted photos, videos, and observations — the showdown couldn't be hidden from the outside world. Although the international connections couldn't physically support the monks and people of Myanmar, they could provide the global attention required to bring such showdowns to slightly better conclusions.

From a Skinny Kid to President

Now, we know the 2008 presidential election got almost no press coverage. The whole thing was a foregone conclusion, with almost no heat in the primaries, and certainly no voter interest in the general election. (Did we lay it on thick enough? We're just joshing you . . .) Well, if you can handle one more interesting look into how the presidency was won, regardless of your own personal vote, you need look no further than Facebook. As reported in *The Washington Post* about a month after Barack Obama's win, it turned out the president-elect had a massive following on Facebook (see Figure 19-1).

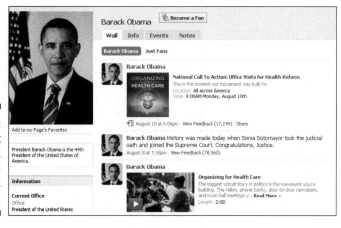

Figure 19-1:
President
Barack
Obama's
Facebook
page.

With more than 3.2 million listed supporters, Barack Obama was able to use the page he had created to drive traffic, organize rallies, and collect donations. He distributed content from the campaign trail on his page, and his supporters were able to interact with his team (and a little bit with him) directly. No one's saying that he couldn't have won the presidency without Facebook, but Facebook is one of many technologies that changed the way politicians campaign. Across the world, politicians can be found on Facebook, connecting with their constituents and trying to keep their jobs.

Index

• A •

abortion, 172
About (tab), 216
About Facebook link (Footer), 50
About Me section, 93
Abram, Carolyn (author), 27
Access My Profile information (link), 238
Access My Public Information (link), 237
Account. *See also* Event administrator;
　Group administrator
　administrative actions, 43–44
　applications settings, 254–256
　deactivation, 17–19, 308, 312
　dealing with problems, 307–308
　Events, 187
　flagging, 149
　navigating to settings, 43
　Page, signing up for, 207
　Page Manager, 210
　Privacy Settings, 71–79
　Profile, signing up for, 29–31
　removal of offenders, 67
　social plugin, signing up for, 243–245
　verification, 37–39
Action links. *See also* dashboard
　Events, 186
　Fan Page, 199
　Groups, 167
　Inbox, 147
　Profile, 96–97
active users, defined, 27
activism
　combating terrorism, 314
　global support of, 317
　political dissent, 315–316
activity partners
　finding, 24
　as friends, 52
Add <*Name*> as a Friend, 96–97
Add More (link), 127
Add Photos (link), 159
Add to My Page (link), 218

Administrators. *See* Event administrator;
　Group administrator; Page
　administrator
adoption, 26, 300, 315
advertising
　attention from, getting, 275–277
　business promotion and, 16–17
　campaigns and pricing, 284–286
　controlling spam, 289–290
　creating, 279–281
　engagement units, 277
　on Facebook, 23, 208
　Facebook rules, 278
　Home page links to, 49
　managing, 287–289
　promoting your Page, 222–223
　removal of Groups for, 172
　reviewing, 286–287
　social actions, 277–278
　social ads, 277
　targeting, 281–284
Advertising link (Footer), 50
age. *See* Birthdays
age restrictions
　advertising, 282
　am I too old?, 31
　am I too young?, 1, 18
　keeping in touch with students, 297–298
　Page, 219
　protecting minors, 82
AIM (AOL Instant Messenger), 59–60
albums. *See* Photo albums
Allow (application prompt), 121
Allow Admins (prompt), 176
Amazon (web site), 296
answering Questions, 126
Application Directory, 218–219
Application Fan Page, 254–256
Applications. *See also* Facebook Platform
　account settings, 44, 254–256
　action links, 239
　adding tabs for, 216
　common features, 118
　creating, 15–16

Applications *(continued)*
dashboards and bookmarks,
48, 239–240, 251–252
default settings, 47–48, 215
Events, 183–184
Fan Page, 198–199
Groups, 164–165
Home page link to, 47–48
invitations, 242, 310
More Applications box, 218–219
Notes, 134
Page, 215–219
Photos and Videos, 118–119
photo-sharing, 89, 118, 235
privacy controls, 75–79, 103, 118, 256–257
privacy protection, 218
Profile boxes, 98–99
reporting inappropriate content, 80–81
Reviews, 216, 218
social plugin, 243
third-party, 235, 258, 293–296
touch screen devices, 250–251, 272–273
trustworthy, 253
Windows as platform for, 234
Applications Settings (page), 254–256
Approve (application prompt), 121
Ask a Question (link), 89, 126, 159
assumptions about you, 2
attachment options
messages, 144
Page Updates, 226–227
attendance status (Events), 185
audience engagement. *See also* advertising;
business promotion
about using Facebook for, 1–2
creating a Page for, 205
user statistics, 210, 227–229
authentication, identity, 37–39
Autism Awareness Month, 314–315
autocomplete, 93

• B •

Barack Obama (Page), 317–318
Basic Directory Information
biographical information, 92–94
Preview My Profile, 73

Privacy Settings, 71–74
public information, 237
basic information
Events, 185–187
Fan Page, 198–199
Groups, 166, 167, 173–175
Page, 212
Profile, 93
Bassock, Brett (student), 316
Beatles Fans Around the World (Group),
164–165, 166, 168
Bebo (social networking site), 19
best practices, applications, 258
BFF (best friends forever), 52
Big Events, creating, 189–192
Bio box (Profile), 97
biographical information. *See* basic
information
birth families, finding, 26, 300, 315
Birthdays
default settings, 105
as Events, 185
on Facebook Mobile, 269
hiding, 30, 159
Home page link to, 46
notification, 91
privacy controls, 76, 104–105, 256
signing up for an account, 30
using Groupcard, 294
Wall posts, 99, 159
Blockbuster (Page), 217, 243
Blocking/block list
applications, 257
privacy controls, 76–78, 103
blogging. *See* Notes
blue navigation bar
bottom of the page, 49–50
top of the page, 41–44
bookmarklet, 152
bookmarks
applications, 47–48, 240, 255–256
Facebook Mobile, 269
sharing, 152
Boxes tab (Profile)
about, 34
Action links, 96–97
adding applications, 240–242

Applications, 98–99
an "at-a-glance" look at you, 36
Bio box, 97
Friends box, 97–98
Profile picture, 96
browser. *See* Web browser
*Building Facebook Applications for
Dummies* (Wagner), 233
business Profiles, 205
business promotion. *See also* advertising;
    Fan Page; Page
applications, 250
becoming a fan, 24
categories of Profiles, 205
creating a Page, 99, 201–202, 207–210
LinkedIn, 19, 309
targeted advertising, 16–17
Wall posts, 108–109
buying merchandise, 294

• *C* •

campaigns, advertising, 284–286
Canada, 28, 265, 315
CAPTCHA (security check)
confirmation of account, 30
identify verification, 37–39
preventing spam, 82
captions (photos), 128
Careers link (Footer), 50
Carpool by Zimride (application), 295–296
category/type
business, 205, 210
Events, 186
Groups, 166, 169, 174
Causes (application), 237–243
celebrity connections
joining Groups, 164–165
MySpace, 19, 309
Pages for, 206
using Suggestions for, 13
cell phones. *See* Facebook Mobile; mobile
    phones; texting/text messages
censorship, 18–19
Change Picture link (Profile), 96
charitable causes, 316
Chat
components, 153–155
Facebook links to, 48, 152

finding friends with, 59–60
options, 155
Pop In/Pop Out option, 154–155
sending flirting messages, 22–23
Choose a Thumbnail (link), 150
Chrome web browser, 152
city of residence
Friend List, 64
Groups, 175
privacy controls, 73
setting up your Profile, 32
classmate search, 61–62
Clicks and Impressions, 286, 288–289
closed Groups, 167, 169, 177
college networks, 19–20, 21, 27,
    31–33, 37, 61–62
Comment box, 246–247
comments
notification of, 139
on photos and videos, 131
on posts/posting, 118
as public communication, 160
social plugins for, 245–246
on status updates, 88
communicating. *See also* public
    communications
all about Facebook for, 1–2, 141
Chat feature, 152–155
Comments, 160
"Facebook Me!", 303
finding people, 13–14, 298–300
keeping in touch with family, 300–301
keeping in touch with people, 297–298
messages, 142–149
Notifications, 156–157
Poke feature, 155
Publisher, 160
Requests, 156
Share feature, 149–152
using a Page for, 203–204
Wall posts, 158–160
Community Page, 199–200
computer platform, 234–235
computer viruses, 67, 82, 305–306
confirmation of account, 30–31
Connect Web sites, 243–250
Connelly, John and Molly (adoptive
    parents), 315

contact information
  default settings, 34, 74, 104
  Groups, 166
  Page, 212
  privacy controls, 94, 104
  Profile, 35
contacts
  advertising targeted to, 283
  friends as, 52
  importing e-mail addresses of, 58–59
  sending friend requests to, 56–58
content ownership, 311–312
conventions, *Dummies*, 2–3
copyrighted materials, 18–19
costs
  advertising, 208, 284–289
  Facebook Page, 202
  Facebook payment plan, 10
  Sponsors help to cover, 49
  text messaging fees, 220, 265
country
  Page restrictions, 219
  user statistics, 229
coworker search, 62–63
Craigslist, 294
Create an Album (option), 120–123
credits balance, 44
cropping (photos), 127
CTR (click-through rate), 288–289
Custom Privacy settings
  limiting visibility with, 70–71
  options, 102–103
  photos and videos, 132–134

● *D* ●

dashboard
  applications, 239, 251–252
  Events, 183–184, 190
  games, 47, 76, 252
  Groups, 173
  music, 294
  Notes, 136
  Photos, 119–120
  privacy controls, 256–257
  Questions, 126
date of birth. *See* Birthdays
dating site, Facebook as, 93, 148,
      298–299, 313–314

deactivation, account, 17–19, 308, 312
default settings
  albums and videos, 133
  Applications, 47–48, 254
  Birthdays, 105
  contact information, 34, 74, 104
  Events, 190
  Groups, 172, 176
  News Feed, 111
  Page, 210, 214–215
  privacy controls, 71–72
  Profile, 36–37, 96–97
  Wall posts, 109, 169
Delete (albums, link), 127
demographics
  families and friends, 24–26
  interest groups, 26–27
  international expansion, 28
  life after being a student, 23–24
  student, 19–23
  target audience, 281–284
  too old for Facebook?, 31
  too young for Facebook?, 1, 18
  user statistics, 227–229
  workplace networks, 24
desktop application, 250
desktop e-mail client, 58
Developers link (Footer), 50
Digg (application), 295
Discography (application), 218
Discussion Board
  enabling, 176
  Groups, 166, 167, 169, 182
  notification of a reply, 157
  Page, 217, 225
Dogbook (application), 236
Doolittle, Robyn (newspaper reporter), 316
drawing pictures (application), 295
drugs, illicit use of, 172

● *E* ●

Edit Album, 127–130
Edit Info (albums, link), 127
Edit My Profile, 46, 96–97
Edit Photos (link), 127
Edit Thumbnail, 96
Edit Video (link), 130–131

editing
    Events, 194–195
    Page, 211
    Photos, 126–130
    Videos, 130–131
Education and Work
    advertising targeted to, 283–284
    classmate search, 61–62
    coworker search, 62–63
    history, 36
    importance of including, 94
    privacy controls, 73
    Profile tab, 35
Egypt, 315–316
e-mail addresses
    finding friends using, 13, 55–58
    Groups, 174
    identity verification, 37–39
    importing to Friend Finder, 58–59
    network authentication, 33
    privacy controls, 94
    signing up for an account, 29–31, 207
    uploading photos and videos, 261–262
e-mail messages
    Facebook compared to, 142–143
    links to your Page, 223
    subscribing to applications, 237–238
e-mail notifications, 157, 178, 182, 195
employment, finding, 23, 301–302
engagement units, 277
estimated reach, advertising, 283–284
etiquette. *See* rules, Facebook
Event administrator, 187
Event "crasher", 189
Events. *See also* RSVP
    about using Facebook for, 15, 22
    accessing the Home page, 46, 183–187
    canceling/editing, 194–195
    creating, 189–196
    default settings, 190
    example, 20
    on Facebook Mobile, 269
    finding, 188–189
    Groups, 168, 176, 182
    guest list, 195–196
    Home page reminder for, 48
    invitation reminders, 27
    messaging guests, 195
    notification of, 196

Page, 217, 225
    privacy controls, 186
Everyone
    access to public information, 237
    photo and video privacy, 132–134
    privacy options, 68, 102–103
exploring topics (Questions), 126

• **F** •

face books, 27
Facebook. *See also* Sharing on Facebook
    account deactivation, 17–19
    account settings, 43–44
    advertising, 208
    am I too old?, 31
    am I too young?, 1, 18
    birth of, 27
    comparison of Pages, Profiles, and
        Groups, 203–204
    comparison to networking sites, 309
    content ownership, 311–312
    covering the costs of, 10, 49
    deletion of Groups, 173
    demographics, 21–27
    impacts on daily life, 297–303, 313–318
    international expansion, 28
    organizing life with, 9–10
    questions asked about, 305–312
    rights and responsibilities, 311–312
    sharing with non-users, 134
    vanity URL/username, 222–223
    as verified network, 19–20
Facebook Insights, 227–229
Facebook logo, 42, 46
"Facebook Me!", 303
Facebook Mobile. *See also* mobile phones
    connecting with, 49, 260
    downloading to, 274
    Home page, 267–268
    messaging via, 38–39
    Notes, 265
    notifications, 265–266
    Photos, uploading to, 261–262
    real-time implications of, 53–54
    status updates, 220–221
    texting, 262–265
    using touch screen devices, 272–273

Facebook Mobile *(continued)*
  Wall posts, 264
  Web access, 266–272
Facebook Official, 35, 93, 302–303
Facebook Platform. *See also* Applications
  application use outside, 243–250
  application use within, 236, 239–243
  availability to developers, 233
  best practices for developers, 258
  described, 234–235
  finding applications, 251–253
  managing applications, 253–258
  other categories of applications, 250–251
  Request for Permission Page, 236–239
Facebook Plug-In, installation, 123
Facebook User Operations
  evaluates inappropriate content, 81–82
  investigates inappropriate use, 18
fake information
  be real and honest, 100–101
  don't use, 99
  privacy options, 106
fake names/accounts
  Name Change, 307–308
  reporting, 80–81
  signing up for an account, 29
  use for Pages, 209
  violation of Terms of Use, 17–18, 236
fake profiles, 37–39
family
  being real and honest with, 100–102
  finding birth parents, 300
  hiding information from, 25
  keeping in touch with, 24–25, 300–301
  Profile relationships, 35
  using News Feed with, 110
Fan Page, 198–199. *See also* Page
fans
  business promotion, 24
  connecting to a Page, 222–223
  friending a Page, 198–201
  message links to Pages, 46
  posting to a Page, 214–215
  updating, 224–226
  user statistics, 227–229
  Wall posts for, 108–109
FAQ. *See also* Questions
  application, 253
  Facebook, 305–312

FARC (Revolutionary Armed Forces of Columbia), 314
Fattah, Esraa Abdel (activist), 316
Favorite Books, 99
favorites. *See also* Likes and Interests
  privacy controls, 73
  Profile, 35
FBO. *See* Facebook Official
filtering
  Events search, 188–189
  finding and contacting friends, 23–24
  Friend List, 64–65
  Groups search, 170–171
  News Feed, 111, 112–113
  posts on friends' Profiles, 88
  Search terms, 114–115
Find Your Friends, 49
Firefox web browser, 137, 144, 152
Fischkin, Barbara (mother), 314–315
Fischkin, Dan (autistic child), 314–315
flirting. *See* gossip and flirting
Footer (links), 49–50
foreign languages
  <Language> link (Footer), 50
  translating Facebook to, 28
forwarding messages, 143
Fox, Elaine (grandmother), 316
Fox, Michael J. (actor), 316
Friend Finder
  adding friends by way of, 55–57
  classmate search, 61–62
  coworker search, 62–63
  getting started with, 31
  importing addresses, 57–59
  instant messaging with, 59–60
  making connections with, 13
  quick-search, 63
  Suggestions tool, 60–61
Friend List
  creating, 64–66
  editing, 43
  Facebook Mobile access, 271–272
  Home page link to, 47
  housecleaning, 67
  limiting visibility, 70–71
  privacy controls, 73, 104
  restricted lists, 308
  using Chat, 153–154
  using News Feed, 111

friend requests
  from family, 300–301
  ignoring/not accepting, 308
  notification of, 42
  privacy controls, 72
  random requests, 54
Friend Selector
  Events, 186–187, 191
  Groups, 178–179
  for Pages, 222–223
friends
  audience options, 68–69
  average numbers of, 55, 112
  being real and honest with, 100–102
  blind dates as, 298–299
  blocking, 76–78
  connecting with, 13–14, 49
  convincing them to join, 310–311
  counting, 249
  defined, 52
  "Facebook Me!", 303
  on Facebook Mobile, 264
  family as, 300–301
  finding, 31, 48–49, 299–300
  Groups membership, 171
  hiding from, 69, 71, 224
  Home page link to, 47
  ignoring requests, 308
  maintaining privacy, 53
  as members of Groups, 168
  privacy controls, 102–103, 256
  quality versus quantity, 54–55
  random requests, 54
  requests, 49
  school roommates, 298
  tagging notes, 138
  tagging photos of, 129
  unfriending (pruning), 67
  using applications, 253
  using News Feed with, 110
  to young to join Facebook, 297–298
Friends box (Profile), 97–98
Friends' Events
  Home page link to, 46
  viewing, 185, 189
Friends Groups, 171
Friends of Friends
  messaging, 148
  photo and video privacy, 132–134
  privacy options, 69

Friends Online, 153–155
Friends Only
  photo and video privacy, 132–134
  privacy options, 69
Friendster (social networking site), 19
FrontierVille (game), 238, 240, 252
fundraising, 316

• *G* •

games
  account settings, 44
  applications, 236, 296
  dashboard, 252
  Home page link to, 47
  privacy controls, 76, 256
Gawker (blog), 245
gender
  advertising targeted to, 282
  hiding, 30, 72
  Page setting for, 219
  privacy concerns, 72, 313–314
  relationship status and, 93
  signing up for an account, 30
Get Connected, Home page link to, 49
gifting
  account settings, 44
  as flirting message, 22–23
  notification of, 42
"Give My Regards to Broad Street"
    (McCartney), 166
gossip and flirting, 22–23, 158
Graffiti (application), 295
Group administrator
  access settings, 176–177
  basic duties of, 172
  basic information needed, 173–175
  creating Events, 182
  customizing options, 175–176
  designating officers, 179–180
  inviting people to join, 178–179
  managing the member list, 180
  messaging members, 182
  uploading pictures, 181
Groupcard (application), 238, 294
Groups
  about using Facebook for, 15
  access to, 169
  Action links, 167
  Administration section, 168

Groups *(continued)*
  Basic Information, 166, 167
  comparison to a Page, 203–204
  component tabs, 166–167
  creating and using, 26–27
  creating your own, 172–182
  default settings, 172, 176
  deletion from Facebook, 173
  described, 163
  discussion board, 166, 167, 169, 182
  fundraising, 316
  hiding information, 165
  Home page, 165
  Home page link to, 47, 163
  joining, 164–165
  inappropriate content, 80–81, 171–172
  notifications, 178, 180, 182
  Officers, 167–168
  Photos, 166–167
  Profile picture, 167
  searching for, 164, 169–171
  suggestions for, 171
  Videos, 167
  Wall, 166
  workplace networks as, 24
guarantee, money-back, 10
Guest List (Events), 195–196
gun control, 172

• H •

harassment, reporting, 80–81
Harvard University, 27
Help Center
  applications and tools, 44
  dealing with problems, 307–308
  Footer link, 50
  navigating to, 43
Hide/hiding
  birthdays, 30, 159
  from family, 25
  from friends, 69, 71, 224
  gender, 30, 72
  Group information, 165
  News Feeds, 53, 111, 201, 257, 308
  notifications, 157
  Profile information, 201, 302
  Wall posts, 109

high school networks, 19–20, 21, 27, 32–33, 61–62
Highlights. *See* News Feed
Home page (Event), 183–187
Home page (Facebook Mobile), 267–268
Home page (Group), 165
Home page (Profile)
  about what you see on, 44
  application links, 47–48
  bottom of the page links, 49–50
  Chat feature, 48
  left column links, 46–47
  navigating to, 42, 43
  News Feed, 45
  Publisher, 45
  right column links, 48–49
  using touch screen devices, 272–273
Home Stream. *See* News Feed
hometown
  building the Profile, 12, 36
  privacy controls, 73
  using Friend Lists, 111
HTML formatting, 136–137, 216
Hughes, Chris (Facebook founder), 27

• I •

icons
  Dummies use of, 5
  editing (pencil), 32, 34, 36, 93
  Home page, 42
  Messages (speech bubbles), 144–145
  Mobile for Pages, 221
  navigation bar (flag), 42, 146–147, 156
  Notifications (Globe), 156–157
  online status (green dot), 154
  privacy control (gray lock), 75
  Publisher (magnifying glass), 75
  Share (page outline), 150
  Video (camcorder), 126
ICQ Chat, finding friends, 59–60
identity
  lying or falsifying, 17–18
  Profile picture, 36–37
  signing up for an account, 29–30
  verification, 37–39
  verified networks, 19–20
identity theft, 67

iLike (music application), 294
illegal acts, 18–19, 199
illicit drugs, 172
importing, 138
inappropriate content
  Fan Pages, 199
  investigating, 18
  reporting, 80–81, 171–172
Inbox (link), 42. *See also* messages
Info tab (Page), 211–212
Info tab (Profile)
  about editing the fields, 92–93
  Basic Information section, 34–35, 93
  contact information, 94
  Education and Work section, 94
  Personal Information section, 93
  Photos, 94–95
  privacy controls, 94
Information Box, 36
information sections. *See* Basic Directory
    Information; basic information; contact
    information
instant messaging (IM), 59–60
Instant Personalization
  described, 76
  Opt In/Opt out, 249–250
  privacy controls, 257
Intellectual Property, violations of, 199
Interactions Graph, 227–229
Interested In (relationship status), 74, 93
interests. *See* Likes and Interests
Internet. *See* Web browser; Web sites
Internet Explorer web browser, 137, 152
invitations
  applications, 242, 310
  blocking, 77–78
  Events, 15, 186–187, 191, 195–196
  Friend List, 64–65
  guest list reminders, 27
  ignoring, 257
  to join Groups, 178–179
  pending requests, 49
  privacy controls, 257
iPhone/iTouch
  applications, 250–251
  using Facebook Mobile, 272–273

job hunting, 23, 301–302
"John and Molly looking to adopt"
    (Group), 315

Lady Gaga (application), 296
language
  advertising targeted to, 283–284
  translations, 28
<Language> link (Footer), 50
Lexulous (game application), 300
Like/liking
  becoming a fan, 199–201, 211, 226
  comments/notes, 139, 246–247
  Events, 194
  on posts/posting, 118
  social plugins for, 245–246
Likes and Interests
  advertising targeted to, 281–284
  Page, 200–201
  privacy controls, 73
  Profile, 34–35, 93
LinkedIn (social networking site), 19, 309
Links (application)
  avoiding computer viruses, 305–306
  Groups, 168, 176
  Home page access to, 47–48
  Page, 224–225
  reporting inappropriate content, 80–81
  sharing with Publisher, 90
Live Feeds. *See* News Feeds
Live Streams, 247–248
Living Social, Visual Bookshelf
    (application), 296
login
  applications, 243–245
  Facebook Mobile, 267
  Page account, 207–208
  Profile account, 31
logout
  ending your session, 44
  Facebook Mobile, 270
Looking For (relationship), 74, 93, 148–149
lying. *See* fake information; fake names/
    accounts

• M •

Make Profile Picture (link), 132
malicious applications, 218
Manage Pages (link), 43
Marketplace (application), 294
Marx, Groucho (comedian), 169
Match.com (social networking site), 19
McCartney, Paul (singer), 166
McCollum, Andrew (founder), 27
Meebo (social networking site), 19
meetings, planning, 15. *See also* Events
Members (Groups), 168
  invitations to join, 178–179
  managing the member list, 180–181
messages. *See also* Chat; Poke
  attachments, 144
  on Facebook Mobile, 264, 270–272
  Groups, 182
  Home page link to, 46
  to non-friends, 147–149
  notification of, 42
  Page Updates, 225–226
  privacy controls, 73
  as private communications, 142–143
  receiving, 144–147
  replying to, 144
  sending, 143–144
  threads, 145–147
  using Share feature, 149–150
  using the Share buttons, 150–152
  using touch screen devices, 272–273
Michael J. Fox Foundation, 316
Microsoft Docs (web site), 249
Microsoft Entourage, 58–59
Microsoft Outlook, 58–59
minors (under age 13)
  account restrictions, 1, 18
  privacy protection, 81–82
MMS. *See* multimedia messaging service
Mobile for Pages, 220–221
mobile phones. *See also* Facebook Mobile
  account verification via, 38–39
  social plugins, 250–251
Mobile Text, 262–265
Mobile Uploads
  additions and changes, 119
  Home page link to, 46

Morales, Oscar (Facebook member), 314
More Applications box (Page), 218–219
Moskovitz, Dustin (Facebook founder), 27
Most Recent (News Feed), 45, 112–113
moving/relocating, finding friends, 23, 299
multimedia messaging service (MMS), 262
music
  applications, 236
  Groups, 166
  sharing, 152
Music, by iLike (application), 294
My Draft (Notes link), 136
My Uploads
  additions and changes, 119
  Home page link to, 46
Myanmar, 317
MySpace (social networking site), 19, 309

• N •

name
  Group, 173
  Name Change, 307–308
  navigating to a Profile, 46
  selection for Pages, 209
  signing up for an account, 29
  vanity URL/username, 222–223
National Breast Cancer Foundation
      (Group), 166
navigation bar
  bottom of the page, 49–50
  on Facebook Mobile, 269
  top of the page, 41–44
networking, 301–302
networks
  Group, 173
  photo and video privacy, 133–134
  privacy options, 69–71, 102–103
  school, 19–20, 21, 27, 61–62
  types of, 32
  verification, 37
  when you can't join, 17
  why should I join, 33
New York Times (fan page), 198
news applications (Digg), 295
News Feeds (feature)
  as communications tool, 110–112
  default settings, 111

on Facebook Mobile, 269
filtering, 112–113
hiding, 53, 111, 201, 257, 308
keeping current with, 45
navigating to, 46
from Pages, 201
posting Events, 193–194
privacy controls, 257
promoting your Page, 223
real-time implications of, 53–54
status updates, 89, 224
writing a note for, 135–136
Nike (Page), 217
non-Facebook users
    convincing them to join, 310–311
    sharing with, 134
non-friends, messaging, 147–149
non-people entities, Pages for, 99, 197
Norway, 28
Notes
    as blogging tool, 47, 134
    on Facebook Mobile, 265
    formatting, 136–137
    Home page link to, 47
    importing a blog into, 138–139
    inserting photos into, 137–138
    Page, 224–225
    Profile link to, 99
    reading, liking, commenting, 139
    tagging, 118, 138
    writing, 135–136
notification
    birthdays, 91
    comments, 139
    described, 156–157
    discussion posts, 169
    Events, 196
    examples of, 157
    Facebook communications, 141, 157
    Groups, 178, 180, 182
    hiding, 157
    for looking at Profiles, 306–307
    photo upload, 123
    tagged photos, 129
    video upload, 124
Notifications (Globe icon), 42, 156–157
Notifications page, 157
nudity, 172

• O •

Obama, Barack, 308, 317–318
offensive/inappropriate content
    Groups, 171–172
    investigating, 18
    Profiles, 80–81
Official Fan Page, 198–199. *See also* fans
offline relationships. *See* relationships
The Onion magazine (Page), 212–213
open conversations. *See* public
    communications
open Groups, 167, 176
operating system, computer, 234
Opt In, updates, 227
Opt Out, updates, 226
Options link (Wall), 109
Organize (photos, link), 127, 129–130
Orkut (social networking site), 19

• P •

Page
    account, signing up for, 207
    advertising, 287–289
    applications, 215–217, 253–254
    applications, adding, 218–219, 250–251
    business categories, 205
    community pages, 199–200
    comparison to Profiles and Groups,
        16–17, 203–204, 206–207
    connecting to, 200–201
    creating, 201–202, 208–210
    default settings, 214–215
    described, 197
    discussion board, 217, 225
    events, 217, 225
    fan invitations, 222–223
    fan pages, 198–199
    inappropriate content, 80–81, 199
    Info tab, 212
    message updates, 46
    mobile text updates, 220–221
    name, selection, 209
    for non-people entities, 99, 197
    options, customizing, 210–211
    Photos, 217

Page (continued)
  privacy controls, 73
  Profile, 99
  reviews, 218
  rich content, adding, 224–225
  Suggestions for finding, 48–49
  Updates tab, 224–225
  videos, 217
  Wall posts, 108–109, 212–214
  Wall settings, 214–215
  who doesn't need a Page?, 205–206
  who needs a Page?, 205
Page administrator
  identifying the, 207, 209
  as shared responsibility, 221–222
  Wall settings options, 214–215
Page Control Panel
  adding administrators, 221–222
  adding applications, 217–219
  editing settings with, 219
  navigating to, 211
Page Manager, 210
Palo Alto, CA, 27
Pandora (web site), 249
Parkinson's Research (Groups), 316
party planning. See Events
passwords and username
  creating Page account, 207–208
  forgetting and resetting, 308
  logging in with, 208
  signing up for an account, 30
  vanity URLs and, 222–223
Past Events
  Home page link to, 46
  viewing, 185
Pay for Clicks, 286
permission
  accessing personal information, 242–243
  additional privacy controls, 78–79
  applications, 236–239, 255–256
  friend invitations, 55–56
  Name Change, 307–308
  to see/join Groups, 167, 170
Personal Information (Profile), 93
pets on Facebook, 236
Photo albums
  creating, 120–123
  default settings, 133
  privacy controls, 132–134

Profile picture, 95
  sharing with non-Facebook users, 134
  tagged Photos, 22, 94
  uploaded Photos, 95
Photo Publisher, 120–124
Photos. See also Profile picture
  Action links, 97
  additions and changes, 89, 119
  application described, 14–15, 118–119
  editing, 126–130
  Events, 187
  Groups, 168, 176, 181
  Home page link to, 46
  inserting into notes, 137–138
  Page, 217, 224–225
  privacy controls, 132–134
  Profile, 94–95
  removal of tagging, 131
  reporting inappropriate content, 80–81
  sharing with, 94–95
  tagging, 22, 42, 118, 126–130
  uploading, 120–123, 261–262
  viewing, 131
Photos Dashboard, 119
photo-sharing websites, 89, 118, 235
pictures, drawing (application), 295
platform. See computer platform; Facebook
    Platform
plugins. See social plugin
Pokes
  Action links, 97
  described, 155
  on Facebook Mobile, 264
  as flirting messages, 22–23
  Home page link to, 49
  as thinking of you messages, 22
politics
  campaign and election, 317–318
  demonstrations and protest, 317
  dissent and activism, 315–316
  identifying your personal views, 92–93
Pop Out Chat (option), 154–155
pornography
  inappropriate content reporting, 80–81
  investigating presence of, 18–19
  removal of Groups for, 172
Post Link (link), 160
Post to My Wall (link), 238
Post to Profile (link), 150–151

Posts by Everyone, 115
Posts by Your Friends, 114
posts/posting. *See also* Publisher
  add photos, 89
  ask a question, 89
  from friends, 91
  linking, 90
  notification of, 42
  to a Page, 214–215
  Recent Activity, 91
  sharing thoughts by, 13–14
  status updates, 88–89
  user statistics, 227–229
  to the Wall, 86–87
predators
  addressing the problem of, 67
  protecting minors from, 81–82
Presidential politics, 317–318
Preview My Profile, 73
pricing, advertising, 284–286
privacy controls
  about using, 1, 71–72, 311
  applications, 78–79, 118, 256–257
  attention of Facebook to, 67–68
  Basic Directory Information, 72–74
  between friends, 53
  between parents and children, 25
  Block list, 76–78
  customizing, 70–71
  default settings, 71–72
  Events, 186
  Groups, 168
  identifying the audience, 68–69
  Page, 99, 214
  photos, 14–15, 118, 132–134
  Profile, 12, 20, 99
  Search, 72, 114
  Sharing, 74–75, 151
  videos, 131, 132–134
  Web sites, 75–76
Privacy Policy, 30–31, 50
privacy protection
  answering Questions, 126
  Ask Question (application), 89
  computer viruses, 67, 82, 305–306
  friending, 67
  honesty and, 106
  inappropriate content reporting, 80–81
  inappropriate use investigation, 18

malicious applications, 218
messaging non-friends, 149
of minors, 81–82
Pages compared to Groups, 203–204
personal responsibility for, 79–80
Profile, 99
Publisher, 160
random friend requests, 54–55
sharing profile information and, 12
unwanted friend requests, 308
Privacy Settings
  Account link to, 43
  choosing options, 102–103
  date of birth, 104–105
  editing, 250
  importance of learning, 311
  Wall, 91
private Events, 186, 191
Profile, application, 254–256
Profile, beginning your
  account access/settings, 43–44
  account verification, 37–39
  boxes and tabs, 34
  city of residence, 32
  editing, 46
  hometown, 12, 36
  information fields, 34–35
  privacy controls, 20, 53
  relationship status, 22–23
Profile, building your
  adding applications, 240–242
  becoming a fan, 200–201
  birth date, 104–105
  boxes and tabs, 95–99, 240–242
  causes for deactivation, 17–19
  comparison to Pages, 16–17, 203–204,
      206–207
  comparison to other networking sites, 19
  creating a positive image, 101–102
  customizing, 210
  default links, 96–97
  description, 85–86
  fake profiles, 37–39, 236
  hiding information, 201, 302
  Info tab, 92–94
  job hunting and, 23, 301–302
  linked to tagged Photos, 22
  posting to Publisher, 45
  preview, 73

Profile, building your *(continued)*
  privacy controls, 102–103
  reasons for creating, 12–13
  reporting inappropriate content, 80–81
  as a social résumé, 11–12
  strategies for building, 99–102
  updating, 100, 101
  Wall tab, 86–91
Profile, business, 205
Profile picture
  changing, 37, 96
  default settings, 36–37
  Events, 186, 192
  on Facebook Mobile, 270
  Fan Page, 198
  Groups, 167, 181
  importance of, 72, 96
  Page, 212
  selecting, 36
  uploading, 35
Profile Picture Album, 95, 132
public communications
  comments as, 160
  privacy protection of, 160
  sharing albums with non-users, 134
  Wall posts as, 158–160
public Events, 186, 189, 191
public information, 237
Public Search
  privacy controls, 76, 257
  privacy of minors, 81–82
Publisher, 212–213
Publisher (Event), 187
Publisher (Facebook Mobile), 273
Publisher (Fan Page), 199
Publisher (Home page), 45
Publisher (Notes), 135–136
Publisher (Page), 211–214, 217, 224–227
Publisher (Photos), 120–124
Publisher (Profile)
  Ask Question posts, 89
  creating posts, 87–88
  linking to Internet content, 90
  photo sharing, 89
  as public communication, 160
  Recent Activity posts, 91
  status updates, 88–89
  using touch screen devices, 272–273
Publisher (Wall posts), 91, 109, 158–160

• *Q* •

QQ (social networking site), 19
Questions (application), 89, 126, 159
questions to ask yourself
  am I too old for Facebook?, 31
  am I too young for Facebook?, 1, 18
  what is a friend?, 52–54
  who doesn't need a Page?, 205–206
  who needs a Page?, 205
Quick Events, creating, 192–194
quick-search, 63
quiz applications, 236
Quora (web site), 244–245

• *R* •

random friend requests, 54–55
real-time sharing (Twitter), 19, 224, 309
real-time updates, 53–54
Recent Activity, 91, 248. *See also* News Feeds
Recent Albums
  additions and changes, 119
  Home page link to, 46
Recent News (Groups), 166, 174
Recommendations (stream), 248
red flags (navigation bar), 42
red-eye reduction, 127
registering an account, 29–31
Relationship Status, 35, 93
relationships
  about using Facebook for, 1–2
  advertising targeted to, 283
  creating a social graph, 10–11
  "Facebook Me!", 303
  Facebook Official, 35, 93, 302–303
  with friends, 52
  messaging non-friends, 148–149
  with Pages, 200–201
religious views, 92–93
Remember Me option, 44
reporting inappropriate content
  Fan Pages, 199
  Groups, 171–172
  Pages/Profiles, 80–81
Request for Permission Page, 236–239
Requests
  applications, 242
  described, 156

Home page link to, 49
Name Change, 307–308
random friend requests, 54–55
Restaurant City (game application), 296
restaurant game applications, 236
restrictions
  age, 1, 18, 31
  country, 219
  Page status, 219
Reviews
  application, 216, 218
  application credibility, 253
  Page, 218
  Page user-statistics, 227–229
Revolutionary Armed Forces of Columbia
    (FARC), 314
rich content, 117
rich-text editor, 136
rich-text markup, 216
Ride Your Bike to Work Day, 15
Robertson, David (Facebook member), 316
robots. *See* spam/spammers
RSVP (Event), 15, 22, 48–49, 72, 184, 185,
    191, 194–195, 225
rules, Facebook
  friend etiquette, 54–55
  Notes etiquette, 135
  participation, 17–19
  Wall etiquette, 87

• *S* •

Safari web browser, 137, 152
safety rules. *See also* privacy protection
  age restrictions, 1, 18
  fake names/accounts, 17–18
  privacy of minors, 1, 18, 81–82
  profile sharing, 12
  trolling/unsolicited messages, 18
  uploading illegal content, 18–19
school. *See also* Education and Work
  finding classmates, 299–300
  meeting roommates, 298
Scrabble Lovers (Group), 182
Search (feature). *See also* Public Search
  Chat with online friends, 153
  by city of residence, 32
  classmate search, 61–62
  coworker search, 62–63

Events, 188–189
on Facebook Mobile, 269
Groups, 164, 169–171
making connections with, 13
messaging non-friends, 148
privacy controls, 72, 114
quick-search, 63
rekindling relationships with, 26
using touch screen devices, 272–273
ways of using, 113–115
Search box (navigation bar), 42–43
secret Groups, 164, 167, 169, 177
security. *See* CAPTCHA; privacy controls;
    privacy protection; Privacy Settings;
    safety rules
See All Messages (link), 145
See My Friend List (link), 73
Select Guests To Invite (link), 186–187
selling merchandise, 294
Send a Message, 97
Send Me Email (link), 237
Send Me Friend Requests, 72
Send Me Messages, 73
Sent messages, Home page link to, 46
set-up wizard, 31
sex. *See* gender
sexual orientation, 282
Share (link)
  Groups, 168
  icon, 150
  links versus buttons, 150–151
  Photos, 94–95
  Profile, 99
  as public communication, 160
  sending messages, 149–151
  sending photos, 151
  sharing albums with non-users, 134
  Web site links with, 152
Share Bookmarklet, 152
Share the Event, 187, 189, 194
Sharing on Facebook. *See also* Facebook
  biographical information, 92–94
  combating terrorism, 314
  content ownership, 311–312
  political activism, 315–316
  privacy controls, 71, 102–103
  Privacy Settings, 74–75
  Profile strategies for, 99–102
  Publisher, 87–91

Sharing on Facebook *(continued)*
  with students to young to join, 297–298
  Wall boxes, 95–99
  Wall posts, 86–87, 107–109
Short Message Service (SMS). *See* texting/
    text messages
shortcuts. *See* bookmarks
Show Deleted Messages (link), 147
sidebars, how to use, 3
signing up for an account, 29–31
Simple Uploader, uploading photos, 123
Skype, 59–60
SMS (Short Message Service). *See* texting/
    text messages
snippets, message, 147
social ads. *See* advertising
social connections
  power and value of, 10–11
  Profile as a window to, 11–12
  sites other than Facebook, 19
  using Facebook for, 1–2, 9–10
social graph
  Facebook Platform, 234–235
  leveraging the power of, 10–11
  utility and reliability, 21
social plugin
  account creation and login, 243–245
  Comments, 246–247
  described, 243
  Instant Personalization, 249–250
  Likes, 245–246
  Streams, 247–249
social résumé, 11–12
social targeting, 17
soundtracks, video, 130
spam/spammers
  avoiding, 30, 67
  Facebook rejection of, 289–290
  identity verification, 37–39
  messaging Group members, 182
  preventing, 82
  removal of Groups for, 172
  reporting inappropriate content, 80–81
spell checker, 144
Sponsors/sponsored links, 49
Starbucks (Page), 16, 205–206, 217
Start New Topic (Group discussion), 169
Static FBML (application), 216

statistics, user
  advertising, 287–289
  audience engagement, 210
  Interactions Graph, 227–229
status updates. *See also* Updates
  on Facebook Mobile, 263, 270
  Mobile for Pages, 220–221
  from Pages, 201, 214
  from Profile, 88–89
  promoting your Page with, 224–225
  streaming, 248
  types of, 107–109
streams, information
  posting to Publisher, 45
  social plugins for, 247–249
Subscribing
  to applications, 237–238
  common interest Groups, 15
  to a Page, 201, 211
  real-time friend's updates, 53–54
Suggestions (tool)
  finding friends with, 60–61
  Home page reminder for, 48
  making connections with, 13
"Support the Monks' Protest" (Group), 317

• *T* •

tabs, adding, 216, 240–242
Tag People in This Note (link), 138
Tag This Photo (link), 129
tagging
  applications, 118
  defined, 94–95
  HTML formatting, 136–137
  linked to your Profile, 22
  notes about friends, 138
  notification of, 42, 129
  Page user-statistics, 227–229
  photo editing and, 126–128
  photos of friends, 129
  photos of you, 128–129, 131
  removal of, 131
  videos, 130–131
  viewing photos and videos of you, 131
Take a Photo (option), 120
target audience. *See* advertising; audience
    engagement; demographics
targeted advertising, 1–2

technical support, application, 253
Terms of Service, 30–31
Terms of Use
  age restrictions, 82
  fake accounts, 242
  inappropriate content, 81–82
  navigating to, 50
  rights and responsibilities, 311–312
  what you can't do, 17–19
texting/text messages
  account verification, 38–39
  Facebook Mobile, 262–265
  Mobile for Pages, 220–221
  notification, 265–266
  real-time friend's updates, 53–54
thinking of you posts, 22
third-party applications
  Carpool by Zimride, 295–296
  development of, 235, 258
  Digg, 295
  Graffiti, 295
  Groupcard, 294
  Lady Gaga, 296
  Lexulous, 300
  Marketplace, 294
  Music, by iLike, 294
  Restaurant City, 296
  Typing Maniac, 236, 252, 293
  Visual Bookshelf, 296
threads, message, 145–147, 272
32665 (FBOOK), 262–265
thumbnails, 96, 150
Top News (News Feed), 45, 112–113
Toronto Star, 316
touch screen devices
  applications, 250–251
  downloading to, 272–273
Track Your Invites, 49
Translation Application, 28
trolling/unsolicited messages, 18
Trust (application prompt), 121, 123
Twitter (networking site), 19, 224, 309
Typing Maniac (application), 236, 252, 293

• U •

Ultimate Frisbee (Group), 181
"*Un Million de voces contra las FARC*"
  (Group), 314

unfriending, 76–78
United Kingdom, 28
Unlike, 199
unsolicited messages/trolling, 18, 147–149
Unsubscribe
  from applications, 237–238
  friend's updates, 54
  News Feed, 111
  user statistics, 229
unwanted friend requests, 308
Updates (messages). *See also* status
    updates
  Home page link to, 46
  Page, 225
Upload a Photo (option), 120–124
uploading illegal content, 18–19
uploading photographs. *See* Photos
URL
  as advertising destination, 280
  avoiding computer viruses, 305–306
  creating a Page, 222–223
user-engagement statistics. *See* passwords
    and username; statistics, user

• V •

verification (Profile), 37–39
verified networks, 19–20
Videos
  Action links, 97
  additions and changes, 119
  application described, 118–119
  default settings, 133
  editing, 130–131
  Events, 187
  Groups, 168, 176
  Home page link to, 46
  Page, 217, 224–225
  Profile link to, 99
  recording, 125–126
  sharing, 152
  tagging, 118, 130–131
  uploading, 123–124, 261–262
  viewing, 131
View Comments (link), 131
View Photos of <*Name*> (link), 97
View Photos/Videos of Me (link), 131
View Videos of <*Name*> (link), 97
violence, 172

Visible To options (Photos and Videos), 132–134
Visual Bookshelf (application), 296

• W •

Wagner, Richard (Dummies author), 233
Wall. *See also* Publisher
  Events, 186
  Fan Page, 199, 201
  Groups, 166, 168
  Options link, 109
  Page, 212–215
  Privacy Settings, 91
  Profile, 86–87
Wall boxes, 95–99
Wall posts
  from applications, 238, 240
  default settings, 109, 169
  on Facebook Mobile, 264
  as flirting message, 22–23
  Groups, 176
  hiding, 109
  Notes, 135–136
  notification of, 42
  Page, 213–214
  as public communication, 158–160
  sharing with, 86–87
  thinking of you message, 22
  to/from friends, 91
  types of, 107–109
Wall settings (Page), 214–215
The Washington Post (Page), 317–318
Web browser
  applications, adding, 250–251
  Facebook links to, 152
  spell checker, 144
Web sites
  Amazon, 296
  browser spell checkers, 144
  conventions for *Dummies* books, 2
  creating, 15–16
  Facebook Share buttons, 152
  Gawker, 245

Groups, 175
Lady Gaga, 296
Microsoft Docs, 249
Pandora, 249
photo-sharing, 89, 118, 235
privacy controls, 75–76, 103, 256–257
Quora, 244–245
Yelp, 75, 243, 249
YouTube, 150, 152, 250, 306
Webcam, recording and upload, 125–126
Welcome (tab), 216
"When I Was Your Age, Pluto Was a Planet" (Group), 168
"Which literary Heroine are you?" (quiz application), 236
Wiley Publishing
  advertising on Facebook, 277–278
  Building Facebook Applications for Dummies (Wagner), 233
Windows Live Contacts, 60
Windows Live Messenger
  chat, 48
  finding friends with, 59–60
Windows Live Spaces, 19
Windows operating system, 234
wizard, set-up, 31
word scrambles (game application), 236
workplace networks
  coworker search, 62–63
  Groups as, 24
Write on Wall (link), 159
Write Something About Yourself (link), 97

• Y •

Yelp (web site), 75, 243, 249
YouTube (web site), 150, 152, 250, 306

• Z •

Zappo (Page), 217
Zimride, Carpool by (application), 295–296
Zuckerberg, Mark (Facebook founder), 27

Apple & Macs

iPad For Dummies
978-0-470-58027-1

iPhone For Dummies,
4th Edition
978-0-470-87870-5

MacBook For Dummies, 3rd
Edition
978-0-470-76918-8

Mac OS X Snow Leopard For
Dummies
978-0-470-43543-4

Business

Bookkeeping For Dummies
978-0-7645-9848-7

Job Interviews
For Dummies,
3rd Edition
978-0-470-17748-8

Resumes For Dummies,
5th Edition
978-0-470-08037-5

Starting an
Online Business
For Dummies,
6th Edition
978-0-470-60210-2

Stock Investing
For Dummies,
3rd Edition
978-0-470-40114-9

Successful
Time Management
For Dummies
978-0-470-29034-7

Computer Hardware

BlackBerry
For Dummies,
4th Edition
978-0-470-60700-8

Computers For Seniors
For Dummies,
2nd Edition
978-0-470-53483-0

PCs For Dummies,
Windows
7 Edition
978-0-470-46542-4

Laptops For Dummies,
4th Edition
978-0-470-57829-2

Cooking & Entertaining

Cooking Basics
For Dummies,
3rd Edition
978-0-7645-7206-7

Wine For Dummies,
4th Edition
978-0-470-04579-4

Diet & Nutrition

Dieting For Dummies,
2nd Edition
978-0-7645-4149-0

Nutrition For Dummies,
4th Edition
978-0-471-79868-2

Weight Training
For Dummies,
3rd Edition
978-0-471-76845-6

Digital Photography

Digital SLR Cameras &
Photography For Dummies,
3rd Edition
978-0-470-46606-3

Photoshop Elements 8
For Dummies
978-0-470-52967-6

Gardening

Gardening Basics
For Dummies
978-0-470-03749-2

Organic Gardening
For Dummies,
2nd Edition
978-0-470-43067-5

Green/Sustainable

Raising Chickens
For Dummies
978-0-470-46544-8

Green Cleaning
For Dummies
978-0-470-39106-8

Health

Diabetes For Dummies,
3rd Edition
978-0-470-27086-8

Food Allergies
For Dummies
978-0-470-09584-3

Living Gluten-Free
For Dummies,
2nd Edition
978-0-470-58589-4

Hobbies/General

Chess For Dummies,
2nd Edition
978-0-7645-8404-6

Drawing
Cartoons & Comics
For Dummies
978-0-470-42683-8

Knitting For Dummies,
2nd Edition
978-0-470-28747-7

Organizing
For Dummies
978-0-7645-5300-4

Su Doku For Dummies
978-0-470-01892-7

Home Improvement

Home Maintenance
For Dummies,
2nd Edition
978-0-470-43063-7

Home Theater
For Dummies,
3rd Edition
978-0-470-41189-6

Living the
Country Lifestyle
All-in-One
For Dummies
978-0-470-43061-3

Solar Power Your Home
For Dummies,
2nd Edition
978-0-470-59678-4

Internet

Blogging For Dummies,
3rd Edition
978-0-470-61996-4

eBay For Dummies,
6th Edition
978-0-470-49741-8

Facebook For Dummies,
3rd Edition
978-0-470-87804-0

Web Marketing
For Dummies,
2nd Edition
978-0-470-37181-7

WordPress
For Dummies,
3rd Edition
978-0-470-59274-8

Language & Foreign Language

French For Dummies
978-0-7645-5193-2

Italian Phrases
For Dummies
978-0-7645-7203-6

Spanish For Dummies,
2nd Edition
978-0-470-87855-2

Spanish
For Dummies,
Audio Set
978-0-470-09585-0

Math & Science

Algebra I
For Dummies,
2nd Edition
978-0-470-55964-2

Biology For Dummies,
2nd Edition
978-0-470-59875-7

Calculus For Dummies
978-0-7645-2498-1

Chemistry For Dummies
978-0-7645-5430-8

Microsoft Office

Excel 2010 For Dummies
978-0-470-48953-6

Office 2010 All-in-One
For Dummies
978-0-470-49748-7

Office 2010 For Dummies,
Book + DVD Bundle
978-0-470-62698-6

Word 2010 For Dummies
978-0-470-48772-3

Music

Guitar For Dummies,
2nd Edition
978-0-7645-9904-0

iPod & iTunes For
Dummies, 8th Edition
978-0-470-87871-2

Piano Exercises
For Dummies
978-0-470-38765-8

Parenting & Education

Parenting For Dummies,
2nd Edition
978-0-7645-5418-6

Type 1 Diabetes
For Dummies
978-0-470-17811-9

Pets

Cats For Dummies,
2nd Edition
978-0-7645-5275-5

Dog Training For Dummies,
3rd Edition
978-0-470-60029-0

Puppies For Dummies,
2nd Edition
978-0-470-03717-1

Religion & Inspiration

The Bible For Dummies
978-0-7645-5296-0

Catholicism For Dummies
978-0-7645-5391-2

Women in the Bible
For Dummies
978-0-7645-8475-6

Self-Help & Relationship

Anger Management
For Dummies
978-0-470-03715-7

Overcoming Anxiety
For Dummies,
2nd Edition
978-0-470-57441-6

Sports

Baseball
For Dummies,
3rd Edition
978-0-7645-7537-2

Basketball
For Dummies,
2nd Edition
978-0-7645-5248-9

Golf For Dummies,
3rd Edition
978-0-471-76871-5

Web Development

Web Design
All-in-One
For Dummies
978-0-470-41796-6

Web Sites
Do-It-Yourself
For Dummies,
2nd Edition
978-0-470-56520-9

Windows 7

Windows 7
For Dummies
978-0-470-49743-2

Windows 7
For Dummies,
Book + DVD Bundle
978-0-470-52398-8

Windows 7 All-in-One
For Dummies
978-0-470-48763-1